European Values in International Relations

TAPRI STUDIES IN INTERNATIONAL RELATIONS

This series, edited jointly by Dr Vilho Harle and Dr Jyrki Käkönen of the Tampere Peace Research Institute at Tampere in Finland, is based on the work of TAPRI on peace studies. The series will be launched with publications from TAPRI Workshops on 'European Futures: Bases & Choices', concentrating on European issues concerning international relations, security, disarmament, human rights, technology and co-operation.

Vilho Harle and Pekka Sivonen (eds), *Europe in Transition: Politics and Nuclear Security*

Vilho Harle (ed.), *European Values in International Relations*

Vilho Harle and Jyrki Iivonen (eds), *The Soviet Union and Europe*

Jyrki Käkönen, Steven Miller and Lev Voronkov (eds), *Vulnerable Arctic: Need for an Alternative Orientation?*

European Values in International Relations

Edited by

Vilho Harle

Pinter Publishers
London and New York

First published in Great Britain in 1990 by
Pinter Publishers Limited
25 Floral Street, London WC2E 9DS

British Library Cataloguing in Publication Data

A CIP catalogue record for this book is available from the British Library
ISBN 086187 840 X

Library of Congress Cataloging-in-Publication Data

European values in international relations / edited by Vilho Harle.
p. cm.—(TAPRI studies in international relations)
Papers presented at the TAPRI workshops on European values in international relations held May 29, 1987, in Tampere, Finland, and Sept. 22–24, 1988, in Helsinki, Finland.
ISBN 0-86187-840-X
1. International relations—Congresses. 2. Europe—Civilization—Congresses. I. Harle, Vilho. II. TAPRI Workshop on European Values in International Relations (1987 : Tampere, Finland) III. TAPRI Workshop on European Values in International Relations (1988 : Helsinki, Finland) IV. Series.
JX1391.E85 1990
327.1'01—dc20 89-28682
CIP

Typeset by Florencetype, Kewstoke, Avon
Printed and bound in Great Britain by
Biddles Ltd, Guildford and King's Lynn

Contents

Contributors vii

Preface x

1 European Roots of Dualism and its Alternatives in International Relations
Vilho Harle 1

2 Heroism, the Construction of Evil, and Violence
James A. Aho 15

3 The Bomb-Sign: Notes on the Overvaluation of the Object
Jussi Vähämäki 29

4 Burke the International Theorist—or the War of the Sons of Light and the Sons of Darkness
Vilho Harle 58

5 Carl Schmitt's Concept of the State and the 'Enemy'
Alexander Demandt 80

6 Philosophical History and the Third World: Hegel on Africa and Asia
Shiraz Dossa 91

7 Savagery and Neo-Savagery: An African Perspective on Peace
M.A. Mohamed Salih 110

8 The German Question from the Conservative Point of View, the Nuclear–Cosmic Age and Karl Jaspers
Jouko Jokisalo 126

9 Violence—An Israeli Perspective
Gershon Weiler 144

10 In Europe's Shadow: Zionism and the Palestinian Fate
Shiraz Dossa 155

11 European Values after the 'Euromissile Crisis'
Matthias Finger 166

12 Is there a New Germany Coming?
Johan Galtung 192

Index 203

Contributors

JAMES A. AHO Ph.D. (Washington State University, 1971); Professor of Sociology (Idaho State University, Pocatello, 1982); author of *Religious Mythology and the Art of War* (Aldwych Press, 1981) and *The Politics of Righteousness* (University of Washington Press, forthcoming, 1990).

ALEXANDER DEMANDT D.Phil (Universität Marburg, 1963); Professor for Ancient History (Freie Universität Berlin); author of *Ungeschehene Geschichte* (Kleine Vandenhoeck-Reihe, no. 1501, 2nd edn, 1986, Vandenhoeck & Ruprecht), and *Die Spätantik Römische Geschichte von Diocletian bis Justinian, 284–565 n. Chr.* (Handbuch der Altertumswissenschaft III, 6, 1989, Beck).

SHIRAZ DOSSA Ph.D. (University of Toronto, 1987); Assistant Professor of Political Science (St Francis Xavier University); author of *The Public Realm and the Public Self: The Political Theory of Hannah Arendt* (Wilfrid Laurier University Press, 1989).

MATTHIAS FINGER Ph.D. (University of Geneva); Assistant Professor of Political Science and Adult Education (University of Geneva), Research Fellow (GIPRI, Geneva); Visiting Fellow (Syracuse University); author of *Les 10 bonnes raisons pour adhérer au nouveau mouvement de la paix* (Loisirs et Pédagogie, 1989).

JOHAN GALTUNG Dr.hon. causa mult., founder and director (1959–69) of PRIO (Peace Research Institute in Oslo); Professor of Peace and Conflict Research (University of Oslo, 1969–77); Honorary Professor of Universidad de Alicante, Freie Universität Berlin, and Sichuan University; currently Professor of Peace Studies at the University of Hawaii.

VILHO HARLE D.Phil. (University of Tampere, 1975); Senior Research Fellow (TAPRI, 1988–); editor of *Essays in Peace Studies* (Avebury, 1987), and co-editor of *Europe in Transition: Politics and Nuclear Security* (Pinter, 1989).

JOUKO JOKISALO Dr. Phil. (Humbolt Universität of Berlin); Teaching Research Fellow (University of Oulu, Finland).

M.A. MOHAMED SALIH D.Phil. (University of Manchester, 1983); Lecturer in Social Anthropology and Sociology (University of Khartoum, Sudan, 1983–) and Senior Researcher (the Scandinavian Institute of African Studies, Uppsala, Sweden, 1987–1990); editor of *Family Life in Sudan* (Oxford University Press, 1987), *Agrarian Change in the Central Rainlands of Sudan* (Scandinavian Institute of African Studies, 1987), and *Ecology and Politics in Africa* (Scandinavian Institute of African Studies, 1989).

JUSSI VÄHÄMÄKI B.A. in Sociology (University of Tampere, 1989).

GERSHON WEILER M.A. (Jerusalem University, 1952 and University of Dublin, 1960) and B.Phil (Oxon, 1958); Associate Professor in Philosophy (Tel Aviv University, 1973–); author of *Jewish Theocracy* (Brill, 1988) and *Philosophische Parabeln* (Braumüller, 1988).

Preface

In 1987 the Tampere Peace Research Institute (TAPRI) launched international TAPRI Workshops on 'European Futures: Bases & Choices'. The workshops are concerned with European values in international relations; human rights in an East–West perspective; technology, co-operation and political order in Europe; the Soviet Union and Europe; superpower stereotypes; alternative security in the Arctic region; and the political consequences of nuclear disarmament in Europe. The workshops have had two or three meetings, with some sixty scholars taking part.

The TAPRI Workshops have been financed mainly by a grant from the John D. and Catherine T. MacArthur Foundation, to which I wish to extend my warmest thanks. Needless to say, the Foundation bears no responsibility for the workshops' publications or other activities.

The present volume is based on the work of the TAPRI Workshop on European Values in International Relations, which so far has met twice: in Tampere on 29–31 May 1987, and in Helsinki on 22–4 September 1988. The book represents a selection of papers presented at these two meetings; in addition I have solicited contributions from other scholars to fill some gaps and to give a wider perspective.

The present workshop seeks to contribute to the ongoing debate on the identity of Europe by applying various approaches, from political philosophy to more current analyses of contemporary European issues.

Originally the task was to investigate alternative organizing concepts which would form the basis of a European identity. The purpose was to trace European lines of political thought in the fields of diplomacy and international relations, along the lines suggested by Martin Wight in his famous paper on 'Western Values in International Relations'. What we wanted to find out was whether there exist uniquely European conceptions of peace, security, co-operation, neutrality, and so on in theories of international relations.

However, it soon became clear that the suggested European values do not necessarily contribute to a more peaceful world. On the contrary, a more 'negative', a 'darker' side of European international (political) thought emerged from the initial perusal of European values: it was found that the European political thought and cultural heritage, i.e. the European way of thinking, contained a strong element of dualism, a tendency to make a distinction between good and evil, between 'us' and 'them', between 'our' friends and enemies. This aspect has been given no space in the debate on European identity – though the 'enemy' lurks behind many statements in that debate. Therefore the workshop decided to make explicit this hidden, darker dimension of Europeanism. Consequently, the present volume tends to be somewhat critical of 'Europeanism' as far as the total unity of interests and values is concerned.

The contributions can be divided into four parts. The first three papers deal with *theoretical dimensions and applications of dualism and the 'enemy' in European political thought.* Harle's first contribution is an introduction to the present collection; the chapter was distributed as a background paper to the second workshop meeting – therefore, it emphasizes the role of dualism in European thought and gives dualism a uniquely European connotation. Aho and Vähämäki discuss more general aspects of the 'enemy' and its consequences in politics and international relations. It will perhaps remain an open question whether the three contributions deal with strictly and uniquely 'European' phenomena, but it can be suggested that dualistic ideas and the 'enemy' have a central role in European thinking and that European thinking has had, and still has, a similarly central role in a more general 'Western' or 'occidental' world and its values.

Second, three contributions are devoted to the *history of political ideas* – a dimension which was a focal concern of the current workshop. Of course, Burke (discussed by Harle), Schmitt (by Demandt) and Hegel (by Dossa) are only examples, but certainly central figures in the political traditions of dualism and the 'enemy'.

Third, as well as discussing theoretical backgrounds and the history of ideas, the book takes some examples from reality in order to identify the *role of dualism and the 'enemy' in contemporary European issues and debates.* Salih's chapter tries to see what Europeanism looks like from outside Europe; Jokisalo looks at conservative contributions to the debate on German reunification and security – a problem which is certainly central to any idea of a United Europe or 'Common European House'; and Weiler and Dossa deal with the Israel/Palestine issue, which is far too often ignored as a 'European' problem. These contributions should not be evaluated from the point of 'truth'; we cannot determine who is right and who is wrong, but the reader may perceive that all these four papers imply that dualistic ideas and the 'enemy' hardly contribute to the solution of real issues and conflicts. Instead, it is more likely that 'European' thinking contributes to the aggravation of those conflicts.

Fourth, the two final contributions deal with *alternatives to dualism and the 'enemy'*. Finger and Galtung emphasize new social movements, soft or green values, and on the demilitarization of European thinking and politics. Unfortunately, we were unable to give more attention to alternative values and ideas, ways of overcoming dualistic distinctions and the dangers of giving the 'enemy' a central role in political thought. In most chapters this dimension is discussed only in passing, just modestly encouraging new research efforts and thinking towards this more constructive goal. Indeed, it seems obvious that new, alternative values should be given serious attention in future investigations of the identity of Europe and Europeanism.

Geographical, economic and cultural diversity, if rid of the dark side of dualism and the 'enemy', is an integral part of Europe and Europeanism. So it is more easy than usual to say that the contributors to the present volume were encouraged to apply different approaches and emphasize opposing arguments: there was no pressure to reach artificial uniformity – the project members tried to give food for thought to each other and to all participants in the debate on Europeanism.

Tampere, Finland
19 July 1989

1 European Roots of Dualism and its Alternatives in International Relations

Vilho Harle

A quest is in progress for the identity of Europe, a search for common, all-European interests in terms of security and co-operation. However, the idea of Europeanism, or the identity of Europe, remains somewhat diffuse. One may well ask whether European unification is possible? Are there factors that could integrate Europe politically from the Urals to the Atlantic and from the north to the Mediterranean? Experience shows that the answer is likely to be negative. The divisions, differences, unique experiences and conflicting interests of the various states in Europe are formidable obstacles to unification.

Yet it may be possible for the divisions to be overcome. The emerging Europeanists seem to believe in a common cultural basis. Furthermore, it is pointed out that Europe lives in a world of increasing military, and particularly economic, power struggles. Therefore, they say, the intra-European contradictions and conflicts can and must be solved or managed in order to guarantee Europe's future and its welfare and security, as well as a reasonable say in world affairs. Scholars might contribute to this process by investigating alternative organizing concepts which would form the basis of a European identity. The purpose would be to trace European lines of political thought in the fields of diplomacy and international relations. For example, one might enquire whether there are uniquely European conceptions or connotations of peace, security and co-operation, or balance of power, neutrality etc. in theories of international relations. And if such are found, it might be worthwhile to explore how they might contribute to the growth of Europeanism at present or in the future.

The suggested supporting role for scholars takes the idea of Europeanism for granted, as given, as a non-problematic ideal. If however one wishes to follow the lines of critical social research – as peace researchers are expected to do – one must not forget the consequences. Then one should ask whether 'European' conceptions would increase or decrease potentialities for co-operation (*or* conflicts) between the European states—as well as between the European states and their environment (i.e. nations representing other values and conceptions). Do European values contribute to a more peaceful world —or do they rather aggravate violence and the danger of war?

The answer to this question requires application of a historical perspective to the genesis and development of European ideas of international security. Here I can suggest four questions: (1) What have been the basic dimensions of international thought, the dominating and shared modes of structuring the abstract reality called international relations?[1] (2) Through which cultural processes are these modes of thinking transmitted from the past to the contemporary world? (3) What are the implications of the old patterns of thinking for the contemporary world and the future of humankind? And (4) What alternatives are there to the dominating modes of thinking, and how might these alternatives become accepted?

Dualistic modes of thinking

We might envisage several answers to the first question, but I shall deal exclusively with only one of them. It seems clear that an integral part of the European cultural heritage, the European way of thinking, is related to dualism. Dualism appears in other cultures too, but in the European cultural heritage and in the European mind it seems to have a surprisingly central role. As Peter Gay (1978, p. 231) has suggested, the need to experience through polarities seems to have profoundly dominated the mental style of Western man. Polarities appear indispensable, however imprecise, unscientific, evasive and distorting they are. It seems natural to confront radical with reactionary, past with present, private with public, true with false, us with them, friends with enemies, good with bad. In the European mind, the idea of 'one state, two systems' sounds strange and exotic.[2]

Johan Chydenius (1985) distinguishes between an essential dualism (in which the principle of good and the principle of evil are eternally opposed to each other) and an existential dualism (in which actually existing good is distinguished from actually existing evil). He also distinguishes between simultaneous and successive dualism. Essential dualism is always simultaneous: good and evil exist at the same time and eternally. Existential dualism may be either simultaneous or successive. The simultaneous variant of existential dualism implies that at a certain point of time, when part of it lapsed into a lower state, good was given its counterpart in evil. Henceforth good and evil existed side by side. The successive variant of existential dualism implies that a good state is transformed once and for all into an evil state. Good and evil are opposed to each other, but they are separated by a span of time.

It is important to discuss the roots of dualistic thinking in at least three—perhaps overlapping—areas: religion, politics and enemy images, if we wish to understand why contradictions hold such a strong position in current modes of thinking. This is not a comprehensive list; I shall be referring to them as examples. In addition, my discussion will aim at giving some food for thought, at suggesting a larger research programme, instead of conclusive discussion.

The religious idea of contradictions was born in ancient Persia, and was later adopted by Judaism and Christianity. During the earliest documented history, in Persia, Zarathustra singled out *Ahura Mazda* (the Lord of Light, the Wise Lord) as the one true God. However, there also exists his opponent: the Evil Spirit (*Angra Mainyu*). There is a cosmic conflict between the Holy Spirit and the Evil Spirit; the conflict becomes one between the powers of Light and Darkness, good and evil, and human beings align themselves on either side. There will be an ultimate eschatological conflict between the powers of Light and the powers of Darkness. In the end a Saviour (*Saoshyant*) will appear in due season and join the good forces and, in consequence, the powers of Darkness will be overthrown and the earth renewed in unending youth and incorruption. Judaism derived this story and similar religious myths from Persian and other neighbouring cultures. And Christianity (as well as Islam later on) has for centuries carried with it these fundamental elements of Zarathustra's and the Jewish religions.

In addition to these religious roots we find the idea of political contradiction, related not to religion but rather to the struggle for power between and within nations during the ancient Greek era. This contradiction made its appearance in a permanent power struggle between Athens and Sparta and in opposition to Macedonia due to the rise of its power over the other Greeks. A fundamental theoretical and ideological expression of this was related to the differences between tyranny and democracy, and between tyranny and freedom.

Since Homeric times the most important divisive line has been between Athens and Sparta, starting with competition and rivalry for political superiority and culminating in a long and practically never-ending war. Even towards the final end of this violent competition,

Demosthenes in his early speeches was still referring to this distinction. According to him Athens was obliged 'not to allow Sparta to rise to a formidable power before the decline of Thebes, not to allow the desired balance of power to alter unperceived so that a Spartan rise exceeds the Theban decline'. He therefore suggested that the Athenians 'should not take the other line of wanting Sparta rather than Thebes as opponents, which is not what we require, but that neither shall have the power to injure ourselves'. Indeed, the Athenians had to take care of their own interests and not become actual members of the states they support instead of Athenians (*Greek Political Oratory*, 1985, p. 173).

An important suggestion made by Athens in several connections, and by Demosthenes in one of his early speeches, was that Athens was defending *democracy* against *dictatorships*. Athens waged war for *freedom*, it was defending *the weak and the poor* against *the rich and the strong*. Indeed, there could be no peace between democracies and oligarchies; Demosthenes said that it was better that 'all the Greeks should be our enemies under democracy than our friends under oligarchy', for:

> In dealing with free states, in my view, there is no difficulty about regaining peace, while with oligarchy even friendship is precarious. There can be no good feeling between oligarchy and democracy, between the desire for power and the aim at a life of equality. [*Greek Political Oratory*, 1985, p. 183]

The violent unification of Greece was the final solution to the power struggle. This approach was tacitly supported for example by Aristotle, the famous Macedonian (who for decades was looked upon with suspicion in Athens) and tutor to Alexander the Great. But Demosthenes actually acquired his unique fame with the speeches directed against Philip of Macedonia. Demosthenes emphasized, for example, that there is no safety for free states in over-familiarity with dictators, and that Philip's 'very titles are diametrically opposed to' freedom. Indeed, 'every king and every tyrant is an enemy of freedom and an opponent of law'. Therefore, 'take good care that in your eagerness to avoid war you do not acquire a despot'. Demosthenes suggested that if Philip's 'proceedings are peaceable' and 'without any doubts, seriously', then 'we should maintain peace'. But if—as Demosthenes thought—there were any doubts about Philip's intentions, then Athens was obliged to resist aggression. There was therefore no sense in talking about the distinction between war and peace: 'we have no choice' but 'we are left with the one most just and unavoidable course, which speakers like this deliberately overlook. What is that? Resistance to aggression' (*Greek Political Oratory*, 1985, pp. 235–6).

Speaking of the basis of European identity, it is mainly related to the enemy against which Europe is allegedly forced and felt obliged to fight. There have been several such enemies, but I shall concentrate on one of them: the Orient. In many senses, its role has been the most central.

Shiraz Dossa (1987) has suggested that while the East had always been perceived to be different from the West because of evident disparities in language and customs, no Greek in the archaic period attached moral or political significance to the differences perceived. The demarcation was made clear by Herodotus, whose subject was the struggle between Greece and the Persian Empire. However, the original situation was perhaps not so idyllic as Dossa suggests: fear of enemies (barbarians or non-Greeks) and hatred of them had their origins before Herodotus. The heroic defensive wars against the strong Persian power was perhaps the second wave in the crystallization of this opposition: the Trojan war was the first. But it is true that the Persian Empire as the enemy was functional to Greek unity, while the Trojan war was not. The expansion of Persia actually brought the Greeks together for defence, albeit temporarily, while the original unity with Agamemnon as the suzerain over all the other Greeks disappeared, according to Homer, during the Trojan war.

One can agree with Dossa on the point that the classical Greek political philosophy played an important role in the process. Political philosophy came to life as the staunch opponent of things Oriental: its articulation of the genius of the Occident presupposed the Orient as negation, signally lacking in salient respects. Plato and Aristotle created an ideal of politics where the notion of political space was almost sacred: it entailed a distinction between the inside and the outside. According to this picture, inside lay the promise and the possibilities of human accomplishment; on the outside, there were none. Indeed, the outside was not part of the human equation; outsiders were beneath even the underdogs on the inside; outsiders lacked the peculiar sensibility, the natural attributes and the rational talents of those within the circle.

There was a social need for this theory in the quest for Panhellenism. Indeed, the historian Xenophon (1984) and the great political orators Isocrates and Demosthenes argued for the idea of Panhellenism along similar lines. On every page of his *Anabasis*, Xenophon clearly brings out the contrast between Greek and barbarian. According to Xenophon the barbarian world was vast and diverse, feudal and ancient or tribal and savage, while the Greek world was compact, united by the sea, and essentially one in its approach to life. It was thought that the barbarians were, by nature, slavish and the ways of the barbarians were completely unacceptable to the civilized Greeks. More importantly, it was impossible to envisage trustful and solid relations between the Greeks and the Persians. Indeed, it was distrust that forced them to war:

> If, then, we want to make friends with them again, we shall have to be very downhearted indeed, when we consider what happened to our generals, who, because they trusted in their good faith, put themselves into their hands. [Xenophon, 1984, p. 149]

Isocrates refers to the fact that the word 'Greek' is not so much a term of birth as of mentality: it applies to a common culture rather than common descent. Therefore, the war against Persia was a holy war:

> This is the only war which is in fact preferable to peace. It is more like a religious mission than a campaign, and desirable for the advocates both of peace and of war, the former of whom would be enabled to harvest their gains in security, the latter to acquire great wealth from the possessions of others. [*Greek Political Oratory*, 1985, pp. 109, 135]

Later on, we can notice that Western Christendom perceived the Muslim world as a menace along the same lines. The Western image of the Muslim world came into sharper focus in the eleventh century, when it remained alone as the main enemy; warfare against it grew into a mobilization of all of Europe, and the Latin Christian world gradually developed its ideological unity. This produced a sharper image of the enemy's features and focused the energies of the West on the Crusades. In the process, the Islamic world came to be perceived as a hostile political and ideological system, which was also an utterly different civilization, a remote and foreign economic sphere (Rodinson, 1987, pp. 3–8).[3]

It is true that the picture became more realistic in some periods, leading even to an admiration of the Orient, but in any case, by the beginning of the nineteenth century a sense of Western superiority marked by pragmatism, imperialism, and utter contempt for other civilizations became dominant. And from the mid-nineteenth century on, imperialism more than any other factor determined the European image of the Orient. The economic, technical, military, political and cultural dominance of the West became decisive, and Iran and the Ottoman Empire were becoming little more than European protectorates. Outright colonization began to spread chiefly after 1881. This inevitably reinforced an already well-established Eurocentrism, which took on a very markedly contemptuous tinge. In much the same way and at the same time as the Yellow Peril, pan-Islam was becoming a fashionable bogey. Europe saw all resistance to its domination as a sinister conspiracy, inspired by a cruel spirit (Rodinson, 1987, pp. 64–7).

World War I shattered the complacent belief of European civilization in the continuity and limitlessness of its own progress (Rodinson, 1987, p. 71), and this process later continued in waves of anti-colonialism and decolonialization. Since the 1960s there has been a dramatic revolution in the old images, but at least part of the Orient none the less remains the enemy and a threat to Europe. During the 1960s and 1970s this role was played by the Arab countries, but after the revolution in 1979 Iran stole the role of monster. Thus many people in the West felt open sympathies towards Iraq, while Iran was perceived as dangerous to Western interests.

This background gives strong support to recent cultural theories emphasizing the functional role of dualistic distinctions in social life. According to them one must be able to tell the difference between friend and enemy, between those who commit crimes and those who follow the law, and so on. Otherwise there can be no social order. But the required distinctions cannot be based on objective factors, they can only be derived from mythologies and presented mythologically. One must create an illusion of evil and differences, and mythologies are required to make the illusions collective (Girard, 1977, pp. 89–118).

The relevance of the traditions of dualism

At the mention of these traditions of dualistic theories and images somebody may ask whether they have any relevance to the contemporary world? Perhaps earlier generations were not as enlightened as we are, and perhaps they were less rational and more religious than we. And if one refers to more recent phenomena such as the fear and hate of Iran and Islam, it readily emerges that there are many Europeans who think about it in less than stereotypic terms. However, the existence of the dualistic tradition in the contemporary world reveals that the roots of dualism are far from irrelevant.

In the first place, it is not quite impossible to think that religious institutions (the Church), educational processes (school) and general cultural mechanisms have transmitted the traditions to our age. Everybody living within the sphere of European culture (and many outside it, too) know by heart the old myths and stories. And we need not look too far to find philosophers, thinkers and schools transmitting the traditions from the ancient past to their and our contemporary world.

For instance, in the process by which religious contradictions have been handed down through European culture, one notes first of all the role of the Bible; this however is so well known that no further documentation is necessary. But in order to understand the emphasis on dualistic thinking—there are alternatives to it in the very same book—we must refer to the 'gate-keepers', persons and forces who have told us how to read and understand the Bible right. The role of the religious power structures established by Jesus and reproduced by the early Church has been decisive. The process might deserve careful analysis, but here I simply refer to St Augustine (and his relation to Manicheism) as an example.

Notwithstanding his conversion from Manicheism, St Augustine remains a dualist. According to Chydenius (1985) Augustinian dualism begins on the cosmological plane. Part of the angels have become evil, not because of their nature but out of free choice. Hence there has come into existence a society of good angels and a society of evil angels. Thus the opposition between the two angelic societies is not essential and eternal but has come into existence through a Fall which occurred at a certain point in time. But since only part of the angels fell, the rest remaining good, after the Fall the good society and the evil society existed side by side. The Augustinian dualism between the two societies is an instance of the simultaneous variant of existential dualism. With human beings, the story is slightly different. Human nature, too, was originally created good, though corruptible. But humanity fell into sin of its own free will and was corrupted in nature. Having once been good, human nature has become evil. But the new nature, which is an evil nature, is common to all people. Through the Fall, humanity has passed from a good state to an evil state. The dualism between humanity's original nature, which was good, and its fallen nature, which is evil, is an instance of the successive variant of existential dualism.[4]

Among more political transmitters we might refer, for instance, to Edmund Burke. In European political history he was the first to encounter and think about the contradictions between the different political systems in the modern sense. In Burke's opinion, there were no objective conflicts of interest between the two states. They simply represented two different political systems, and for Burke this difference was religious in the fundamental sense. Burke insisted on war, a holy war, aiming at the total destruction of the enemy and final and unconditional victory over it (see chapter 4 in this volume).

The existence of these transmitting mechanisms implies that it should not be too difficult to find expressions of the traditional dualisms in our world. And indeed, among the vast material available we can again take only examples. The first is a brief remark made by Maxime Rodinson:

> From a political and ideological perspective, if one compares the attitudes of Christianity toward Islam with those of Western capitalism toward communism today, the parallels are clear. In each grouping, two systems are at odds: yet within each system, a single dominant ideology unites divisive and hostile factions. [Rodinson, 1987, p. 9]

Rodinson's remark is self-evident; the only comment it may require is that one should not ignore the fact that the dualistic patterns, especially if related to the enemy, are functional to somebody along the lines of the cultural theories mentioned earlier.

My second example comes from Johan Galtung (1987), who discusses an archetype for US foreign policy. That archetype follows exactly the dualistic traditions discussed here. It maintains that the United States is 'a nation closer to God than any other, God's own country . . .'[5] To this way of thinking the construction of world space is simple and predictable. There are four parts of the world, suspended between good and evil. On the top is the United States, surrounded as second layer by the centre of the world, the allies that should satisfy at least two of three characteristics: a free market economy, faith in the Judaeo-Christian God, and free elections. In the next layer is the periphery, practically speaking identical with the Third World countries. And outside these countries is the fourth category of evil countries. The archetypal evil country would have neither a free market economy, nor the Judaeo-Christian faith, nor a democratic system.

In his analysis Galtung maintains that 'Satan might over time change manifestation, but always with a preference for one at a time.' So, 'Satan might, for instance, reject communism as his instrument, for instance, because communism becomes . . . too ineffective' and 'find a new instrument, terrorism, full of vigor'. In consequence, the pattern is 'a Judaeo-Christian construction with the possibility of making even major, quantitative jumps, like Saul becoming Paulus on the road to Damascus'. But the 'basic condition . . . is recognition of the United States as ultimate recognizer'. Galtung discerns two roads to 'salvation'. One is recognition, and submissiveness as its corollary. The other is to take on the 'characteristics of the Center in general and the United States in particular, more particularly free market mechanisms, Judaeo-Christian faith and free elections'.

One might suggest that Soviet political thought too is closely related to the European traditions. Therefore, it is no wonder to find Galtung's approach readily applicable to, for instance, Soviet theories of the class struggle (at the international level). Then of course one might find a mirror image of the American archetypes, reflecting rather similar basic structures of international conceptions.

Our last example is related to the symbolic meaning of nuclear weapons.[6] It has been suggested that symbols, in general, build a bridge between ourselves, with our limited abilities to conceive and understand, and that which by its nature transcends those limited abilities. This bridge-building is an aspect of the human need for structure, differentiation, and orientation in space and time, a sense of distinction between 'me' and 'not-me'. This leads directly to a situation which fosters attitudes of extreme dualism: the quest for security turns into a battle of absolute good against absolute evil. Nuclear weapons add a unique and really powerful feature to this absolutism. If one finds absolute protection and absolute safety in weapons of absolute power, the dualism of 'our side' and 'the enemy' becomes absolute too; it becomes emotionally essential to believe in an absolute enemy. The enemy as a real flesh-and-blood individual disappears, to be replaced by 'the enemy' as an abstraction embodying total and irredeemable evil. This, again, is functional: fear of the enemy is always fear for our world, its order, its stability, its meaningfulness. Even if there is a desire for life, safety and peace, these might be sacrificed in order to preserve the whole—and the fundamental principle governing the whole is absolute dualism, symbolized by and magnified by the bomb. All this may seem to reflect the power of reason. The balance aimed at by means of the bomb and deterrence is to be achieved and maintained through human reason; this vision of perfection seems to assure us that the real enemy, unpredictable irrational instability, can be vanquished for ever. But in fact this vision is mainly mythological as well as apocalyptic: the bomb and nuclear war will deal the enemy the final blow. That is, human reason has given a unique opportunity for God to intercede in the battle as a mighty warrior and to set the world right through violent punishment of evil.

Common humanity as an alternative to dualism

The cultural heritage of religious/political contradictions and related enemy images tends to make the solution of conflicts impossible. A basic tenet of this heritance of dualism is that the opponent must be annihilated: there is no room for compromise. My analysis has thus produced a rather critical and pessimistic answer to the question of European unification: all-European unification is likely to remain impossible; Europe will rather remain divided into two or more opposing 'camps', even if their actual constellation may in the future differ from that now prevailing. And quite different interests may speak for Europeanism but for quite different reasons.

Indeed, if the idea of Europeanism is to be realized, it will inevitably be based on dualism. Europeanism will not be an alternative to dualism, Europeanism is from beginning to end just a new application of dualistic patterns. And in this application, there are candidates for the role of common, unifying enemy: Islam in religion, Japan and the other Pacific–Asian countries in economic competition, and the United States in economics, politics and security. Thus, there remain two roads: either an exclusive West European unification against the USSR, the USA and Japan, or an all-European unification against 'outside enemies'. This gives no encouraging promises of world peace, while within Europe there is a danger that the unification process will require internal enemies—the first signs of racism in Europe are already visible.

If the idea of Europeanism is an inherently dualistic and political concept, as I maintained earlier, Europeanism cannot be accepted in any critical perspective; a more constructive alternative to dualism must be found. This however, is no easy task. Casting about for alternatives which would eliminate the dangerous heritage, make possible the coexistence of different systems, and open up new possibilities of compromise, one must answer an important question: are there any alternatives to the dualistic way of thinking? Unfortunately, the answer may be negative. Suggestions are likely to speak in terms of 'universal brotherhood' or 'world government' and so forth, immediately labelled as unrealistic by the majority of people—the majority take the dualistic pictures for granted, and anything deviating from it cannot be true, realistic or feasible (Chernus, 1987, p. 40). Johan Galtung (1987) likewise emphasizes that 'the basic metaphor' is so deeply ingrained in the US population that the freedom of choice is seriously curtailed: If the American people were to be deprived of their basic beliefs, 'the construction—meaning the USA—might well collapse'. The belief may be false, but its removal might have deeper implications than unhappiness—'some kind of more basic disintegration might follow'. This is also envisaged in the social cultural theories according to which the distinctions between good and evil, between friend and foe, form the very basis of society.

But there are no alternatives to alternatives: the task is to find alternatives which would organize human associations in another (i.e.

more peaceful and constructive) way. Here one might ask, in first place, whether there are any alternatives within the European cultural heritage. Another approach might be to examine ideas from other cultures; this could lead to new insight and expanding understanding, only unfortunately alternatives from other cultures are likely to be irrelevant and unacceptable to the European mind.

The European cultural heritage itself has in fact offered potential alternatives—only they have been forgotten or even suppressed; in power struggles they have been supported only by minorities and, in general, they have been of no significance in winning these struggles.

One source of alternatives is to be found in religious traditions. Jesus Christ, the apostles and the early Christian writers, and to a minor degree the early Church too, replaced dualism with the conception of a unitary and universal community, the *mundus*. We remember, too, the maxim of loving our enemies, even if its introducer was crucified and the message has been taken seriously by 'outsiders' only (by some religious sects and integral pacifists between the twelfth and seventeenth centuries, Leo Tolstoy and some others). More recently Johan Galtung (1987) too has suggested that a key to the future is God:

> Who said that God of the US–God covenant is the God of hard Christianity, a tribal, jealous, revengeful, vindictive, even cruelly aggressive God as reported in the first books of the Old and the last book of the New Testament? Who said that it could not also be the God of soft-line Christianity, compassionate and merciful, with no particular Chosen People or Chosen Peoples—only *chosen human beings*, including *those who claim that they reject Him*? [Galtung, 1987]

In a more political debate, the Stoic *cosmopolis* is well known from the late Greek and the early Roman era. Still later, according to the Gelasian theory (formulated by Pope Gelasius I) 'we are still within the sphere of the universal community, the cosmopolis or *mundus*'. During the Carolingian era the universal community was again 'the Church', but the Stoic cosmopolis was not supplanted by the Christian Church. The cosmopolis was then identified not only with the Empire but also with the Church. It was conceived that there is, in fact, only one universal community (the *mundus-cosmopolis*, the *imperium–res publica* or the *ecclesia–corpus Christi*) and that this universal community had two authorities, the priest and the king, the former taking precedence over the latter (Chydenius, 1985, pp. 33–4).

We also remember humanism as a philosophy which recognizes the value or dignity of man and makes him the measure of all things. It has been and is popular to speak of a universal human nature or essence. A recent contribution in this area is the concept of universal values applying to all human beings, or common human values (*allgemeinmenschliche Werte*), and common humanity (*Allgemeinmenschlichkeit*). Common humanity consists of factors, conditions and values that enhance the development of humankind and co-operation/ peace among human beings.

Criticism, however, should be brought to bear on any alternatives as well. For example, the idea of common human values may be an alternative to dualism, but there are certain dangers inherent in such universalism. Talk of universalism leads all too easily to talk of imperialism. And this holds true within 'Europe' as in the world at large. We know that the cultural area of which Europe is the centre[7] has undergone considerable expansion—through an extremely violent process. In an uninterrupted process, the expansion of Europe from the sixteenth century onward resulted in the occupation by Europe of the whole of the American continent. During the nineteenth century and until after World War I, European imperialism extended its domination over the whole globe, with the partial exception of Japan. The global superiority of Europe in both technology and ideas was at the time total—and this tends to be the case in the contemporary world as well (Chaliand & Rageau, 1986).

Notes

1. Johan Galtung (1987) speaks of archetypes, which 'are raw material out of which the social cosmology of a people is made, the assumptions built into deep ideology and deep structure, never to be questioned'.
2. This expression was coined by Deng Xiaoping, along the traditional lines of the cyclic images of *ying* and *yang*, at the beginning of the 1980s to justify and make possible the reunification of China and Taiwan. The slogan was applied to the Hong Kong Treaty of 1984 and the Macao Treaty of 1978. Hong Kong and Macao will be joined to China, but they will retain their social and political systems at least fifty years afterwards. Deng has promised that Taiwan will even have an independent foreign policy and armed forces of its own.
3. While Edward W. Said (1978) sees 'Orientalism' in a clear-cut negative light, Maxime Rodinson (1987) gives a more detailed and many-sided picture of this phenomenon. See also Arkoun (1987).
4. The dualism of St Augustine is quite consistent with his conversion to Neoplatonism, too. Neoplatonism certainly differs from Manicheism inasmuch as it does not regard evil as a substance but as the privation of good. But it nevertheless implies a dualism between the principles of good and evil (Chydenius, 1985, pp. 11–13).
5. Galtung quotes President Taft, who said in 1912: 'We are not going to intervene in Mexico until no other course is possible, but I must protect our people in Mexico as far as possible, and their property, by having the

government in Mexico understand that there is a God in Israel and he is on duty. Otherwise they will utterly ignore our many great complaints and give no attention to needed protection which they can give.'

6. My summary is based on Chernus (1987), whose study belongs to comparative religion. However, these ideas reflect many other fields as well; for instance, similar notions have been suggested in peace research dealing with language and culture and their relationship to armaments.
7. The concept of Europe and European should be seen to transcend the 'European' geographical area and manufactured maps: the roots of the European mind stretch far back into non-European soils. And the influence of European culture has even wider extensions; the European cultural heritage can be found all over the world (especially in the United States).

Bibliography

Arkoun, M., 1987. *Rethinking Islam Today.* Washington: Center for Contemporary Arab Studies, Georgetown University, Occasional Papers Series.

Chaliand, G. & J-P. Rageau, 1986. *Strategic Atlas.* Harmondsworth: Penguin Books.

Chernus, I., 1987. *Dr. Strangegod–On the Symbolic Meaning of Nuclear Weapons.* Boulder: University of South Carolina Press.

Chydenius, J., 1985. *Humanism in Medieval Concepts of Man and Society.* Commentationes Humanarum Litterarum 77. Helsinki: Societas Scientiarum Fennica.

Dossa, S., 1987. 'Political Philosophy and Orientalism: The Classical Origins of a Discourse', *Alternatives*, vol. 12, no. 2.

Galtung, J., 1987. *United States Foreign Policy: As Manifest Theology.* IGCC Policy Paper, no. 4, University of California Institute of Global Conflict and Cooperation.

Gay, P., 1978. *Freud, Jews and Other Germans.* Oxford: Oxford University Press.

Girard, R., 1977. *Violence and the Sacred.* London: Johns Hopkins University Press.

Greek Political Oratory, 1985 (trans. A.N.W. Saunders). Harmondsworth: Penguin Books.

Rodinson, M., 1987. *Europe and the Mystique of Islam.* Seattle: University of Washington Press.

Said, E.W., 1978. *Orientalism.* New York: Pantheon Books.

Xenophon, 1984. *The Persian Expedition* (trans. Rex Warner). Harmondsworth: Penguin Books.

2 Heroism, the Construction of Evil, and Violence

James A. Aho

Warfare is an occasion of calculated mutual violation. The violation of human beings requires their social construction into certain kinds of things, namely, embodiments of evil. The sociology of reification elucidates the procedures groups use to manufacture evil-doers. The sociology of heroism explains why groups undertake such constructions in the first place. Together, the two theories constitute an emerging, comprehensive social anthropology of collective violence.

The sociology of heroism

The general theory of heroism and its relationship to violence was first articulated by the late Ernest Becker (Becker, 1968; 1973; 1975). Its axioms can be succinctly stated: All organisms want to 'feel good', to maximize pleasure and minimize pain. But human beings are not merely their bodies; human needs are more than just biological. They are also symbolic and spiritual. Human beings yearn to 'feel good about themselves'. They need to know their existences are somehow significant in the cosmos, that they are justified. To use Becker's phraseology, human beings need to know themselves as heroes.

The tactics used throughout history publicly to display and solicit acknowledgement of human greatness constitute a thesaurus of cultural anthropology. They vary from the accumulation of riches to having numerous progeny (who as they extend one's life germ, symbolically extend one's self), from gathering degrees and honours to completing projects and expeditions, from ascetic denials of one's biological appetites (including as in *hara kiri* and suttee the denial of life itself to obtain greater life) to what interests us here: the heroic redemption of the world.

The cultural motif of heroic world redemption is not unique to European culture. Not only can the Islamic *jihad* (the struggle for *jihada*, righteousness) and the *peregrinatio pro Christi* (the armed pilgrimage to the Holy Land to cleanse it of the Antichrist) be understood as elaborate, violent ceremonies conducted in the service of order and sanity; so too can the Aztec *guerra florida* (the object of which was to secure a harvest of 'tuna flowers', human hearts, for the nourishment of the god of light in his fight against chaos), Hinduism's 'conquest of regions', to preserve the world from moral anarchy (*apattikala*), and even the sublime martial arts of China and Japan.

Nevertheless, it is also true that social order and the heroic labour to save it have been conceived differently in various civilizations. In the Orient, for example, anomy is experienced as a rupture in the unchanging impersonal cosmic order – call it Tao – and world-redemptive gestures typically take the form of egolessly realigning private and public affairs with this eternal Way. As Confucius teaches: To 'hit the mark' in archery is not the same as to go through the leather target. That, he says, is a measure of brute strength, and that is the 'old way', the way of the barbarian. Rather, the goal is stylistically, but effortlessly, to shoot in accordance with the rules of the ceremony, including shooting in harmony with flute and drum. In this sense, the true hero or 'superior man' (*chün tzu*) does not stand out in the manner of the prototypical blustering warrior hero of the West who, like Samson the Nazarite, screams his outrage at injustice, and then in God's name, rips down houses, burns vineyards, and slays sinners by the score. Instead, he becomes silent and invisible; he is absorbed into a cycle infinitely larger than himself.

In civilizations that have come under Judaeo-Christian and Muslim influence – which is to say, among others, modern Europe – chaos is experienced as the product of disobedience of ethical duties, not mere ritual infractions, as these are revealed through prophecy. Here, then, the heroic task becomes one not of passively yielding to the Way, but of energetically taking up weapons to reform the world after the personal commandments of the holy one. The Occidental holy war functions to sterilize the world of an alien darkness or disease, not to reconcile people to its inevitability, particularly its inevitability in themselves. It is this type of world-saving effort that is the focus of concern in the following pages.

For adherents of either traditional or secularized versions of Occidental faiths, the earthly world is 'fallen' and susceptible to heroic intervention. But no social movement can transform the world all at once in its entirety. Therefore it focuses its righteous indignation and redemptive energy on a 'fetish' of evil: a despicable act, a heretical belief, a foreign place, an alien people or a criminal individual, which is placated, imprisoned, expulsed or exterminated. The word 'fetish' implies the largely fantastic, sometimes hysterical, almost always capricious nature of bestowals of the title 'evil-doer'. Collective fetishism is tragic, says Becker, 'precisely because it is sometimes very arbitrary: men make fantasies about evil, see it in the wrong places, and destroy themselves and others by uselessly thrashing about' (Becker, 1975, p. 148).

The dialectic of heroism

As applied to the work of world redemption, the dialectic of heroism can be seen as comprising three moments. In the first, an ideal is imagined: democracy, equality, peace, brotherhood, universal love, freedom, racial purity, moral perfection, the conversion of all peoples to the 'true' faith, and so on. In the second moment the actuality of the real world is counterpoised to the ideal. This is the inexorable *Is* in opposition to the *Should Be*: inequality, tyranny, mistrust, cynicism and indifference, miscegenation, corruption, the babel of faiths, heresy, apostasy and violence. From the experience of contradiction issues suffering, pathos, and *com-pathos*, compassion for others. To eradicate his own pain and what is suffered for others sympathetically, the hero embarks on the third and decisive moment in his quest: transformative labour, courageous, persistent effort to embody the ideal in the concrete. This is the doubt-filled, exhausting, morally risky toil to reconcile 'essence' with existence.

To use Hegelian imagery, the successful completion of the heroic task may be spoken of as the realization of the ideal and the idealization of the real. In it the hero appropriates the alienated object world back to himself, making it his own. He reconciles his 'insides', his ideals, with what is outside himself, and in so doing experiences a sense of joy in the union of subject and object. But the heroic quest does not always end happily. While the more formidable the contradiction between real and ideal the greater the psychological reward in reconciling it, the greater too are the hazards of compromise and failure. Emotionally the most compelling heroic struggles take place at the very point where fulfilment and tragedy meet. Holy war, war to reform the world after a transcendent ideal, employs the most craven means. Hence as the Old Testament, the *Mahabharata*, the *Iliad*, the Eddas, and the Sagas, indeed all the world's great mythic literature understands, it is the pre-eminent stage for heroic dramatization.

Heroic violence and reification

The prototypical warrior hero needs a fetish of evil, without one there is nothing against which to fight, nothing from which to save the world, nothing to give his life meaning. What this means, of course, is that if an evil-doer is not ontologically given in the nature of things, one must be manufactured. The Nazi needs an international Jewish banker and conspiratorial Mason to serve his own purposes of self-aggrandizement, and thus sets about creating one, at least unconsciously. By the same token, the radical Zionist is locked in perverse symbiosis with his Palestinian persecutors, the Communist with his imperialistic capitalist running dogs, and the capitalist with his Communist subversives.

It would be the height of insipience to deny that there are bona fide conflicts of interest out of which mutual hostilities emerge. Part of the impetus of the peace studies programme is to reduce international hatreds that threaten war by demonstrating to national leaders that in light of the self-destructive consequences of building and deploying modern weaponry, they share an interest in peace. Without disrupting the validity of this programme, the theory presented here suggests, on the contrary, that groups also sometimes fabricate conflicts of interest with convenient evil-doers in order to struggle against them, so as to dramatize their own significance.

However this may be, the sociology of reification describes the steps in the social manufacture of evil-doers. These steps are analogous to those first articulated by Peter Berger and Thomas Luckmann in their ground-breaking classic, *The Social Construction of Reality* (Berger & Luckmann, 1967). Briefly, this book rests on the familiar Kantian distinction between noumena and phenomena. The first refers to the world-in-itself (as seen, so to speak, by God); the second to the world-as-it-appears, or as it is experienced by human beings. The idea is that in so far as human beings can never directly know things-in-themselves, we should henceforth redirect our attention to phenomenology, that is, to the study of the experience of things. Phenomenological sociology has since taken upon itself two tasks: describing in detail the contents of the world as it is experienced by differently situated people, and second, analysing how that world experience has come into being, how it was 'constructed'. In essence, the world is said to be constructed stepwise through the process of reification.

The process of reification

'Reification', literally, means the way in which figments of the imagination, words and ideas return to haunt their makers by coming to be experienced as objects with independent lives. Indeed, a commonly used equivalent to reification is the term 'objectivation'. Whatever word is chosen, it refers to the manner by which people come to experience their created social world in an incorrect or false way (false consciousness). To say it in another way, it is the manner by which people come to experience the social world as *sui generis*, a thing for which they have no responsibility, over which they have no power, and which they must passively suffer as victims do their fate. God, says Ludwig Feuerbach, is originally a projection of Mankind's own image and likeness. But this divine Project quickly assumes a life of its own, presenting itself to human consciousness as mankind's Creator, the Lord to which they must pay obeisance. This is the theoretical basis of the Marxian notion of commodity production and alienation.

Peter Berger and Thomas Luckmann itemize the process by which reification occurs: naming, legitimation, myth-making, 'sedimentation', and ritual. No claim is made that these steps occur in this particular sequence. Furthermore, later research may find that more than these five steps are involved in the process. In any case, thus far the theory has been profitably used by social psychologists to understand how, for example, death and dying are 'accomplished' in hospitals (Sudnow, 1967), how illness (as opposed to disease) is socially 'constructed', how insanity is 'manufactured' (Szasz, 1970), how criminality, delinquency (Cicourel, 1968), addiction (Szasz, 1974), and even incapacitating blindness (Scott, 1969) are collectively fabricated by the sometimes well-intended, sometimes cynical collusion of physicians, courts, social scientists, families and well-doers at the expense of unwitting victims. The theory can easily be extrapolated to the field of evil-doers and evil-doing generally, to the whole panoply of witches, commies, Nazis, terrorists, micks, niggers, Japs, gooks, pigs, fags, and pushers, and the myriad of 'Others', *harbies*[2], and aliens that have been selected throughout recent history to play the role of foil to the world-redeeming hero in the theatre of self-aggrandizement.

Naming

Jack Douglas says 'Our motto must be, "The world of social meanings is problematic until proven otherwise" ' (1984, p. 13). Phenomenological sociology begins with the observation that what is ordinarily taken as unproblematic and absolute—for example, good and evil—are in fact subject to negotiation. Persons, acts or situations are in and of themselves neither good nor evil. They come to be seen as such, when they do, by virtue of the meanings given them in the course of everyday social life.[1]

One of the crucial steps in the negotiation of meanings is naming or, as it is more popularly known, 'labeling' (Becker, 1963). As applied to the subject at hand, it is not uncommon in the course of public (journalism) and private (gossip) discourse for defamatory labels to be imposed flippantly on persons, acts or situations that are not quite as they supposedly 'should' be. At times such labels are bestowed on the basis of a loose, intuitive 'fit' between the person, his or her actions and background, and the formal criteria for its usage. At still other times, particularly during moments of mass hysteria, defamatory labels are bandied about arbitrarily and fix on anyone who by chance happens in the way.

Furthermore, while 'nut', 'slut', 'fag', and categories of far more dangerous import—'heretic', 'terrorist group', 'Communist', 'soft-core fascist'—may be used innocently, with the labeller unconscious of any malicious intent, they are even more often used cynically to destroy careers and enhance political and national causes. Whichever is the case, the point is that defamatory words rarely, if ever, simply describe things; they also rhetorically 'accomplish' them. And what they accomplish is a victim, an evil-doer, ready for violation. In short, the child's ditty—'Sticks and stones may break my bones, but words will never hurt me'—is patently untrue. Defamatory language prepares audiences cognitively and emotionally to take up sticks and stones.[3]

Legitimation

It is one thing to defame others; it is another for such labels to 'stick'. If labels are to adhere to the intended victim they must be validated. One vehicle for effecting this is the public degradation ceremony. This is a formal hearing, trial, inquisition or tribunal presided over by presumed experts licensed to issue disparaging judgments on their fellows (Goffman, 1956). As analysed by Irving Goffman, however much such ceremonies may differ in detail, those that actually 'work' in reconstituting people into beings appropriate for exile or destruction must meet several necessary and sufficient conditions: (a) They must be held in extra-ordinary, hallowed precincts, on sacred ground, at sacred time, with the victim and executioners alike arrayed in special costumery. All the actors, including the victim, must in addition assume an attitude of solemn reverance toward the proceedings. (b) The accusers called to testify against the victim must show themselves to be motivated by patriotic concern for 'tribal values' alone, not by private considerations of vengeance, envy, greed, etc. (c) These tribal values must be made explicit. (d) The accusers must demonstrate that nothing in the victim's life is accidental, but is part of a uniform *Gestalt* or action type, 'evil', however this is conceived—for example, 'dirty red'. (e) This type must, furthermore, be rhetorically counterpoised to its opposite, let us say, 'Christian American', of self-evident virtue and dignity (and of which the accusers must be examples).

Research on ceremonies meeting these conditions, *regardless of their formal outcomes*, indicates that they have unanticipated, pernicious consequences for the accused (Schwartz & Skolnick, 1964). They have the effect of contaminating the accused and of confirming in the eyes of the masses the accused's guilt, insanity, addiction, subversiveness, apostasy or satanism. That is to say, the ceremony itself, if properly conducted, serves a latent social function of victimization. Each society, it has been argued, keeps a stable of mostly poor, uneducated and diseased aliens either within or outside its gates, to appear as the accused in rites of degradation. Seen as people of little other social utility, this is their primary function in life. They are used in successive re-enactments of degradation rites during which the tribal values of the community are revivified in the eyes of the spectators, and by which (through their degradation) the community is symbolically repeatedly 'saved' (Irwin, 1985).

Myth-making

'Myth-making refers to the provision of retrospective biographical or historical accounts of defamed persons that show why it is inevitable, necessary and predicted that they be and act as they do, namely, as evil-doers. It is a second device groups use to validate the labels they bestow on others.

Sometimes myth-making occurs after the 'successful' outcome of a public degradation ceremony, as in a pre-sentencing report (Shover, 1974). In such cases their composition must also be written in bureaucratic jargon, and must show how the victim's case fits the official 'scientific' theory of evil in favour at the time, whether genetic, psychological or sociological. For example, the victim is said to have come from a broken home, was abused by his parents, had a 'culture of poverty', or had a genetic propensity for evil as indicated by his body build, facial features or skin colour (Ryan, 1971).

Where no ceremonial judgment has been passed on the victim, myth-making may proceed outside official channels, the reconstruction of the past lives of evil-doers becoming even more fanciful and fablistic. Every reform movement keeps for this purpose a staff of fablists, nowadays trained in the use of a variety of media, including moving pictures and television docudramas.

In the Christian world perhaps the most notorious example of a fictional literature that reifies human beings into evil objects is that concerning its archetypal enemy, the Jew. Included in this are *The Talmud Unmasked* and *Der Talmudjude*, written by the nineteenth-century Catholic priests Justin Pranaitis and August Rohling, and used by generations of anti-Semites as authentic sourcebooks of Jewish belief and practice (Katz, 1980). Still another is the infamous *Protocols of the Learned Elders of Zion*, a plagiarism of a novel by an obscure German, Herman Goedesh, who himself evidently stole the plot from an earlier anti-Napoleonic tract by Maurice Joly. It pretends to detail the tactics used by the High Jewish Council, the Sanhedrin, in its quest for world domination (Cohn, 1967).

Sedimentation

Once experience has been formulated in word and myth it is capable of being transmitted from one person to the next or, more significantly, across generations. In its linguistic transmission the original experience becomes available to those who have never had it. This is what is meant by 'sedimentation', a particularly powerful stage in the process of reification (Berger & Luckmann, 1967, pp. 67–72). Through it word and myth come to have lives of their own. They become detached from the original act of naming or myth-making and evolve into anonymous parts of the everyday taken-for-granted 'stock of knowledge' of a society. What was at first a defamatory label, perhaps nonchalantly thrown out in the course of idle gossip or irresponsible editorializing, becomes with each retelling 'common sense', what everybody 'knows' to be true about 'them', the evil-doers.

As the sedimentation (inculcation) of a defamatory myth in the minds of a new generation occurs, several things follow: (a) Its subtleties and qualifying details are abstracted and it becomes more concise. (b) The essential defamatory points of the myth are sharpened for recall. (c) It is stylized into a mnemonic formula.

One example: Jacob Katz, the author of *From Prejudice to Destruction*, sketches the development of the Judaeophobic mythos of Christian Europe that prepared it for its genocidal crusade, from the erudite scholarship of Lutheran professor Johan Eisenmenger, who flourished in 1700, down to the pious, mechanical cant of Nazi fablists.

Another example: The celebrated geneticist Theodore Dobzhansky carefully describes how genotype and environment jointly influence IQ test scores, and illustrates his argument by pointing to the relatively low mean IQ scores for Black American conscripts in World War I (Dobzhansky, 1962, pp. 10–22). One of Dobzhansky's statements is lifted out of context by University of Alabama racist biologist Wesley George (retired) in his tract, *The Biology of the Race Problem*, to support the claim that intellectual ability is not distributed equally between races (George, 1962, pp. 46–8). George, in turn, is cited in Ku-Klux-Klan literature to validate the inflammatory formula that the 'negroidal race' is closer to the ape than to man.

Ritual

Human memory is fickle and the mythological lessons imprinted on new minds must be continually reimpressed. The pre-eminent pedagogy for this is ritual, the vivid re-enactment of the myth's essential themes. In its dramatization the 'truth' of the myth is reconfirmed. What is collectively believed and was momentarily at risk of being forgotten is recognized. Society is preserved from chaos (Durkheim, 1954).

Looked at broadly, most of society's practices—its folk-ways, conventions and laws—are little more than ritual re-enactments of its cultural myths. Social life as a whole is a perpetual motion machine: its rituals feeding its myths, its myths informing its rituals. Viewed this way, ritual is probably the most seminal stage in reification, in the rendering of ideas and thoughts into tangible things.

The culminating step in the social construction of the evil-doer proceeds as follows: The 'good guys', as they honour themselves, ritualistically respond to those they have designated evil in the 'appropriate' way, that is, with secrecy, caution and cunning and, if necessary, with cruelty. To act in any other way is to be unrealistic; after all, it is of their nature that evil-doers prey on the non-vigilant. Any mercy extended them would only invite their aggression, any openness would only reveal our own mortal weaknesses, and our trust would only be repaid with duplicity. But being rational in their own right, evil-doers respond to these gestures precisely as expected, which is to say, 'evilly—with conspiratorialism, distrust, wiliness and savagery. In this way the prophecy of the good guys concerning the diabolism of the bad is uncannily fulfilled. The truth of the myth is sustained.

Routine combat against society's internal and external enemies (respectively, the judicial system and warfare) clearly illustrates this maddeningly vicious cycle. Both institutions endlessly generate the very evil-doers they are supposedly set up to protect society against. In trying to engineer an end to this cycle, peace studies faces a formidable problem: war, preparations for war, imprisonment and execution have the effect of reconfirming dearly held myths concerning evil others, relative to whom we are good. Despite their terrible costs, then, they provide a perverse sense of security. History teaches that human beings sometimes choose to die in heroic combat against evil-doers rather than contemplate the unsettling possibility that their beloved myths might be fundamentally wrong.

Transcending Manicheism

> Imagine the 'enemy' as conceived by the man of ressentiment [that is, the heroic world reformer]—and here precisely is his deed, his creation: he has conceived 'the evil enemy', '*the evil one*'—and indeed as the fundamental concept from which he then derives, as an afterimage and counter-instance, a 'good one'—himself. [Nietzsche, 1967, part 1, sect. 10]

In these words Friedrich Nietzsche summarizes our argument: fetishes of evil are socially constructed and then systematically destroyed so that the world is saved and that executioners might sense their heroic significance. In ancient times, this was accomplished by ritualistically placing upon the head of a goat the community's sins and then exiling the goat, with the sins, into the desert. Having the advantage of distance we now see this for what it truly was, a magical practice of collective delusion. Our first task as devotees of peace studies is to realize that while clothed in scientific garb and armed with nuclear bombs and satellite laser beams, we are like the ancients: ethical primitives. Our second task is to begin composing an ethics for our age, an ethics transcending evil fetishism. For it is not enough simply to illuminate our moral blindness. We must also propose remedies. Failure to do so can only result in nihilism.

What, then, might a non-fetishistic ethics look like?

First, to the extent that Ernest Becker's claim is accurate—that the yearning for cosmic significance is built into human nature—then a non-fetishistic ethics will take this as a starting point for its deliberations. In other words, a non-fetishistic ethics will also be a realistic ethics. And this means it will place humanity's most idealistic cravings for heroic transcendence in the forefront of attention. To do otherwise would be to relegate it to the realm of whimsy (Becker, 1975, pp. 46–75).

Second, a non-fetishistic ethics will acknowledge that the strategy of sensing one's greatness by saving the world cannot be dismissed out of hand as misguided. After all, the very concept of peace studies is predicated on the hope and conviction that we can put under conscious control our destructive powers and 'save the world'. As we saw earlier, a fundamental archetype of European culture, if not of the human psyche, is to nominize human affairs, to create *nomos* where before there was *anomos*.

Third—and this is crucial—given the immense dangers posed by unreflective heroic posturing in a technological age like ours with its destructive potential, a non-fetishistic ethics will require that redemptive gestures be uncompromisingly conscious. That is, it will tirelessly point out how evil-doers and evil things are generated again and again to serve the interests of well-doers. But this is to say that a non-fetishistic ethics will begin by acknowledging that the righteous are always and inevitably in some essential way responsible for the evils against which they so assiduously labour. The evil they fear and loathe is in themselves, just as it is 'out there' embodied in the 'Other'. To feast on our own subjective evil instead of reflexively projecting outward is a precondition of civilized conduct towards the enemy. What such conduct might consist of in specific conflict situations cannot be answered here.

This is not the place to trace in detail the appearance of this kind of ethical discourse in our times (but see Neumann, 1969). It is enough to make the following cursory observations:

First, this new way of ethical thinking is a basic component of what has been called 'feminist' metaphysics, which begins by rejecting hackneyed 'patriarchal', absolutist divisions between spirit and matter, mind and body, God and man, and most importantly, us and them. In other words, it begins with consciousness of the subtle and complementary unity of all things.

Second, this new way of ethical thinking is not the monopoly of a few cloistered academicians, but has evolved into something approaching a *Zeitgeist* in which we all, Europeans and Americans, knowingly or not, increasingly participate. It finds expression both in the ecological movement and in the world citizenship movement, of which peace studies is a minor offshoot.

Third, the disavowal of fetishistic ethics is not so novel after all, but is a collective reappropriation of our own European (including Muslim) cultural heritage. It is a drinking more deeply from the well of our own received tradition of wisdom. It is found both in the Occidental religious notion of all humanity's Fall from grace and in the 'pagan' Indo-Aryan appreciation that the opposition between enemies is in part illusory. In the Indo-Aryan epic, the *Mahabharata*, for example, the great battle of the Bharatas is fought between what appear at first to be diametrically opposed forces, the righteous white-skinned Pandus and the infamous, black-skinned Kurus. As the tale proceeds, however, it is shown how the Pandus conquer their foes through resort to diabolical means, urged upon them by the Lord Himself, Krishna. In the end the righteous are shown for what they truly are: blood-brothers of evil, with the Kurus offspring of the same father Vyasa, himself son of the daughter of truth, Satyavati. Absolute good and evil is, we are taught, *maya*, an illusion.

(It should be added that the point of the *Mahabharata* is not to discourage struggle against moral anarchy. On the contrary, elsewhere it is taught that he who out of fear of sinning fails to resist evil commits thereby an even greater wrong. Rather, the point is that Manicheistic dualism, as emotionally satisfying as it might be, is both intellectually dishonest and morally hazardous.)

Fourth, it is ironic that our recent glimpse of these ancient truths has come to us not in friendly guise, garbed in life, light and beauty, but in the most despicable form imaginable; the death, darkness and horror of our penultimate technological creation, the bomb. Again, this should not surprise us. The righteous Pandu brothers are likewise provoked into recognizing their own unavoidable complicity in evil only when, after a post-battle victory celebration, a disgusting apparition visits their camp one evening:

> The warriors in the Pandu camp beheld Death-night in her embodied form, black, of bloody mouth and bloody eyes, wearing crimson garlands and smeared with crimson ungents, attired in a single piece of red cloth, with a noose in hand, and resembling an elderly lady, employed in chanting a dismal note and standing full before their eyes. . . . [Quoted in Aho, 1981, p. 222]

Fifth and most importantly, development of a non-fetishistic ethics, an ethics for our age, an ethics transcending Manicheistic political routines, has not come from cool logical deduction of specific prescriptions from abstract theoretical principles. Instead it has arisen from a deeply personal, painfully shocking awakening of Europeans and Americans from our ego-identification with moral purity. Psychologists speak of this as a 'psychic wound' which has seared us with grief, guilt, shame and terror. In ancient times, this wound was symbolized in Indo-Aryan mythology by the *vajra*, the diamond-lightning bolt of insight that slashes through even the most obdurate illusion of self-righteousness. Perhaps today's equivalent to the *vajra* bolt is 'the light brighter than a thousand suns', the illuminating flash of the bomb. With the Pandu brother we too cry out, 'Although victory hath been ours, O Krishna, our heart, however, is yet trembling with doubt. . . . The foe who were vanquished [i.e. evil] have been victorious! Misery looks like prosperity; and prosperity . . . like misery.'

Notes

1. It should be understood that this is an axiom of phenomenological sociology only. Once the present author takes off his sociological glasses, so to speak, he experiences the world as others ordinarily do, namely as a place wherein, among other things, good and evil are entirely unproblematic and given in the 'nature' of things. Following the suggestion of Edmund Husserl, the practice of phenomenological sociology involves the systematic 'bracketing' or suspension of belief in the taken-for-granted world.
2. *Harbie* is the Islamic archfiend.
3. For the political murder of a Seattle, Washington family of four mistakenly labeled as Jewish Communists, see Aho (1987).

Bibliography

Aho, J, 1981. *Religious Mythology and the Art of War.* Westport, Conn.: Greenwood.

Aho, J, 1987. 'Reification and Sacrifice: The Goldmark Case', *California Sociologist,* vol. 10.

Becker, E, 1973. *The Denial of Death.* New York: Free Press.

Becker, E, 1975. *The Structure of Evil.* New York: Free Press.

Becker, H, 1968. *The Outsiders.* Glencoe, Ill.: Free Press.

Berger, P & Luckmann, T, 1967. *The Social Construction of Reality.* Garden City, NY: Doubleday-Anchor.

Camus, A, 1956. *The Rebel.* New York: Vintage.

Cicourel, A, 1968. *The Social Organization of Juvenile Justice.* New York: Wiley.

Cohn, N, 1967. *Warrant for Genocide.* New York: Oxford University Press.

Dobzhansky, T, 1962. *Mankind Evolving.* New Haven, Conn.: Yale University Press.

Douglas, J, 1984. *The Sociology of Deviance.* Boston, Mass.: Allyn & Bacon.

Durkheim, E, 1954. *The Elementary Forms of the Religious Life.* New York: Free Press.

George, W, 1962. *The Biology of the Race Problem.* New York: National Putnam Letter Committee.

Goffman, E, 1956. 'Conditions of Successful Degradation Ceremonies', *American Journal of Sociology*, vol. 16.

Irwin, J, 1985. *The Jail*. Berkeley: University of California Press.

Katz, J, 1980. *From Prejudice to Destruction*. Cambridge, Mass.: Harvard University Press.

Neumann, E, 1969. *Depth Psychology and a New Ethic*. New York: G.P. Putnam's Sons.

Nietzsche, F, 1967. *Toward a Genealogy of Morals*. New York: Vintage.

Ryan, W, 1971. *Blaming the Victim*. New York: Vintage.

Schwartz, R and Skolnick, J, 1964. 'Two Studies of Legal Stigma', in H.Becker, *The Other Side*. New York: Free Press.

Scott, R, 1969. *The Making of Blind Men*. New York: Russell Sage.

Shover, N, 1974. 'The Official Construction of Deviant Identities', *Crime and Delinquency*, vol. 20.

Sudnow, D, 1967. *Passing On*. Englewood Cliffs, NJ: Prentice-Hall.

Szasz, T, 1970. *The Manufacture of Madness*. New York:Dell.

Szasz, T, 1974. *Ceremonial Chemistry*. Garden City, NY: Doubleday-Anchor.

Weber, M, 1964. *The Sociology of Religion*. Boston, Mass.: Beacon Press.

3 The Bomb Sign: Notes on the Overvaluation of the Object

Jussi Vähämäki

Introduction

In the following text I use both Freudian and Heideggerian argumentation in order to eliminate the tendency or 'tradition' of forgetting the primarily collective functioning of the nuclear weapons as objects and their constitution as 'social' objects, i.e. symbols. Works by René Girard and Walter Burkert are used mainly to elucidate more clearly the culturally defined role of weapons as objects and the mythological and psychological issues involved.

The specific object or sign here is the 'hydrogen bomb' and the conglomerate of objects called 'nuclear weapons'. My primary purpose is to illustrate some of the ways in which these weapons constitute social, meaningful objects with a specific symbolic character or 'Being'. I also examine some of the images that we create in our attempt to assure ourselves that those weapons possess some inhuman and utterly foreign properties. In short, my purpose is to describe the process whereby we merge their symbolic character with their actual existence as beings and see them as the basis for our problems, a mental process which substitutes for real analysis. Other closely connected questions which I take up here are: How do the weapons designate something different from what they actually are? What is the 'history' of their paradigmatic, or designative, function? Is it possible to discover any development in our relation to nuclear weapons?

I perceive that in addition to the 'nuclear exchange' there is another exchange, more fundamental to our cultural production and that this exchange influences the armaments industry in general. This is also an 'exchange' that we try to avoid in an effort to keep weapons at a distance. The symbolic character of nuclear weapons, then, can also be regarded as a road which leads beyond the weapons, i.e. those weapons can be seen as symptoms of, or as substitutes for this more fundamental 'exchange'.

The turning from symbol to symptom is closely related to the process of 'recollecting' or uniting the symbol, as well as also to the dissolution process, wherein the proper symbolic character is lost and the symbol becomes the symptom. These processes can be observed in the context of the European peace movement and the so-called deterrence theory. Both peace movement activists and deterrence theory proponents share the assumption that nuclear weapons are symbols of the new 'nuclear' era. For both groups these are 'absolute weapons'; the 'Bomb' is a transcendent, autonomous sign which guarantees a firm and common ground for reasonable international politics and communication. It makes little difference whether the participants in the nuclear weapons debate argue in favour of the bomb, as the deterrence theorists do, or against it, as the peace activists do. In any case both sides share between them the object which designates the common space for debate.

The history of the belief in the 'absolute weapon' is a chronicle of changing representations of nuclear weapons, embedded in the history of the 'absolute'. This chronicle consists of the erection and construction of the 'absolute's' power, its changing status as it metamorphosed from the good 'absolute' to the bad 'absolute', and all the possibility of restoring of this goodness to the 'absolute' by collective mobilization.

My 'political' argument is that both the peace movement activists and the deterrence theory advocates have overvalued nuclear weapons, which has led them, especially after Gorbachev's challenge and the Intermediate Nuclear Forces (INF) treaty, to their present crisis of belief. This crisis, caused by the rapidly changing role of nuclear weapons, has embarrassed Western European politicians as well as peace activists and deterrence theorists. Until recently, nuclear weapons have constituted a firm ground on which to build political analysis and military strategy. Now that the superpowers themselves are losing their interest in these weapons as a positive base on which to build security, it is no wonder that confusion arises among strategic analysts and peace activists. The familiar paradigm is missing, but apparently there is not yet a new one around which to organize actions and ideas. It is understandable, therefore, that the research community is as confused as the congregation of peace preachers, since their common object of interest has been expropriated. They are unable to decide on a new course of action or rules of communication.

The thieves in this case are the superpowers—the United States and the Soviet Union—that scorn to play the game according to the rules which have been in force until now. They have betrayed the peace movement by assuming a negative attitude toward the nuclear weapons, but they have not done this with an intention of surrendering any of their power and influence in world affairs. In a way they have also betrayed the deterrence theorists by changing from a positive to a negative attitude with regard to the 'absolute weapon' as a deterrent. This change was not made, however, for the purpose of letting disorder into international relations, as theorists are willing to believe, but in order to strengthen the superpowers' role in the world, a role which was slowly being subverted by the changing representations of nuclear weapons.

In this context I also believe that the INF treaty and the future hypothetical reduction of the nuclear arsenal have as their logical basis the changing role of the representations of the nuclear weapons, that is, the degeneration of nuclear weapons from symbols to symptoms. The superpowers are reducing their nuclear arsenals not merely for cosmetic purposes or for the purpose of keeping the situation stable, but mainly for strategic reasons: to strengthen their own international roles. They are moving towards an active reinterpretation in the sphere of world politics, especially where Europe is concerned. That is why the INF treaty is not an exception to the old rules of the game, as almost every analyst of international relations seem to believe, but rather the initial promulgation of new rules for the old game.

The problem of tradition

The birth of the peace movement, its fight for a durable, firm identity, its apocalyptic efforts to cope with what it sees as a coming crisis, are also parts of a larger, mainly unconscious, 'tradition' which guides all of us in our efforts to achieve security, establish order in our social life, and create a predictable and familiar world. One of the main tendencies in twentieth-century European thought has been to render explicit our debt to this tradition, to show that the tradition is not eternal and omnipotent. Analysts have pointed out that its strategy is based on fear, dependence and ritualization rather than on real sovereignty and emancipation. It has been shown that we are actually suffering from this tradition because it accentuates and aggravates our problems. This theme was already exemplified in the nineteenth century by Friedrich Nietzsche when he wrote:

> One repays a teacher badly if one remains only a pupil. And why, then, should you pluck at my laurels? You respect me; but how if one day your respect should tumble? Take care that a falling statue does not strike you dead! [Nietzsche, 1980, p. 36]

Later Sigmund Freud articulated the position explicitly in his theory of the unconscious. I am rather critical of his 'modernist' revisions of the theme, especially concerning the renunciation of the so-called seduction theory. That renunciation transferred tradition, and ritual as its (dream)work, into the patient's unconscious, into his/her fantasy, as it were. Thus guilt was shifted from the sphere of community (fathers and uncles, the law and religion) and tradition to the sphere of 'ruling conventions' or social prejudices. Freud ascribed the patient's troubles to his or her 'own' particular misundertandings or fantastical elaborations and in a way absolved the community from the guilt.

In some sense one may understand, however, that this had to be done in order to make possible a 'cure' or a 'translation' from the patient's individual speech to the universal language of the human collective, that is, in order to open a way for making restitution or atonement for the crime of tradition and thereby liberating the community from guilt. This restitution could only be made in some space separate from the reality of crimes committed against the individual by others. It is impossible to accept this space, where the victim and victimizers confront each other, as a starting point for a 'cure'. Restitution there is impossible, because it would merely lead either to siding with the victim against the victimizers, or to siding with the victimizers against the victim. In either case results are catastrophic for theory of the unconscious and lead only to uncontrollable, formless violence. Therefore Freud invented a space that was beyond both the victim and his victimizers, the patient and his/her relatives. It is a space situated directly between the two, and makes possible an agreement between society and the individual. He called that space the unconscious. It would then become a starting point for a new autonomous scientific theory that he named psychoanalysis. It is only this chance for a 'cure', the possibility of translation, which is guaranteed by the unconscious and designated by the body of the neurotic, that provides psychoanalysis with its autonomous status as a science. That was, after all, what Freud was fighting for.

Likewise, tradition also haunted Martin Heidegger. It is well known that he fought consistently against the tendency in Platonic tradition that he called the 'forgetting of Being', and against its consequences: overvaluing objects as autonomous beings and forgetting that they are 'socially' constituted.

Heidegger held the view that Western philosophy or metaphysics was a tradition of trying to forget the communal, collective nature of each object, the debt or inheritance that each being traces back to the primal scene of its 'concretization'. Contrary to that tradition of forgetting, Being was thus a specific 'social' property, something more than just separate beings or objects. It was something that tied the individual beings together as symbols; it made them symbols and gave them their existence. Specific beings could only designate Being and function as its *paradeigma* or *exemplum*, but they never are Being itself.

Western metaphysical thought since Plato has tried to forget this paradigmatic character of beings, by confusing Being with beings, confusing the truth of Being with the existence of beings. In this context forgetting is mainly a process of overlooking the 'social' or 'communal' character of every being. It is the specific symbolic element, that ties objects together and shows that they are something recognizable and useful.

The social nature of individual objects is also fundamentally tragic because every object contains within itself a debt to Being as its Other. Heidegger finds no escape from this tragedy or debt. Every attempt to forget the debt would only increase it, render the tragedy more powerful and violent than ever and threaten the planet with intellectual and ecological catastrophe. That is the reason why he was forced to translate the tragedy to a kind of aesthetic experience. The only way to save the planet is by defining the debt explicitly, to recognize it and give it a particular space where it may be admired, thereby diminishing its power over the people. That is, in order to ensure the survival of the planet, the debt must be made explicit, not in order to restitute it but to save it as a constant appeal in everyday life. It could be said that the space of restitution, on which Freud grounded the institution of psychoanalysis, is in Heidegger's interpretation in constant danger of losing its substance and form. For example, the borders between art and philosophy tend to evaporate in Heidegger's later writings. This evaporation process threatens life (and philosophy) again with the problem of guilt and atonement without any sovereign or autonomous ground where wrongdoing could somehow be resolved. It is then a situation which threatens the ordered life of humankind with uncontrollable violence. This is the situation which René Girard calls a 'mimetic crisis'.

Behind the tragedy of collective human nature there is the problem of violence and aggression which the Western philosophical tradition tries to forget. This position has been argued most convincingly by René Girard and Walter Burkert.

Walter Burkert articulates the problem of tradition and its effects on our actions in the context of violence and aggression in the following terms:

Aggression and human violence have marked the progress of our civilization and appear, indeed, to have grown so during its course that they have become a central problem of the present. Analyses that attempt to locate the roots of the evil often set out with short-sighted assumptions, as though the failure of our upbringing or the faulty development of a particular national tradition or economical system were to blame. More can be said for the thesis that *all orders and forms of authority in human society are founded on institutionalized violence.* This at least corresponds to the fundamental role played in biology by intraspecific aggression . . . [Burkert, 1983, p. 1; emphasis added]

The problem of tradition is tied to the problem of human violence. Until now tradition has unsuccessfully tried to push violence back, but on the contrary it has only escalated violence, ultimately making it the most central problem of humankind.

For René Girard the history of Western culture has been the history of the mythicization of human violence, that is mythologization of the real history of scapegoating and killing victims. Humanity has tried to resolve and restrict its aggressive and violent character by transferring it to a victim and then turning the violence into the property of this victim. The victim is seen as an entity totally different from a normal human being. Unfortunately, however, this is not enough, the transfer does not succeed and new victims are always needed. Substitution and transfer have so far only enhanced violence and put it at the centre of human affairs. In Girard's view, humanity must confront its own violence in order to resolve its accumulating problems and must not rely on the expedients of substitution and transfer. The structures of violence must be demythologized (Girard, 1987b, p. 117).

In Girard's opinion, only Christianity contains scandalous elements that demystify the mythological tradition of substitutive violence, and only Christianity consciously sides with the victim. For the first time in human history, Christianity has made it possible to see the operation of the scapegoating mechanism behind the mythologies (cf. Girard, 1985). The only way to reduce the role of violence and tradition in our lives, and to prevent the statue of tradition from falling and striking us dead, is to identify with, and side with, the victim, so that no new victims are sought for. Girard makes a forceful, convincing 'conservative' critique of the tradition of modern times, defining it as a tradition which destroys all other traditions, thereby escalating violence throughout society.

There are at least three different modern strategies for dealing with tradition.

The first is Freud's 'classical strategy' (in a full military sense of both words) which builds a kind of objective metalanguage for the translation, the space of justice where the cure is possible. This space is the unconscious, which constitutes a sovereign third party. It is not, strictly speaking, either in the possession of a patient or a society or a tradition. The unconscious is the sovereign body politic that establishes or accepts the claim made by the individual on tradition. The unconscious settles the debt by its very being. It collects interest on the debt, that is it acts as an intermediary between the two parties. In that way the unconscious receives all the violence and guilt and, after assuming its burden (wrongdoing and guilt, i.e. the unpalatable remains and relics which are turned into symbols) and accumulated interest, returns them as 'translated' into harmonious relations between the individual and society.

The second is Heidegger's properly modern and sublime strategy which emphasizes constant awareness of a crisis in relation to the body politic, as a sovereign principle of restitution. The body politic or the unconscious is in perpetual danger of losing its sovereignty. It threatens to explode the unsettled guilt and violence throughout society.

The third is Girard's 'scandalous' strategy of demythologization that unveils 'the founding mechanism of all worldly prestige, all forms of sacredness and all forms of cultural meaning' and 'discredits and deconstructs all the gods of violence, since it reveals the true God, who has not the slightest violence in him' (Girard, 1987a, p. 429). Following this true god means giving up 'mimetic desire'—the desire which leads to violence and its substitution or transfer through a victim. The Girardian problem tackles the mystery of restitution in a most unexpected, 'scandalous' and also 'Christian' way, when it recommends giving up interests, abandoning the whole body politic, and settling our problems without a victim as the substitute object. In the Girardian context the bomb is only one of the false gods of human violence, an euphemism of the fundamental fact of human violence, a substitute object.

The Girardian 'scandal' has also a specific ironic relation to a mimetic crisis. It imitates the threat of unbound violence in order to unveil its mechanism and not to escalate it. Imitation serves to curtail and reveal the mimetic mechanism. In a way the 'scandal' functions as a healing *pharmakon* or prescription. It toys with the idea of the 'cure', not in order to make the cure possible, but in order to show that

> what is important above all is to realize that there are no *recipes*; there is no *pharmakon*, not even a Marxist or a psychoanalytic one. Recipes are not what we need, nor do we need to be reassured—our need is to escape from meaninglessness. However large a part of 'sound and fury signifying nothing' there may be in public and private suffering, in the anguish of mental patients, in the deprivations of the poor and in the rivalries of politics, these thing are not lacking in significance, if only because at each moment they are open to the ironic reversal of the judgement against the judge that recalls the implacable functioning of the gospel's law in our world. We must learn to love this justice,

which we both carry out and fall victim to. The peace that passes human understanding can only arise on the other side of this passion for 'justice and judgement', which still possesses us but which we are less and less likely to confuse with the totality of being. [Girard, 1987a, p. 446]

This 'less and less' expresses Girard's concept of modernity as an opportunity to suspend judgement and as an opportunity to withdraw from a decision.

Animal stories within the ritual

Tradition is not a *perpetuum mobile*. In reality it does not work endlessly although in theory, especially in political theory, people dream of tradition without time and the erosion which is caused by time. Tradition needs restoring and rebuilding, new rules that revive and refresh it. These new rules make it interesting again, even if they involve only minor changes and adjustments. They push tradition back to its work, which is to guide the construction of our representations of reality and shape our actions.

The problem of tradition is a difficult one, which should be dealt with in the context of ritual. It is ritual that keeps tradition intact, renders it transmissible and protects it from extinction. Ritual contains the set of rules and tools that support tradition, and to 'destroy' tradition means to eliminate these tools. Eliminating ritual, however, is not an easy task. Ritual returns even in the shape and construction of the very tools that were to be employed in criticizing it.

The following parable from Franz Kafka should make explicit some of the problems involved:

> Leopards break into the temple and drink the contents of the sacrificial vessels; this happens over and over again; eventually it can be reckoned with, and it becomes part of the ceremony. [1981, p. 7]

If we leave out all the speculations of the parable's literary elements and take it as it is, as a story, what do we have?

We could imagine the leopards that broke into the temple and the fear that these fierce animals aroused in the people attending the sacrificial procession. At first, when the animals broke in, there was evidently a moment of terror and destruction for the people inside. After the action had been repeated several times, however, the people became accustomed to it, maybe even forgot that the leopards were dangerous, and they continued the ritual as before. After a while they were so used to it that they began to wait for the leopards and felt anxious if the animals did not come in time. What was in the beginning something disastrous and frightening, something disturbing and noisy, was transformed into something essential for the ritual, namely into information. The leopards had metamorphosed into signs that have a definite place in the ritual. In the context of the ritual they had a meaning.

The parable is an example of that power through which tradition and ritual transform violence and chance, through which they (ex)change them into order. It illuminates some of the problems involved in criticizing tradition.

For example, if there were too many leopards the result would be the total destruction of the temple and the ritual. That would be, from the viewpoint of the ritual, an unbearable and 'unthinkable' situation. Correspondingly, if the leopards were weak, perhaps too young or too old, they would not break in or at least the people inside the temple could drive them out and tell a mythic story about the fight. In that case the leopards would be only a marginal or even unnoticeable phenomenon in relation to the ritual. Their roaring in the jungle or their scratching on the outer wall of the temple would be heard inside only faintly or not at all. As leopards they would fail to take their proper place. That would mean that nothing would have taken place, not even the place would exist, no matter how stubbornly we might believe that there was something innocent in what took place. There is no exception, no pure space without noise, even an exception is nothing other than an exception, your individual share, your lot from that which has taken place.

Therefore it is difficult to be a wild animal in human society and especially in human narratives. You have no alternative but to come when the master says you should come. You have been chased very far from the centre. As a matter of fact you do not even have an existence of your own, not before the master orders you to come and appear, orders you to come to life within the sphere of the ritual, to take your place in a cleared space on the sand or on the pure black of the chalkboard and orders you to appear as a sign. That is the only thing that counts. You must stay and wait, like a statue: a leopard figure, a stone guest at the supper offered by tradition. As a matter of fact you are the one being eaten by the hosts, you provide the food for the ritual, you perpetuate the ritual and that is the reason why they hunt and capture you. Now, however, you are the stone guest whose silent figure tells the onlookers that everything is going well. You must not move or fall because that would break the order of the ritual and make a new hunt necessary. It happens after all, though; the statue falls, it must be put back into its place, that is, where the place exists as you and through you, and you exist as the Other.

The leopards are forced to come just at the right moment, not sooner or later, with proper force and in a suitable condition. They have to be strong and aesthetically admirable animals, otherwise nobody would pay attention to them and they would remain irrelevant, producing only a disturbing noise. No wonder that they prefer the darkness of the jungle outside the light of the temple.

In a way Kafka's parable illustrates how the destiny of these leopards had been written long before the leopards were even born. It was written by the people who built this temple for the sake of their community and their security. One day, they gathered together to hunt leopards in order to bring some food and warmth into their temple, to obtain some meat and to burn some bones. The leopards just happened to be there. It was not for the sake of the leopards that the hunt was prepared. The leopards and their predetermined appearance are an integral part of the social constitution of the 'temple'. They are the awaited ones, the saviour and Messiah, the ones who provide warmth and food. The fire burns and gives its glow and warmth; the meat is roasting, there is no need to eat it raw, and in the mean time the hunt is recounted in stories and acted out in the light of the fire.

The difference between human and beast then lies in the fire and in the bones, in the leftovers of the cure and translation, in the incurable and untranslatable. The difference lies in that which cannot be eaten and consummated, i.e. in that which has no Being. That which is without Being can only denote the Being of the others by its very absence of Being. The bones and the teeth of the common meal are turned into signs because they are unpalatable. They are vehicles of translation. They have the required negative and differential character. It is unclear, though, where exactly they acquire this capacity to denote something other than they are. What is the secret of the translation and cure, or the secret of the human collective? Maybe the science of translating and curing is something like a social alchemy?

Everything is so simple and yet so complicated. The animal's teeth are transformed into a necklace and its hide into a mantle. The necklace designates the share or lot of the hunter, his individual Being and his collective being together with the others. It shows his Being beyond the teeth, his transcendental Being as a collective animal. The mantle, on the other hand, provides a shape for the community in which the hunters live, the leopard land inhabited by the leopard-men.

Later on the teeth are transformed into numbers and letters as the collective develops the science of food-sharing into mathematics. Mathematics is the only true 'social science' because it bestows rationalism on (it 'gives reason') the community by giving each of its members his/her proper individual ratio and share of collective property. Rational science indeed! The collective nature of mathematics and all rational sciences, however, does not stop in this rendering reason (*rationem reddere*), this returning or exchanging of gifts. The sciences also have a 'second' first principle, the principle of non-contradiction, that is, the principle of unanimity. Before reasoning can begin, the mathematician must be sure that everyone agrees, that there are no complaints, claims or particular interests, that everyone is interested only in sharing in rationalism, that all strife and every disturbance is wiped away for that reason (Serres, 1983, pp. 65–133).

Ritual is a sphere of human activity where nothing ever happens accidentally. Every act, every movement, every utensil and every animal has a significance in the context of ritual (Smith, 1982, p. 54). It seems that the existance of ritual and tradition is a necessary precondition for critiques of ritual and tradition, and that every critique of tradition has its potential place in tradition even before that critique is born. In that case, to criticize tradition and ritual means only to enlarge the area of the ritual, to extend the space of the temple and to throw more wood and bones into the fire. Indeed, it is difficult to be a leopard. Men chase and kill you, and after that take your pelt to use it as a costume in their rituals. There is no escape from being either destroyed or forced into silence or caught up as an object. There are few hiding places left, it would be easier to live as a little insect or a creature that no one would notice.

Is there an eternal meaning in the leopards and their part in the ritual? What will happen when people are so familiar with the animals that they do not notice them any more? What will happen when the ritual slows down and becomes monotonous, when the worshippers become absent-minded, sleepy and dizzy? When there is nothing interesting, nothing meaningful to wait for? When the jungle does not break into the temple in the guise of the leopards but in the guise of the minute insects, like commonplace, tedious material, just plain and ordinary rubbish? When doubts about the ritual's significance emerge gradually? This slackening is the greatest threat to the temple. Suddenly the jungle is everywhere, no longer confined to any particular location, and it devours the temple from every possible direction. Theoretically or philosophically it might be impossible to criticize the temple, but in reality it happens every day.

This dangerous situation is also solved in a practical manner. The priest of the temple, referred to as a 'politician' (from a Greek word meaning fortress or citadel) in the language of contemporary discourse, has invented a tool, a procedure to counteract this slowing down of the ritual, this invasion by insects which inflict wounds in the sovereign body of the temple, in the body politic. This tool or procedure is dignified by the name 'politics'. Politics is nothing but the art of hunting big animals in order to obtain food and strengthen the temple. The priest–politician knows that it is useless to fight against the minute insects and vermin. You can eat them or they can eat you. The difference between hunter and prey, the one who eats and the one who is eaten, nature and culture, the raw and the cooked, evaporates here. Insects are always dangerous to healthy and normal social life, because they eliminate the difference. As is well known, struggling against mosquitoes and other small pests does not provide the same effect as hunting for the bigger animals. Therefore the situation calls for opening a wound that is bigger than the one inflicted by mosquitoes, and applying a remedy that heals the body and drives the insects out. The temple needs rebuilding and the participants in the ritual require sustenance. Bigger animals are needed. That is why the hunt is organized and why the hunting ritual is instituted. Only bigger animals can provide the necessary food to keep the temple and the ritual functioning. Therefore when the temple is in a crisis, when there is no food and there are only insects invading and devouring the wounded body politic, the prophet comes. He tells a story. He has seen, somewhere near the temple, the shadow of the leopard, the sign of salvation, maybe the shadow of the bomb. It is time for a hunt to begin. The time of incertitude and hesitation, the time of modernity is over.

It is generally acknowledged truth that the history of Western civilization has been a history of secularization, of the loss of belief in God's transcendence as a force for social cohesion. It is said that we no longer live in a religious society, that we no longer believe in anything, that God is dead. God may very well be dead, if there ever was a living God, but all the other statements are invalid. The truth is that the space of the temple is today more capacious than ever. There is no accident, no meaningless word or action, nothing occurs by chance, everything is ritualized. Observe the field of so-called strategic studies! There is no accident, only ritual. Consider nuclear war! In the context of modern technology it would be only an accident, the last wild animal in existence, a slight mistake; when that mistake is cleared we will live in perpetual peace. Contrary to the common belief one could argue that modern, secular human beings constitute so far the most religious community of believers that has ever existed. The process of modernization is a process of ritualization, a process of sacralizing every single object and giving it significance in the context of the ritual. At the same time, however, there is a subversive tendency contained within the ritualizing and sacralizing processes, slowly consuming the temple and the ritual, rendering them monotonous and insignificant, even while expanding their area of operation. This tendency forces the ritual to rebuild and recollect itself, it forces the priests to organize a hunt. It places tradition in a state of uncertainty by wounding it and affords people the opportunity to criticize tradition, while simultaneously enabling them to dispense with ethical judgements concerning the decision to kill the prey.

The overvaluation tendency and the peace movement

I am convinced that the present problems of the peace movement have their origin in these basic questions of tradition and ritual. The future of the movement might depend on its capacity to articulate itself consciously in contrast to tradition, that is, it must see itself in a certain kind of relation to tradition and see the problems that arise from this relation. These problems also affect the theory of deterrence and the investigations of peace researchers where there has been a common starting point and ground for debate, shared with the peace movement, that is, where deterrence proponents and peace activists have shared a common object of concern.

Hence it is my general thesis that peace activists and deterrence theorists have overvalued their object, especially in the case of nuclear weapons. This overvaluation is already implicit in the use of terms such as the 'nuclear era' to imply that the post-war era is something utterly different and specific in the history of civilization. This concept of a new era is shared by a variety of researchers, politicians, writers and peace activists as well as by psychoanalysts. Nuclear weapons have become symbols of this new era, they mark its unique and autonomous place in human history. They are signs that function as *exempla* of something different and new. This special 'newness' requires that the *exempla* have no antecedent and no history.

As symbols the weapons have been perceived as something given, beyond which is impossible to go because beyond them there is nothing but 'total annihilation'. They are understood as real objects which have a truly different, transcendent nature. The idea that they are socially constituted substitute objects, which have a special function in society, the idea that they are denials of reality or even 'victims' has not been very popular so far. There have been few efforts to enquire into the role played by weapons in human communication and in the establishment of social order, that is, their special function in society. At most, many leftist researchers have seen weapons only in narrowly technical terms, in the terms of political–military power and strategic interests, as objects which are used by one group to oppress another, as something foreign, repressive and incidental to fundamental production of social relations.

Overvaluation has led to a certain spiritual, intellectual or psychological dependence on these weapons, which in turn manifests itself easily in political voluntarism and at best in minute, laborious descriptive analyses of international relations. When there is no deeper understanding of phenomena, all minor changes on the surface tend to assume an extremist, all-or-nothing, 'either/or' aspect. One of the problems of peace research is that it so easily translates into a thinly veiled, superficial analysis of international politics. Researchers neglect their obligation to analyse the general role of violence in all cultural activity and to see the problems of international relations in the context of that activity. Analysts should regard political processes as ways of building reality and not as reality itself.

Usually political problems and also prospects for solutions arise only when the overvalued object begins to lose its value, when it becomes disembodied and dissipates. The loss of a common object as a shared focus for debate opens the way for a conflict in which different interpretations may contend for power and the right to determine the direction of political tendencies. In this situation the rules of the political game are themselves at stake (Weber, 1987, p. 28). I think that we are living in just such a situation at present.

The bomb and its degeneration as a deterrent

Since World War II, weapons (especially nuclear weapons) have been for peace movement and defence intellectuals or deterrence theorists the 'thing', a matter of life and death. The bomb has provided a solution to the problems of peace. It has guaranteed peace either by its presence or by its potential absence. At the same time nuclear weapons have guaranteed the legitimacy and integrity of the peace movement and the deterrence theory. Because the bomb exists, there is and must be a peace movement and its struggle for peace; because the bomb exists there is and must be deterrence theorists who tell what the bomb means when it speaks.

Since Hiroshima and Nagasaki, nuclear weapons have been clearly different and identifiable objects; they have had an unmistakable form and shape. At the same time, it has also been easy to see the peace movement and all that it represents as something totally different and identifiable. There has been no danger of confusing these various representations with each other. The bomb has aroused enough interest on all sides to keep the ritual going.

What if weapons lose their form and shape, though? What if they degenerate into something unidentifiable and, in that sense, to something monstrous? How could we then safeguard our identity, our form and our altogether different character? In a way that is just what has happened to weapons, especially to nuclear weapons, as they have constituted the true object and true guarantee of the peace movement's identity.

The story of that degeneration is almost mythic. We can trace it through at least three different phases, which establish a kind of genetic order to this development.

The 'classical' phase

The first phase is that of the 'absolute weapon' and heroic struggle concerned with the presence and absence of nuclear weapons as dangerous objects. This phase is characterized by efforts to restrict the accumulation, proliferation and use of these weapons. It is the era of defining and clearing a space for the nuclear exchange, making the rules of the game and keeping the form and shape of an object clear and intact. In that phase there is an honest struggle for peace, as there is for war as well; it is clear to everyone who is an enemy and who is not. The enemy is not a shapeless, disembodied, unidentifiable monster that lurks behind every corner. Nuclear weapons are horrible, but at the same time they are desirable. They could conceivably be used to safeguard national security; they create a sense of order and keep the world recognizable. They are perfect and useful objects that bring predictability to international strategic relations, they are genuinely artistic creations that can gather people together and unite them in a collective struggle for survival. In short, they are meaningful and beautiful objects, objects in their proper and ordered place. By their very meaningfulness they give people a sense of identity, place and perspective, be it positive, as the deterrence theorist thinks, or negative, as the peace activist thinks. They are classical creations in the true sense of the word.

The 'sublime' phase

The second is the uncanny and sublime phase, the phase of 'exterminism' (cf. Thompson, 1982). In this phase the heroic struggle is in constant danger of turning into ruthless and unrestricted violence, into chaos and total destruction as doomsayers have so often stressed.

The process of fighting for the object's presence or absence, the struggle to assert the right of ownership, wears down the object. The object begins to lose its form and objectivity. It is transformed into a monster that does not fit very well within the framework of the rules with which it is surrounded (Ferguson, 1984, p. 9). It cannot be used for playing the familiar game, because it seems to lose its contents and change its shape, nature and direction all the time. Theories of militarization of the state, civil society and culture abound. Within this phase we can also find support for the thesis that modernization is militarization, or at least closely connected to it. The world is supposedly threatened by a plague of total militarization, total bureaucratization, and so on.

The uncanny, monstrous element is so acutely present that serious, objective analysis turns out to be ridiculous or perverse. It is worth imitating this analytical tendency in order to demonstrate its futility. It is a process reminiscent of the theatre or carnivals. In reality the bomb cannot be used in calculations but it can be admired. It is beautiful, dangerous and sublime. It is something altogether new. It is a growing monster that is constantly fighting the way out from its place of concealment into society. It is not desired, because it is of no use, but it must be kept in its secret place, for only in a specific space does it possess the beauty and power to draw its admirers together.

This is first and foremost a phase of collective mobilization, a phase of rallying people around the bomb-monster so that they may laugh at it and hate it. It is the phase of the peace movement as a mass campaign, as a unanimous mobilization against the bomb. It is also a strictly ritualistic phase which prepares and directs an act of collective violence against the monstrous and at the same time godlike object.

When it is kept under cover in its secret place, the monster is threatening, dangerous and fascinating. Brothers and comrades do not fight against one another for the possession (presence or absence) of such an object. On the contrary, they fight in order to render the object objective, to make it something different, identifiable and unmixed, to keep the monster in its place.

In this way the monstrosity of nuclear weapons can act as a uniting device, hence providing security. As weapons they are useless, they can only be used as topics for debate. As devices for communication (uniting people all over the world in a campaign against nuclear disaster) they are still unsurpassed (cf. Kerckhove, 1984; Thompson, 1982). This change from the local and heroic struggle, from the sphere of rationality and politics, to the global struggle for survival, for an established order and identifiable rules, that is for communication, is the second phase in the degeneration of nuclear weapons as objects.

The 'scandalous' phase

The third stage in this degeneration begins when the monster emerges from its hiding place, when it loses its form and becomes involved in everyday life. To the people living in the era of this monstrosity, the degeneration means utmost chaos and disaster. Contrary to their nightmares there is, however, this non-phase. This could be called the 'rubbish' phase or a 'scandalous' phase (Girard, 1987a, p. 429). Nuclear weapons then lose their sublime and artistic character, they lose their meaningfulness and change to something unattractive, dull, ordinary and undesirable. Hence people are not in the least interested in fighting to possess them, and are not even afraid of them. As useful armaments and/or as devices of global communication, nuclear weapons have lost their potential for uniting people in a common cause. In short, they have degenerated to something less potent, like rubbish or scrap.

From within the monster's hiding place emerge the whole stage setting, the whole creation of its identity, the ruins of the ritual. When revealed, they arouse little curiosity, at least not at this point, because they have not yet turned into collectors' items. The clearly recognizable object (the bomb) was, in the past, useful in uniting people and giving them broader horizons for activity, a predictable, familiar order of things and a sense of security. The weapon/object was a means of communication and made possible the exchange of information. It has changed into something ambiguous and contradictory, something unrecognizable, like a noise that hinders communication and interferes with people's efforts to understand reality.

From the global device of communication (the universal, united perspective either against or for nuclear weapons) nothing has emerged but a heap of rubbish, a rattling noise and perhaps a smell of saltpetre. Like every other object, these weapons turn out to be stillborn. As objects they were thought and dreamed about. Stories of their advent and destiny were told beforehand over and over again, cradles were built and clothes made while people waited for them to come. They were portrayed as vehicles laden with death, as containers of violence. They promised to bring with them eternal security and peace. In fact violence and death were supposed to be exchanged for these weapons, but the transaction was not altogether honest. It turned out that somebody cheated us. Those weapons contained nothing and they were incapable of carrying violence away; their concealed interior, thought to be full of chaos and wildly careening atoms, was completely empty and silent. Nothing ever happens there. (Nothing ever happens in the obejcts, they are always beaten to death.) Instead of being embodied within these dangerous weapons, chaos and violence are again contained within ourselves. They are everywhere and perhaps noisier and more menacing than ever.

After all, the truth is that we received nothing genuine or substantial, only some eloquent speeches and sophisticated advertising. Our senses were overwhelmed with illusion, seduction, persuasion and jokes, but not the thing-in-itself, no peace or security, no bases for our identity; no sovereignty, as was promised, only servitude and dependence. We had to come back to the starting point that we thought we had left behind long ago. Perhaps we never really left it at all.

Re-establishing the body politic

The degeneration of the object brings with it a situation which could best be described as a moment of indecision or formlessness. It is a situation where there are no distinct boundaries and identities and when the potential interpretations are not established as a definite set of rules, where the future interpretations have not yet salified and condensed, and where it is difficult to locate and recognize the opponent. We are now in a period before the new rules have been firmly established and before people have fashioned a new and secure object as a focus for their identity.

Re-establishing the rules, solidifying the object, is made possible by reversing this 'genetic order of degeneration' and starting from left-overs, from this heap of rubbish and noise, this commonplace material. We acquire an order which constructs a secure and autonomous identity for itself and apparently for the world as well, and for the political theorist and maybe for a kind of a 'peace movement' too. First, select a piece of rubbish, analyse it, see in it the reasons for your embarrassment or crisis, make a monument of it or a work of art. Thus you have a durable mark for your identity, for you are not the 'guilty' one. Afterwards you can reverse the story and say that the monument made you, that it is the symbol of a god who created us, the human race, out of formless clay.

It is a fact, though, that the old peace activists as well as the deterrence theorists have missed the point. They failed to see or hear the opening act of the new era, because they were waiting for something extraordinary to take place. Maybe they were expecting thunder and failed to notice what actually happened. As a matter of fact they insist that such an opening is impossible because of the 'absolute weapon', the bomb. They love the old leopards, those pure, tedious and evil-smelling beasts, and fail to see that a new hunt is being prepared.

We could very well interpret the summit at Reykjavik between Reagan and Gorbachev as a moment of indecision or formlessness, a kind of 'breach in the pure war script' as has been suggested by Mehan & Skelly (1988, pp. 35–66). This breach was mainly due to the degeneration of nuclear weaponry as a legitimate and convincing deterrent. This degeneration forced the superpowers into the situation where continuing the game of world politics with the old rules was becoming difficult and even dangerous.

In Reykjavik both parties were unsure what course of action they were to take to rebuild their eroding influence, what interpretation to share, what object to take as their common focus of interest, after it had become clear that the nuclear deterrent could no longer function as such a focus. The explanation or interpretation was at hand, as it always is. There they were, the noisy nuclear weapons, like a swarm of insects whose presence seemed to obstruct all normal and rational politics, arousing uneasiness, mistrust and panic in people. They attacked and infected the body politic itself, which is for modern society the only entity which guarantees that people can live together without destroying one another.

The first signs of the new interpretation, its most basic dimensions, are sketched in the INF treaty. There the superpowers try to reverse the degeneration in the role played by the nuclear arsenal. Nevertheless, the new interpretation, the new set of rules for the old game played by the superpowers as before, is not yet fully in force. Since the rules are not yet instituted, there is still room for conflicting interpretations and deconstruction of the old order, though it is difficult to see where the conflicting interpretations would come and what their content might be.

The bomb and revelation

Throughout history, people who have struggled for peace have never for a moment suspected that someone is cheating them, offering them promises instead of real answers. Weapons, and after World War II, nuclear weapons, had seemed real devices for controlling chaos and violence, real answers. It is an ironical paradox that soon after World War II, which proved with so many deaths that weapons are not a guarantee against uncontrolled violence, people were willing to forget its lessons. Suddenly, they believed again in weapons, in the bomb, as a device that could bring either total order and security or disorder and death.

What or who has blinded us? Some say it is the evil influence of bad politics and politicians, their thirst for power, some say it is the Cold

War and its advocates in East and West. Maybe it is evil in the guise of international communism or capitalism, and so forth.

The fact remains that it is easy to cheat and scare us and thereby to buy our approval and participation both in the creation of the danger as well as in its possible cure. In order to acquire some sense of identity, our own sovereign piece of territory, and security, we are willing to buy everything that is offered. An 'offering' means, in this case, she who comes forward to present herself as an example, as a sacrificial sheep, as a victim. This victim is thought or dreamed of as a being that will make our boundaries clear and distinct, and hence will make it impossible for us to doubt our identity.

I leave these speculative questions of identity open and return instead to the problems of nuclear weapons and the peace movement. As I see it, the most fundamental questions in this context are: is it possible to free ourselves from nuclear weapons, is it possible to destroy them? Usually the answer is: yes, it is possible, but only by using them, only by destroying the whole world with them. That is why, in contrast to the frightful perspective of destroying weapons by using them, the peace movement's task until now has been to keep those weapons disguised and hidden, to keep them outside our own world in their hidden mausoleums, to take care of them and to worship them. As weapons in particular or as objects in general they are (or until recently have been) sacred and too dangerous to touch. Touching them means death and disaster.

As weapons, they have changed the whole modern era to the 'nuclear age', established it as a completely different and autonomous epoch in the history of humanity. The weapons may be controlled but not dismissed, conserved but not forgotten. We may worship or hate them but we are not allowed to forget them. It is amazing that people after all do forget them, lose their interest in them, and that this forgetfulness is real and not pretended. Perhaps the greatest achievement or sin of humanity today was not to kill God but to lose interest in him?

It is unrealistic and sacrilegious to say that nuclear weapons are old-fashioned, that they are unworthy of interest, that they need not be regarded in principle as different from other weapons, that they are not signs of a new era, but quite the contrary, and that they do not merit our worship, even now when some of missiles are turning into rubbish. It is not a view that any peace activist, military professional, strategic thinker or peace researcher could share. At best it is only a utopian dream—a long term goal. In normal circumstances, it would be taken as a childish viewpoint, rather unreasonable, perhaps even adventurous and dangerous at worst. It would deprive us of the very force of the 'absolute weapon', the power that has prevented World War III from breaking out.

If someone challenges the sacred character of nuclear weapons, insists that as weapons they are not radically different from conventional armaments and not actually autonomous or eternal, contends that staring intensively at them only prevents us from asking more fundamental questions about our cultural production, he is accused of belittling the weapons' massive and disastrous potential. As different and autonomous objects (as signs of a totally new era), nuclear weapons define our 'own', proper and specific place in the history of humanity. Without them, we would be far more uncertain of our being, of our place and identity. To phrase it differently: if those weapons did not exist, we presumably would have to invent them.

Indeed, it is possible that as objects and as weapons they exist only as something to be spoken about. They are in some sense imaginary, supported by fanciful stories of their utterly transcendent character. There are both military stories using them to win a war, and extremist stories of touching them and destroying the whole world.

These supportive stories or mythical narratives all point to some kind of consent and harmony for which the bomb is a terrible but necessary precondition. This is extremely clear at the 'second phase' of the object's degeneration, when stories abound of collective mobilization against the bomb. Furthermore, these stories bear a strange resemblance to the classical political narratives of the sovereignty and autonomy of the general will, especially that of Rousseau's rage against all the enemies of general will. The narratives usually regress to addressing the need of collective mobilization against all the enemies of the bomb's sovereignty and autonomy. It does not matter if the storyteller is a peace movement activist or theorist, a defence intellectual or the Secretary of Defence, even a psychoanalyst who tries to analyse the bomb's role ends up in mobilizing forces against this utmost evil (cf. Volkan, 1987). The bomb is a precondition for the modern equivalent of 'the social contract'; without it there would be no collective covenant, no mutual consent and no international exchange of ideas. Without it (if the bomb were abolished) people would be scattered all over the world not knowing each other, unable to differentiate between friends and enemies, human and animal, culture and nature. Without a bomb there would be two possible scenarios. An undifferentiated violence would reign, a 'natural state of war', such as Hobbes described:

> In such condition there is no place for industry; because the fruit thereof is uncertain: and consequentially no culture of the earth; no navigation, nor use of the commodities that may be imported by the sea; no commodious building; no instruments of moving and removing such things as require much force; no

knowledge of the face of the earth; no account of time; no arts; no letters; no society; and which is worst of all, continual fear and danger of violent death; and life of man, solitary, poor, nasty, brutish and short. [Hobbes, 1946, I. 13]

Otherwise an undifferentiated harmony would prevail, a golden age like paradise before original sin; the natural state of *liberté* and *perfectibilité*.

The bomb is in Rousseauistic terms a tragic but necessary precondition for society, or 'saving our planet from total annihilation'. It is a ground and reason for the creation of a covenant, a real lawgiver and sovereign, the body politic which guarantees the social pact (Rousseau, 1979, pp. 59–60).

The bomb has no history other than that of revelation. We do not know how it came about, we cannot detect its slow evolution, record its history. It opens up the space for which there is no anterior. Enquiring into the origin of the bomb would be as futile as to ask: who was the first man that built the fence or dug the ditch to define and segregate private property? When came the first floods that cleared the space for (agri)culture? Or to ask of God: what is your name? What name shall I tell to the people of Israel? The answer would always be something unpronounceable, maybe something full of sound and fury but still totally beyond comprehension. Kafka has depicted this uncanny situation well in his story 'A Leaf from the Past':

I own a shoemaker's shop in the square fronting the imperial palace. Hardly have I pulled my shutters up at first light when I see that the mouths of all the streets around the square are occupied by armed men. They are not our troops, though, but clearly nomads from the north. How they have done it I do not know, but they have pushed right through to the capital, which is a very long way indeed from the frontier. Anyway, there they are; there seem to be more of them each morning . . . [1981, p. 191]

The bomb is here as the Other, the sovereign, a palatable body politic. It is a sign. It is 'not me', or better still, it de-signates that 'it is not mine'. This de-signative and abortive gesture makes it an instrument of communication and collectivity. It restricts 'the nature of man' wherein we find 'three principal causes of quarrel. First competition; secondly diffidence; thirdly, glory', as Hobbes wrote (1946, I. 13). All these natural human characteristics could be represented by one word only: *mimesis* (Girard, 1987a, pp. 26–7). Mimesis leads to tyranny and violence; hence the body politic, the sovereign and the victim are needed to restrict its appropriative character.

As we are so often admonished, it is useless to ask why the sovereign is needed, why there must be a body politic; without them there would be only violence and chaos. That is the case with the bomb too; it is here and there is no need to ask why and where it comes from. It simply is. Its very being donates the power of life and language to everyone.

Yet every kind of mythological revelation story flourishes around nuclear weapons (see Dowling, 1987). There are stories about people's heroism in inventing or resisting them, stories of the bomb coming to earth like lightning and showing the way for humankind. There are stories about clearing a space and building a temple for worship which must be kept distinct and separate in order to commemorate the revelation, as in Hiroshima. All these stories point to the necessity of preserving these weapons as a guarantee of our being, as a sacred sign of revelation. These stories are necessary for enshrining and perpetuating the bomb as an object of interest, something desirable, something that stands in between order and chaos and separates us from the 'natural state of war'. Only as intriguing, desirable objects are weapons capable of inspiring individuals' collective mobilization, capable of drawing people together. Only then they can function as a device for communication and global understanding, either positively, providing by their presence security, or negatively providing security by their very absence.

What if nuclear weapons lose their attractive character as objects, if they begin to show the erosion of history, and lose their revelatory and eternal character? What if the body politic guaranteed and sanctified by the bomb is full of worms and offers nothing to eat? That would be a catastrophe for those people who believed the weapons to be eternal. For these people there would be nothing left but the desert and apocalyptic silence. No God, no society, no order. For them the modern apocalypse is nothing but this desert and the desert is nothing but the death of desire, and desire dies when it loses its interest in the object, when it forgets the object.

It seems that this is just what has happened to the European peace movement. It is, after all, possible to abolish nuclear weapons. As a matter of fact, part of the nuclear arsenal is in the process of being destroyed, although nuclear warheads are being saved, a factor to which the peace movement activist or deterrence theorist clings, as though to a lifebelt. This process did not begin because of any conscious action undertaken by the peace movement, but because the very castles of rationality, the Soviet Union and the United States, have lost their interest in nuclear armaments.

For the peace movement, for peace research institutes and military think-tanks, the situation is bewildering and embarrassing. It borders on the incredible that something which a moment ago was believed to be a sacred instrument of global communication, which united all the people and was arousing everybody's concern, has suddenly been transformed into rubbish which only the superpowers have to deal with, by hiding it in their back yards or destroying it. We, the general public, feel that it is no longer our business. Our attention has already been directed elsewhere.

Reactions are illustrative. Now that the symbolic value of nuclear weapons has decreased, the European peace movement is in crisis. It is a phenomenon of the past and should be relegated, with its no longer sacred ritual objects, to a museum. Peace researchers, for their part, insist that what is happening is not real, that it cannot, will not, or should not happen. There must be some hidden agenda, God must still be there, there must be food left for the ritual, but the priests try to hide God by speaking in some foreign language, abruptly changing the old rules and the old grammar.

We can talk in terms of disappointment, sadness and shock, as if we had suddenly lost our true love. In short, a while ago millions of people hated the bomb, yet now it seems that this hate was nothing but love and affection:

> After they had got rid of him, had satisfied their hatred and had put into effect their wish to identify themselves with him, the affection which had all this time been pushed under was bound to make itself felt. It did so in the form of remorse. A sense of guilt made its appearance, which in this instance coincided with the remorse felt by the whole group. The dead father became stronger than the living one had been. . . . What had up to then been prevented by his actual existence was thenceforward prohibited by the sons themselves. . . . They revoked their deed by forbidding the killing of the totem, the substitute for their father. . . . [Freud, 1983, p. 143]

Maybe it is an exaggeration to claim that nuclear weapons are being destroyed against the will of peace activists and deterrence theorists. It would be more accurate to say that the activists and theorists were deprived of their autonomy when their opinions were exploited and they themselves were integrated into superpower politics. It seems evident, though, that the peace activists and many researchers, at least after World War II, have created their identity and oriented their activity around the different and autonomous character of nuclear weapons. That is why it is quite understandable that when these weapons begin to lose their unique character, when they have become counterproductive in world politics, they can no longer act as an *exemplum* of the special need for a nuclear resistance movement or for research that takes the nuclear arsenal as its object and institutional ground.

This crisis for the peace movement and deterrence theory has become aggravated because nuclear weapons have shifted from the public domain to the superpowers' private spheres. The United States, and especially the Soviet Union, have tyrannically absorbed all the slogans of the old peace movement: total annihilation, saving the planet, the nuclear winter, the supreme value of survival. There seems to be no sovereign place for a special movement fighting against weapons that threaten the whole world with destruction. The superpowers have occupied the space formerly claimed by the peace movement for its own activity, they have deprived the movement of its autonomy, and Soviet–American initiatives in this environment seem to bring more results than the political campaigns of the peace movement.

Conclusion

Those waiting for peace are not waiting, not at all. There's less and less reason for not having any news. Peace is visible already. It is like a great darkness falling, it's the beginning of forgetting. You can see already: Paris is lit up at night. . . . It had suddenly struck me that there might be a future, that foreign land was going to emerge out of this chaos where no one would wait any more. There is no room for me here anywhere, I'm not here, I'm there with him in that region no one else can reach, no one else can know, where there's burning and killing. . . . The lit up city means only one thing to me: it is a sign of death, of a tomorrow without them. [Duras, 1986]

The peace movement cannot solve its crisis by stubbornly clinging to the past. That would merely result in building a museum of kitsch, remembered with affection, a museum whose host of fanatic attendants would diminish year by year. This resembles what has happened, for example to the so-called labour movement. There is no reason at all for allowing random objects to arrest our attention, becoming substitutes for reality, excuses for denying reality, or channels for anxiety.

It is difficult to say whether there is one simple solution to that crisis. There is not just one kind of peace. That may not even be desirable, if we take 'peace' to mean 'openness' and not 'forgetfulness'. A world at peace has so far meant an orderly world, an instituted peace in which people try to forget the violence that generated it. Order has meant violence at the borders of our world, walls built of corpses preserving this peace called security. The idea of peace must somehow be freed of its alliance with the state and territoriality, if it is to mean something other than just order.

A special problem for the European peace movement in particular and also for the European population in general is that Europe after World War II, after Hiroshima and Nagasaki, has lived in the cool shadow of the bomb, in a pocket of quiet water, making Europeans believe that the order is eternal. The bomb has provided a good shelter against the burning excess of the nuclear sun, a resting place, a hearth (*hestia* as Greeks called it), where we may live. It is thanks to nuclear weapons that we did not have to come to terms with the causes of World War II. Those weapons have spared the whole of Europe from a painful self-analysis and transferred its violence and guilt to a cause somewhere outside the true Europe, to fascism, something transcendentally evil and in principle non-European, to Communism, a specific case of Eastern despotism, and so on.

Now there are signs that nuclear weapons are losing their transcendent character and can no longer indicate the difference between good and evil. There seem to be no clear and distinct boundaries between Self and Other, good and evil, we and they. Europe, the peace movement as a European phenomenon, as well as all the theories that preach about the inflexibility of the world order, are faced with a certain crisis of their specific identity which was based on the autonomous character of the bomb as the Other. The bomb of course is only a particular *exemplum* of the general functioning of the Other in our cultural production, a kind of a 'convention' or habit of speaking of the Other. It is a trace or a mark of the Other, not the Other itself as a psychoanalyst or structuralist would say. So, when the old sign becomes inefficient, when it ceases to function, and when the old habit of speaking is inadequate, we must change the sign and our habit of speaking. Only then there is a need for new interpretation and new rules.

Therein lies the possibility for a kind of a 'psychoanalytic' cure or translation. Though I think that no one should take this specific cure seriously, as a general recovery of health. It is more like adjusting oneself to illness through common delirium. During such a cure we could realize that what is most important is not the specific sign nor our imaginary involvement with that sign (the bomb). The sign, the bomb-sign as a sign of death, must exist and mark the difference between life and death no matter what its contents may be. This sign constitutes the common world for living. The act of speaking, remaining within the language, is more important than the words of the speech. This is called moving from the world of imaginary involvement to the world of symbolic, to the world of the 'pure' exchange of symbols, something dreamed of by everybody since Rousseau and Marx.

After your old symbol has become useless and non-productive, pick another one, but do not believe in it, only pretend to do so. Use it only as a device for keeping your world together, as a transference-object which drives you to act, speak and be with others. This procedure is nothing else but the old 'god-stuff' in a new guise. It does not solve the problem of violence to say that God is dead; but for our own sake we must act as though God still existed. The substituting continues as before, but now with a certain amount of 'reflection' and 'bad consciousness' in it.

The situation also brings forth both opportunities and dangers in research as well as in politics, especially concerning Europe, possibilities for new constellations of power which might well include fascist efforts to establish closed and fixed forms of identity, efforts to move again beyond doubt, or 'synthetic' tendencies toward what I would like to label an open sovereignty or the ethics of sovereignty.

There are two possible, very general solutions to the crisis of the sign or the *exemplum*, that is, the crisis of the symbol and its capacity to provide a common ground for debate.

The first is a sovereignty which does not search for an exemplum able to bring everything into a state of order again. It is not a question of separate identity but of openness and quarrel: openness of boundaries, ideas, economy, even an openness of conflict. Sovereignty does not mean identity under the illusory and false idols and signs of security. It is something like a parasitic identity, if a parasite can have a fixed identity and recognizable form (see Serres, 1983). This sovereignty meticulously misreads 'facts' to deceive us and contrives inventions to lead us astray, slowly distancing us from the 'classical' culture of order and beautiful form.

The second is the discovery of a new symbol as quickly as possible, a new *exemplum* for identity, a new focus for collective mobilization. That is the easiest way, a way given to us by our tradition in its mythologies, statues and rituals.

For example, in Europe there are signs of racism. Racism, as a hunt after the leopards, is indeed a very 'good' way building up a solid and frigid identity. There are also frightening ecological problems that could lead to very similar results. To speculate further: we could think that racism on the one hand and the new ecological movements on the other, on the general level of the search for identity, have much more in common than activists in both parties might suppose. They share common features in their origin, although the focus of these movements is rather different. It is also arguable that the peace movement, especially its way of mobilizing people around a specific, urgent social problem, has stimulated these movements.

To use psychoanalytic jargon: for the peace movement nuclear weapons have constituted maternal figures and the movement has refused to mature under the emotional warmth of these figures. The bomb, as an all-embracing mother, has blocked their view, so that the peace activists fail to see beyond the relations that produce the bomb. So far the only properly ethical, and—in the psychoanalytic sense—imaginary question has been: is the mother absent or present? There have been no doubts about the mother's power up until recently. Now these doubts are arising. Maybe the greatest impact of the INF treaty—and the situation of indecision that began at Reykjavik—is that it made a break, however small, in this intensive mother–child relationship. It let in the first beams of light, creating a contrast and showing that even the mother is not all-powerful, even she has a particular locality and function.

This may lead to a cure, in the sense that we may hunt for a new *exemplum* around which to build the old temple, or it may lead to a deeper cultural analysis of the social relations and forces that produce these feminine figures of death, and force us almost unconsciously to hunt and dream about the difference. Even a dream is not innocent, or just a story told for fun, as is well known. Perhaps that dream, as Samuel Weber writes, 'for once will allow us to care about something other than just winning' (Weber, 1987 p. 58).

Bibliography

Burkert, W., 1979. *Structure and History in Greek Mythology and Ritual*. Berkeley: University of California Press.

Burkert, W., 1983. *Homo Necans: The Anthropology of Ancient Greek Sacrificial Ritual and Myth*. Berkeley: University of California Press.

Burkert, W., 1987. 'The Problem of Ritual Killing', in Hamerton-Kelly, 1987.

Cohen, A. & S. Lee, eds., 1986. *Nuclear Weapons and the Future of Humanity*. New Jersey: Roman & Allanheld.

Derrida, J., 1982. *Margins of Philosophy*. Chicago: University of Chicago Press.

Derrida, J., 1983. 'The Principle of Reason: The University in the Eyes of its Pupils', *Diacritics*, vol. 13, no. 3.

Derrida, J., 1984. 'No Apocalypse, Not Now (full speed ahead, seven missiles, seven missives)', *Diacritics*, vol. 14, no. 2.

Dowling, D., 1987. *Fictions of Nuclear Disaster*. London: Macmillan.

Duras, M., 1986. *La Douleur*. Glasgow: Collins/Flamingo.

Ferguson, F., 1984. 'The Nuclear Sublime', *Diacritics*, vol. 14, no. 2.

Freud, S., 1983. *Totem and Taboo*. London: Ark Paperbacks.

Freud, S., 1984. 'A Note on the Unconscious in Psychoanalysis', in *The Pelican Freud Library*, vol. 11. Harmondsworth: Penguin Books.

Freud, S., 1985. *The Intervention of Dreams*. Harmondsworth: Penguin Books.
Girard, R., 1977. *Violence and the Sacred*. Baltimore, Maryland: Johns Hopkins University Press.
Girard, R., 1985. *The Scapegoat*. Baltimore, Maryland: Johns Hopkins University Press.
Girard, R., 1987a. *Things Hidden Since the Foundation of the World*. Stanford, Calif.: Stanford University Press.
Girard, R., 1987b. 'Generative Scapegoating', in Hamerton-Kelly, 1987.
Girard, R., 1987c. *The Scapegoat*. Baltimore, Maryland: Johns Hopkins University Press.
Hamerton-Kelly, R. ed., 1987. *Violent Origins: Ritual Killing and Cultural Formations*. Stanford: Stanford University Press.
Hegel, G.W.F, 1977. *Phenomenology of Spirit*. Oxford: Oxford University Press.
Heidegger, M., 1962. 'Plato's Doctrine of Truth', in W. Barret *et al.*, eds. *Philosophy in the Twentieth Century*. New York: Random House.
Heidegger, M., 1969. *The Essence of Reasons*. Evanston, Ill.: Northwestern University Press.
Heidegger, M., 1974. 'The Principle of Ground', *Man and World*, vol. 7.
Heidegger, M., 1975. *Early Greek Thinking*. New York: Random House.
Heidegger, M., 1985. *Being and Time*. London: Blackwell.
Hobbes, T., 1946. *Leviathan*. Oxford: Oxford University Press.
Kafka, F., 1981. *Stories 1904–1924*. London: Macdonald/Futura.
Kerckhove, D., 1984., 'On Nuclear Communication', *Diacritics*, vol.14, no. 2.
Lifton, R., 1986. 'Imagining the Real: Beyond the Nuclear End', in L. Greenspoon, ed. *The Long Darkness*. London: Yale University Press.
Mehan, H. & J. Skelly, 1988. 'Reykjavik: The Breach and Repair of the Pure War Script', *Multilingua*, vol. 7, no. 1/2.
Nietzsche, F., 1980. *Ecce Homo: How One Becomes What One Is*. Harmondsworth: Penguin Books.
Rousseau, J-J., 1979. *The Social Contract*. Harmondsworth: Penguin Books.
Serres, M., 1982. *The Parasite*. Baltimore, Maryland: Johns Hopkins University Press.
Serres, M., 1983. 'The Apparition of Hermes: Don Juan', in J.V. Harari & D.F. Bell, eds. *Hermes: Literature, Science, Philosophy*. Baltimore, Maryland: Johns Hopkins University Press.
Smith, J., 1978. *Map is Not Territory*. Leiden: E.J. Brill.
Smith, J., 1982. *Imagining Religion: From Babylon to Jonestown*. Chicago: University of Chicago Press.
Smith, J., 'The Domestication of Sacrifice', in Hamerton-Kelly, 1987.
Thompson, E., 1982. *Zero Option*. London: Merlin Press.
Volkan, V., 1987. 'The Need to Have Enemies and Nuclear Weapons', in H.B. Levinen *et al.*, eds. *Psychoanalytic Explorations of the Nuclear Threat*. New York: Analytic Press.
Weber, S., 1987. *Institution and Interpretation*. Minneapolis: University of Minnesota Press.

4 Burke the International Theorist[1]—or the War of the Sons of Light and the Sons of Darkness

Vilho Harle

Edmund Burke (1729–97) is known first and foremost as a British politician and political theorist. According to the generally accepted view,

> critical response to the French Revolution produced the pamphlets by which his posthumous reputation was transformed from that of a thoughtful writer on matters relating to the British Constitution to that of the acknowledged major exponent of the conservative reaction to the French Revolution. [Miller, 1987]

This image, however, overlooks at least one important aspect of him; it entirely ignores his ideas on international relations. The picture ties Burke exclusively to the history of political theory. Everything outside that domain is put aside and belittled. For example, Macpherson (1980, p. 71) refers to the well-known problem of Burke's inconsistency in being both 'the defender of a hierarchical establishment', and 'the market liberal' exclusively as a problem for political theory. For Macpherson the alleged discrepancy between Burke's positions on the American and the French revolutions is only a 'seeming inconsistency', which 'can be dismissed very quickly' (Macpherson, 1980, p. 6). In similar vein Burke's sustained attack on the arbitrary rule of the East India Company receives but scant attention in Macpherson's work.

Greenleaf explicitly discusses the international dimension in Burke's thinking, but again in exclusive relation to political theory, ignoring the existence of distinct nations and the problem of relations between them. We thus read that 'Burke was not one to deny the crucial importance of political power but he was always aware of the need to impose limits on it.' Greenleaf hints that 'this meant stating the nature and responsibilities of imperial power', but the basic questions still remain within the traditional field of political theory. According to Greenleaf's interpretation Burke was asking whether power is wilful or irresponsible; whether its use may be justified in terms of expedience or state necessity; or whether it is always the duty of the ruler to conform to law in the exercise of authority (Greenleaf, 1975, pp. 550–4).

There is nothing surprising in this construal of Burke exclusively in terms of classical political theory. As Michael Donelan has pointed out, classical political thinkers have rather little to say about international relations. Political theorists did not handle international issues explicitly in their writings; 'as theorists they say nothing because there is nothing to say' (Donelan, 1978, p. 75); or:

> International relations is concerned with a mere space between states, a desert of crude power, mitigated at best by a network of pragmatical customs and by pragmatical, unstable co-operation. This is a place for great intelligence and the highest qualities of character but only on the part of practical statesmen and their attorneys and historians and commentators. There is no international theory to be done. [1978, p. 90]

For my own part, however, I would suggest that the 'international' aspects of Burke's thinking and career deserve serious theoretical discussion. Furthermore, I would claim that the international dimension will reveal his influence on the later Cold War images of the enemy. Burke the international theorist is also related to the traditions discussed in Chapter 1: Burke constitutes a direct link between the ancient traditions of dualism and the Cold War discourse (cf. Dalby, 1988; Nathanson, 1988).

Burke the international theorist

Burke the international theorist was introduced by Wight (1966), who, in considering where international theory is to be found, suggests political philosophers, philosophers and historians as the most rewarding source in the quest. Furthermore, he suggests that the only political philosopher who has turned wholly from political theory to international theory is Burke. Indeed, Burke's major publications deal with foreign affairs and relations between nations.[2] Much, then, is to be gained by discussing him as an international theorist, not instead of but in addition to a political theorist. This can contribute not only to an understanding of Burke's ideas, but specifically to an understanding of his 'use' in various times.[3]

During the nineteenth century Burke was regarded as a utilitarian liberal but not as a prophet of reaction (Kramnick, 1977, p. 41). Even after World War I Harold Laski could still applaud Burke as a liberal utilitarian, while noting and deploring his darker undemocratic side. Burke was made over into a Natural Law man and a conservative only during and after World War II. As Macpherson (1980, p. 4) maintains:

> Coincidentally, the new portrait filled a new need in the 1950s: in reviving Burke the crusader against radicalism, it discovered a welcome ideological support for the Cold War crusade against the apprehended threat of Soviet communism.

I suggest that this 'new Burke' was Burke the international theorist, and that, therefore, the new portrait served political needs not at all coincidentally: there was an identified quest for a Burke-like international theorist and the tradition he represented and transmitted to modern political thinking. The Cold War was the Christian crusade against Communism. This was why Burke's texts were perceived, after World War II, to convey the holy creed inspiring the defence of 'Western Christendom' against the 'Moscow enslavement of 1917'. Cold War anti-Communists saw Burke's defence of Christian Europe against French revolutionary fanaticism as a stirring example to the Western democracies engaged in ideological warfare against atheistic Communism. Burke was the inspiration America needed in the Cold War: as he saved Christendom then, so his words could do it now. As Kramnick suggests, Burke was functional to the Cold War conservatism of the 1950s and early 1960s, and to the more recent new conservatism of the late 1960s and 1970s (Kramnick, 1977, pp. xi, 3–4, 45–7). The new revival of Burke during the 'second' Cold War in the 1980s corroborates this picture.

This chapter aims at documenting the role of dualistic distinctions in Burke's thinking. Hence my discussion will be somewhat selective. A more comprehensive analysis of Burke's international theory will require additional research in the future.

Burke for peace

The Indian question[4] is related to 'the Manner in which India is connected with' England. And we know that according to Burke (1981b, p. 222),

> The Two great Links by which this Connection is maintained are, first, the East India Company's Commerce; and next The Government set over the Natives by that Company, and by the Crown.

Burke had a great respect for the Indian social and political organization as well as for Indian religion (Marshall, 1981, p. 14). He did not adopt an air of superiority towards people outside Europe (cf. Said, 1979). On the contrary, he supports the principle of equality instead of dominance as the basis of British–Indian relations. The 'Natives' were for Burke human beings:

> This multitude of men does not consist of an abject and barbarous populace; much less of gangs and savages ... but a people for ages civilized and cultivated; cultivated by all the arts of polished life, whilst we were yet in the woods. [Burke, 1981a, p. 389]

Burke perceives a natural harmony of interests in British–Indian relations. The stability and prosperity of India would contribute to the prosperity of Britain. In a properly ordered British–Indian relationship, from which 'British greed and corruption' had been eliminated, there could be no conflict of interests. The interests of the natives of India and those of Great Britain 'are in Effect, one and the same'. Burke gave some indication that he was aware that harmony between Britain and India might be more difficult to attain than he usually implied, but he still insisted that, even if Britain's national interest rather than the interest of individuals was at stake, there could still be no compromise with the duty to put the well-being of India first (Marshall, 1981, p. 24). If parliament could not

> contrive some method of governing India well, which will not of necessity become the means of governing Great Britain ill, a ground is laid for their eternal separation; but none for sacrificing the people of that country to our constitution. (Burke, 1981b, p. 383)

Equality and harmony led to a special interpretation of mutual interdependence: the British policy in India would have an important influence in England: 'I am certain that every means, effectual to preserve India from opression, is a guard to preserve the British constitution from its worst corruption' (Burke, 1981b, p. 383).

Burke criticized the excesses of colonialism, because he saw that the English had foolishly lost much of their great empire in the West; only a wise policy would keep intact the empire in the East. In his campaign against the East India Company, Burke, in effect, worked out theories relating to the relationship between any imperial power and any subject people (Marshall, 1981, p. 1), implying various criticisms of imperialistic practices. Burke was not seeking to develop *a* theory of imperialism, but as Greenleaf has in passing suggested, he tried to state the nature and responsibilities of imperial power (Greenleaf,

1975). Burke raised issues which have since become the staple of debates on the economic effects of imperialism.

Exploitation had nothing to do with chance, it was a system—as imperialism has come to be seen (Marshall, 1981, p. 195). In relation to the ideas of equal interdependence Burke refuted the idea of imperial dominance; according to him the prosperity of the natives must be secured, 'before any Profit from them whatsoever is attempted' (Marshall, 1981, p. 23). Attempts to seek unilateral advantages for Britain at India's expense were self-defeating. A reform of India through colonial rule was unthinkable to Burke; direct British rule could do a great deal of harm. In no instance that Burke knew of had the condition of the inhabitants been improved by British occupation. The famine, war and economic decline in southern India arose not from defects in Indian society, but from abuses by Europeans. A prosperous, self-sufficient society had been disrupted by British misconduct (cf. Marshall, 1981, pp. 15, 20): 'When all the countries . . . came into our possession, they were all eminently peopled, and eminently productive; though at that time considerably declined from their ancient prosperity. But since they are come into our hands!—!' (Burke, 1981a, p. 389).

Burke believed that, for example, 'the fertility of Bengal, the skill of its artisans, and the wealth of its merchants had until recent years produced a flourishing trading system based on a free market'. But once the British East India Company had acquired political power, it had used this power to curtail the freedom of the market, with catastrophic results (Marshall, 1981, p. 21). According to Burke:

> . . . there is not a single prince, state, or potentate, great or small, in India, with whom they have come into contact, whom they have not sold. . . . there is not a single treaty they have ever made, which they have not broken. . . . there is not a single prince or state, who ever put any trust in the Company, who is not utterly ruined. [Burke, 1981a, p. 391]

Burke's solutions to the problem of unequal dominance are fairly well known today. He maintained that the British must use ultimate authority with the utmost restraint (Marshall, 1981, p. 20).[5] Furthermore, he supported the idea of free trade. He maintained that artisans must be free to sell to the highest bidder and Indian merchants must be encouraged to compete freely with Europeans, including the Company itself (Marshall, 1981, p. 21).[6] And Burke recommended even more radical measures. He maintained that authority is a trust and that 'it is of the very essence of every trust to be rendered accountable; and even totally to cease, when it substantially varies from the purposes for which alone it could have a lawful existence' (Burke, 1981a, pp. 385–6). And finally,

I therefore conclude . . . that this body (the East India Company), being totally perverted from the purposes of its institution, is utterly incorrigible; and because they are incorrigible . . . power ought to be taken out of their hands; just on the same principles on which have been made all the just changes and revolutions of government that have taken place since the beginning of the world. [Burke, 1981a, p. 440]

Burke was a vigorous opponent of the English government during the period leading to the declaration of independence by the North American colonies and the subsequent war. Burke's position on this question was undeniably related to politics in England, but he was conspicuously explicit in speaking of international questions, not only domestic politics:

I have ever wished a settled plan of our own . . . wholly unconnected with the events of the war, and framed in such a manner as to keep up our credit and maintain our system at home, in spite of anything which may happen abroad. I am now convinced, by a long and somewhat vexatious experience, that such a plan is absolutely impracticable. [Burke, 1887e, p. 138]

It is true that Americans were, to Burke, Englishmen. To him the people of the colonies were descendants of Englishmen, faithful to English political ideas and principles (Burke, 1887c, p. 120), the King's 'English subjects in America'. Conceptions of civil war were thus applicable to the situation. It was British blood that was spilled by British hands; the British were continuing the effusion of English blood. Burke could not agree to 'unite in new severities against the brethren of our blood for their asserting an independence' (1887b, pp. 169–73). He advised the colonists not to 'think that the whole, or even the uninfluenced majority, of Englishmen in this island are enemies to their own blood on the American continent' (1887a, p. 184). But, in fact, this point of view, in Burke's mind, led to acceptance of the American independence, rather than to its domination by the English force.

In Burke's opinion, the American revolution had been made inevitable by the policies of the English government, not by the behaviour of the colonies. The colonists must have been faced with 'horrible calamity': they had suffered gross personal insults from the British power (1887e, p. 138). England had started the war on the colonies, and had made this war 'not by arms only, but by laws' before open violence and armed conflict broke out. There was a 'long array of hostile acts of Parliament by which the war with America has been begun and supported' (1887f, p. 202). Burke maintained that 'discontent will increase with misery' (1887c, p. 133): 'That grievance is as simple in its nature . . . as it is powerful in affecting the most languid passions: it is—"AN ATTEMPT MADE TO DISPOSE OF THE PROPERTY OF A WHOLE PEOPLE WITHOUT THEIR CONSENT" ' (1887b, p. 164).

Indeed, Burke was convinced that the disorders of the people were 'owing to the usual and natural cause of such disorders at all times and in all places, i.e. the misconduct of government' (1887b, p. 163). This misconduct was reflected particularly in the debated taxation. Burke called attention to the fact that 'the great contests for freedom' in England had been 'from the earliest times chiefly upon the question of taxing' (1887c, p. 120). Therefore any solution to these problems implied the right to independent finances. Burke advised the British government to 'leave America, if she has taxable matter in her, to tax herself', but not to 'burden them by taxes: you were not used to do so from the beginning' (1887h, pp. 72–3).

Burke did not accept the dominating convention that the Americans had no right to revolt against their parents, for 'when children ask for bread, we are not to give a stone'. The relations between England and America could only be based on unsuspicious confidence: 'When confidence is once restored, the odious and suspicious *summum jus* will perish of course'. The acceptance of liberties, and the application of conciliation would lead to relations where mutually beneficial trade appears and the partners could live 'with an open and flowing commerce between us' (1887a, p. 187). From another angle Burke proposed to be 'content to bind America by laws of trade: you have always done so'. Therefore, the duties upon glass, and paper were to be removed 'upon consideration of such duties having been laid contrary to the true principles of commerce (1887h, pp. 21, 71–4, 187, 235). If this solution is not accepted, 'instead of a standing revenue, you will . . . have a perpetual quarrel' (1887c, p. 174).

The misconduct of government and the exploitation of the people in the colonies by the English government is closely related to the question of liberties. The theme of liberty is one of the most frequently repeated ideas in Burke's texts on the colonies. He maintained that

> . . . a spirit, that, unhappily meeting with an exercise of power in England, which, however lawful, is not reconcilable to any ideas of liberty, much less with theirs, has kindled this flame that is ready to consume us. [1887c, p. 127]

Burke suggested that the 'fierce spirit of liberty' was stronger in the English colonies 'than in any other people of the earth'—probably including the English in England. The spirit of liberty had been reared, according to Burke, from six capital sources: 'of descent, of form of government, of religion, of manners, of education, and of remoteness' (1887c, pp. 120, 127). So,

> Your Majesty's English subjects in the colonies . . . know that to live under such a plan of government is not to live in a state of freedom. Your English subjects in the colonies, still impressed with the ancient feelings of the people from whom they are derived, cannot live under a government which does not establish freedom as its basis. [1887b, p. 164]

Therefore, the relationship between England and the colonies could be properly arranged solely on the basis of liberty: 'peace, order, and civilization followed in the train of liberty'. Freedom, and not servitude, is the cure of anarchy if only England was ready to comply with the American spirit or to submit to it as a necessary evil (1887c, pp. 150–2, 189).

Burke not only suggests conciliation, or conflict resolution through submission, he also explicitly rejects conventional and violent alternatives. He saw no possibilities for conventional representation by the colonists in the English parliament for geopolitical reasons: one cannot remove the 'eternal barriers of the creation'. And similarly, concerning the use of English governmental power in the colonies, 'no contrivance can prevent the effect of this distance in weakening government' (1887c, pp. 126 and 153). In consequence, Burke did not suppose that the Americans might submit themselves to British power: 'Respecting your wisdom, and valuing your safety, we do not call upon you to trust your existence to your enemies' (1887a, p. 193).

Furthermore, he disapproved the use of force; in its stead he chose 'prudent management'. Force might be justified only if 'fighting a people be the best way of gaining them'—but the use of force would be counterproductive; it was to him 'temporary', 'uncertain', 'impairing the object', and against 'experience in favour of force as an instrument in the rule of our colonies' (1887c, pp. 118–19). Burke also objected to 'harsh laws and feeble armies', for him 'mercy, as we conceive, consists, not in the weakness of the means, but in the benignity of the ends' (1887b, p. 168). Against the opinions of realists of the later days, Burke explicitly dismissed military force as the basis of international order: 'the character of judge in my own cause is a thing that frightens me' (1887c, p. 137). Neither did he hold that all things are lawful in war; on the contrary, everybody in England was fully responsible for 'every barbarity, in fire, in wasting, in murders, in tortures, and other cruelties, too horrible and too full of turpitude for Christian mouths to utter or ears to hear' (1887a, p. 189).

Burke justified non-violence by the negative consequences of the use of force which would ensue for England. Here again, foreign policy was likely to have consequences in domestic affairs. Burke refers to economic losses the American war caused for people in England (1887e, p. 140). However, he emphasizes moral consequences more. According to Burke, attempts to prove that the Americans had no right to their liberties implied that 'we are every day endeavouring to subvert the maxims which preserve the whole spirit of our own' (1887c, p. 130). A military government in America was the only substitute for civil liberty, but the establishment of such a power in America would become 'an apt, powerful, and certain engine for the destruction of our freedom here'. Burke eloquently cries: 'What, gracious sovereign, is the empire of America to us, or the empire of the world, if we lose our own liberties?' Indeed, 'victory would only vary the mode of our ruin'. He advised not to become 'the instruments in a design, of which, in our turn, we might become the victims' (1887b, pp. 176–7). In conclusion:

> Knowing the inestimable value of peace, and the contemptible value of what was sought by war, we wished to compose the distractions of our country, not by the use of foreign arms, but by prudent regulations in our own domestic policy. [1887b, p. 162]

Finally, Burke's conception of peace, as implied by some of these quotations, deserves our attention. The conception he supported was clearly rather unconventional. Peace was not mere non-existence of armed struggle, but something more. If armed hostilities are ended by force 'we may call the effect of our victory peace', but still 'the war is not ended: the hostile mind continues in full vigour, and it continues under a worse form'. That kind of peace is 'nothing more than a sullen pause from arms'. For Burke, peace was 'a blessing' not obtained 'through the medium of war; not peace to be hunted through the labyrinth of intricate and endless negotiations' (1887f, pp. 194, 230). It was to be 'peace sought in the spirit of peace, and laid in principles purely pacific' (1887c, p. 106). Peace was not domination by one party over the other, nor the threat of force, it was a precondition for permanent connection through commerce and equal exchange. The peace and union of the colonies were 'the very foundation' of his plan (1887c, p. 175).

If we stopped here, Burke might look like a representative of the so-called idealist school in the study of international relations.[7] And, in the full spirit of the idealist school, Burke's campaign against Warren Hastings, and the more successful position on American independence, were conscious efforts to educate the public. It is also conspicuous that

Burke envisaged a linkage theory (introduced in the 1960s by scholars in international relations), according to which the effects of policy in one country (India, America, France) will be diffused into other countries (England) through several mechanisms (linkage groups).

Burke's ideas are rather similar to later anti-imperialist claims. However, it must be pointed out that Burke also enjoys a reputation as one of the most advanced imperialists in British history. He was far ahead of his time not in anti-imperialism but in his thought on benevolent imperialism, suggesting 'positive' applications of the imperialist rule. In Burke's view the benefits of imperial citizenship far outweighed any disadvantages accruing from it. For Burke, England was the eldest brother who guards the family possessions for a number of younger brothers, on whose help he also depends. Burke's positive imperialism was a system of mutual help: it was in the interest of the whole to see to it that all parts of the Empire were fairly treated. In short, Burke acted not only to correct an injustice to an oppressed people but to strengthen the British Empire at a time of crisis. Burke was willing to vest in the imperial parliament, to be used whenever needed, the kind of power necessary for upholding imperial unity: Britain had to be constitutionally supreme over the parts of the Empire, but in exercising her supremacy must be generous (Mahoney, 1960, pp. 51, 57–8, 111, 312–15).

Burke for war

Burke wrote several pieces on the French revolution, the best known among them being the *Reflections on the Revolution in France*. However, the conventional picture of Burke suggested at the beginning of this chapter maintains that he was only interested in the revolution in France and its consequences in England. The international aspect is again ignored. In fact, Burke's 'French' texts were in several ways related to international relations, particularly between England and France. Burke's four letters *On the Proposals for Peace with the Regicide Directory of France* (1796–7) are especially important in this respect. The new political system in France had existed for six to eight years before the letters were written. The letters continue to criticize the French system, but the major aim is now to consider how the relationship between the Regicide Directory and England could and should be arranged; in particular, was there any possibility for peace between the different political systems? Burke's answer was a clear-cut no: peace with the Jacobins was no better than defeat by them. Attempts at peace with France were out of the question, the allies had been, in Burke's opinion, 'miserably deluded' by a dramatic error: 'that it was in our power to make peace with this monster of a state' (1887d, I, p. 245). England was obliged to wage war—together with, or even alone for, its allies in Europe—until the Regicide power was destroyed and eliminated altogether.

According to Burke the 'usual relations of peace and amity in civilized Europe' had disappeared as a consequence of the French revolution. France was not involved in normal international relations; the relations of France were no longer to be found 'among the rest' (Burke, 1887d, II, p. 360). While Burke saw that England should make free trade possible for India, and that American independence was a precondition for free trade (and, in consequence, peace), he understood that France after the revolution would be a danger to free international trade. Burke maintained, indirectly or directly, that France was not interested in normal international relations, that is, trade between equal partners, but only in the increase of her power over other nations. This would suggest one reason why Burke was widely accepted after World War II, when the United States had to find a theoretical justification for free trade in the American-dominated Bretton Woods regime.

Burke warned that it would be dangerous to have peace with a system which in its essence was 'inimical to all other governments'. The acknowledgement of any kind of superiority in this new power would completely ruin the old governments. The Regicide Directory was an expanding power that would not stop 'until they have accomplished our utter and irretrievable ruin' (Burke, 1887d, I, pp. 250, 258). The enemy plans 'an invasion, which at one stroke may complete our servitude and ruin and expunge us from among the nations of the earth' (1887d, III, p. 446).

According to Burke the balance of power had been the common law of Europe 'at all times and by all powers'. But the Regicide Directory had, he maintains, constantly rejected the very idea of a balance of power, and treated it as the cause of all the wars and calamities that had afflicted Europe. The alternative suggested by the Directory is a 'sort of impious hierarchy, of which France is to be the head and the guardian'. Therefore, France 'means to form an universal empire, by producing an universal revolution', and 'pretends to secure eternal peace to the world, guaranteed by her generosity and justice, which are to grow with the extent of her power' (Burke, 1887d, III, pp. 441–3). The regicide power, 'usurped at home', is to be erected 'into a legislature to govern mankind' (1887d, I, p. 268). In brief, 'to talk of the balance of power to the governors of such a country was a jargon which they could not understand even through an interpreter' (1887d, III, p. 443).

Peace negotiations were, therefore, in vain. The Regicide Directory could never been reduced to reason. The Directory's peace offer was delusive, 'the design of cheating' the people of England and the allies (1887d, I, pp. 275, 292). The enemy did not show 'the smallest indication of a desire for peace' but 'rather the direct contrary' (1887d, III, p. 442). It was thus impossible to negotiate in good faith with a power that assumed 'the ill faith and treachery of those they have to deal with'. The enemy sought to deceive the defenders into disarming themselves; the Regicide Directory only wished to gain time (1887d, I, pp. 252, 274, 287).

Therefore it was not wise to make peace without previous knowledge of the terms, for without that knowledge peace became a surrender (1887d, I, p. 283). Or again:

> Has this empire nothing to alarm you when all struggle against it is over, when mankind shall be silent before it, when all nations shall be disarmed, disheartened, and truly divided by a treacherous peace? [1887d, IV, p. 31]

Burke asks everybody to note that the Regicide meant to dictate a pacification (1887d, IV, p. 18). So one should not leave 'the moment of negotiation, a most important moment, to the choice of the enemy' (1887d, III, p. 409).

The war of the Sons of Light against the Sons of Darkness

In the Indian and American cases Burke spoke for peace, in the French case for war. Indeed, Burke the international theorist has a Janus face. This is fully compatible with historical experience and earlier studies on Burke the political theorist. For example, Paine, who had known Burke for some three years, simply assumed that since they had taken rather similar positions on events in America, Burke would share Paine's enthusiasm for events in France; Paine wrote excitedly to Burke, still then his friend, that the revolution in France was certainly a forerunner of other revolutions in Europe! And it is usual to speak of two Burkes in political theory: the Tory prophet and the ambivalent radical (Kramnick, 1977, pp. 4, 143).

A conventional explanation is to suggest that behind the two Burkes there is only one: Burke the politician. Burke was a practical politician who was not speaking of international relations and war in general (his ideas may have general implications, but that is another matter), he was always debating on concrete phenomena: India, the North American colonies and France. In some specific situations (India,

America) he thought that peace and commerce were best. But in the case of France, he accepted and supported *specific* war against it. It is not so rare to find similar patterns in other politicians, or for that matter scholars. Some may well think that a specific war is inevitable and supportable, while war in general is not, or that other specific wars are disputable. A specific war is always assessed through the existing value structure of the individual: if a specific war is required to make the important values safe against a perceived threat, that specific war is accepted (Airas, 1978).

A more interesting alternative is to consider Burke's conspicuous inclination to make a clear distinction between good and bad. Burke had rather strong feelings about good and bad: to him the good always represents the absolute truth. The distinction between good and bad (as equal to true and false or right and wrong) emerges everywhere in his texts, including his general political writings.[8] Concerning the East India Company he felt 'bound to declare against those chartered rights which produce so many wrongs'. Burke should have deemed himself 'the wickedest of men, if any vote of mine could contribute to the continuance of so great an evil' (Burke, 1981a, p. 401). The East India Company and Warren Hastings were the evil against whom Burke felt himself obliged to struggle. Hastings' fundamental crime was the 'assault on the age-old social structure of India and on its traditions in general'. Kramnick puts it perfectly in noting that for Burke the trial of Warren Hastings took on the character of a 'crusade' for Burke and that it 'transcended the particulars and became an assault on virtually all the corruptions of Burke's time (Kramnick, 1977, pp. 26, 127). Also in the American case, 'wicked and designing men' were responsible for the 'misconduct of government' (Burke, 1887a, p. 184; cf. Kramnick, 1977, p. 23).

After the French revolution Burke received a strong personal, moral obligation from God, indeed, a gift from God: 'A kind Providence has placed in our breasts a hatred of the unjust and cruel, in order that we may preserve ourselves from cruelty and injustice' (Burke, 1887d, IV, pp. 89–90). Burke had a strong feeling of duty; he knew that participation in the struggle was to change the balance in the struggle between good and bad in the first's favour. This divine inspiration was to lead his pen: 'If I had but one hour to live, I would employ it in decrying this wretched system, and die with my pen in my hand' (1887d, IV, p. 28).

Concerning India and America the bad were found in England (or among the representatives of the British government and authority in the colonies). As we found in the Indian debate, the 'Natives' were good people, as were the 'Englishmen' in America. The line of division went within a nation, dividing Englishmen into two opposite groups:

Those who have and who hold to that foundation of common liberty, whether on this or on your side of the ocean, we consider as the true, and the only true, Englishmen. Those who depart from it, whether there or here, are attained, corrupted in blood, and wholly fallen from their original rank and value. They are the real rebels to the fair constitution and just supremacy of England. [Burke, 1887a, p. 190]

But as to France, the distinction between the good and the bad became mainly international. Now, Burke contrasted the virtuous English and the radical French. This at the same time was to contrast virtuous English and radical millenarian English (Kramnick, 1977, p. 29): there were, as we know from Burke, some followers of the French revolution in England, but without revolutionary France they could not survive. They did not represent central political power, but were located in 'certain societies in London'.

Burke's conceptions of good and bad are derived from religious bases. As a youth he was deeply religious, and the passing years served merely to strengthen his religiosity (Mahoney, 1960, p. 316). Throughout his career he was preoccupied with the devil. Burke's diabolism was linked to the literary and philosophical use made of the devil in the Christian myth, rendered most profoundly for his world by Milton. Burke's preoccupation with the Jacobins as demonic is related to the devil's ambitious striving, his tampering with 'The Great Chain of Being'. The Jacobin was for Burke the devil, because the devil was the rebel *par excellence* (Kramnick, 1977, pp. 182–4).

The influence of religion can be perceived everywhere in Burke's ideas. His political thought rests on a moral basis, and the source of moral truth is for him an eternal moral order derived from God. Man is a religious animal, and religion is the foundation of civil society (Parkin, 1956, pp. 1, 131). That is, Burke saw society as an organism embodying a divinely given moral order (Macpherson, 1980, p. 4). The 'commonwealths' were 'not physical, but moral essences' (Burke, 1887d, I, p. 234); God had structured the universe in a hierarchy of descending orders (Kramnick, 1977, p. 21). Burke insisted that the Christian religion was the indispensable basis of political stability and peace (Macpherson 1980, p. 3). The basis of a monarchy can only be secured by religion: there can be no unchristian monarchy (Burke, 1887d, IV, pp. 81–2). Atheist institutions strike at the root of social nature by violating the sacraments and by making social order impossible. If religion perishes, 'disorder', and 'a great evil, that of a civil war will emerge (Burke, 1887d, IV, p. 112). Therefore the French revolution was not a revolution in government, but a 'destruction and decomposition of the whole society' (1887d, I, pp. 325–6). So Burke could not countenance the importation of the Jacobin ideas into England: the Christian religion could never coexist with such a 'fraternity'.

Burke's position is similar to old dualistic traditions such as religious ideas dating back to Zoroastrianism, Judaism and later Christianity, and dualistic political debates in Ancient Greece. Burke identifies himself with the Sons of Light in their struggle against the Sons of Darkness, and with the opponents of Spartan, Persian and Macedonian suzerainty. Burke himself referred to these traditions in the Christian and Greek versions, and revealed in addition a full understanding of the specific historical situation in which he was living and in which he had received the call to join the Sons of Light. One may best understand the specific nature of Burke's 'French' crusade by keeping in mind that he respected the Indian religions and saw that religion gave strength and power to dissidence in the American colonies (Burke, 1887c, pp. 122–3): the form of religion did not count, its non-existence did. Burke was personally beyond the earlier European division of religions: his mother, and originally also his wife, was a Catholic. And in the campaign against the Regicide Directory Burke understood that the Roman Catholic religion represented the most effectual, if not the only, barrier against Jacobinism—the Catholics comprised the vast majority of the lower classes, and people from this segment of society were the special objects of the Jacobins (Mahoney, 1960, p. 244).

According to Burke, the declaration of a 'new species' of government represented a crisis in the politics of Europe. He refers to certain earlier divisions, particularly to that between Catholic and Protestant and that of the Guelfs and Ghibellines (Burke, 1887i, pp. 319–20). 'But in the modern world, before this time', Burke maintained 'there has been no instance of this spirit of general political faction, separated from religion, pervading several countries, and forming a principle of union between the partisans in each' (1887i, p. 320).

For Burke, France was not a state, but a faction. That faction was not local or territorial but represented a general evil. It was 'the evil spirit that possesses the body of France' (1887d, II, pp. 342–3). Paris is described as nothing less than hell where orderly civility has been turned upside down: children cut the throats of their parents, and mothers cruelly abandon their offspring (Kramnick, 1977, p. 185).

Indeed the new situation, in Burke's opinion, was a 'chaos, where *light* and *darkness* are struggling together' (1887d, III, p. 451; emphasis added). France was now 'the synagogue of Antichrist'. Burke cultivates, indeed, several direct or hidden allusions to the Book of Revelations. According to Burke the enemy 'will make his public entry into London on one of the pale horses of his brewery'. The description of the Regicide Directory makes it similar to the Beast: France is 'a double-natured monster, republic above and monarchy below'; there is 'no centaur of fiction, no poetic satyr of the woods, nothing short of the hieroglyphic monsters of Egypt, dog in head and man in body, that can give an idea of it' (1887d, IV, pp. 80, 102). The regicides are the Evil Spirit, the angel revolting against God; they have disconnected themselves from God through 'Regicide', 'Jacobinism' and 'Atheism' (1887d, I, p. 308). They transcend their God-given size, their place in His creation. Jacobins are the most dreadful calamity that can rise out of hell to scourge mankind (Kramnick, 1977, pp. 36, 182).

Typical of early religious conceptions of the final battle, Burke points out that 'we are not at an end of our struggle, nor near it' (1887d, I, p. 240). The battle is almost a draw, and causes extreme dangers to the Sons of Light: the first struggle with evil will also be the last (1887d, II, p. 343). Just like his predecessors in the tradition, Burke accuses the English supporters of Jacobinism, saying that 'their hearts are abroad', and that nothing that the Regicides do can 'alienate them from their cause' (1887d, IV, pp. 92, 106).

The ambassadors meeting the Regicide Directory 'will come out of it sad and serious conspirators, and such will continue as long as they live'. Burke strikes the very chord of religious belief in saying that 'they will become totally indifferent to good and evil' (1887d, I, pp. 259–60). He emphasizes that the new power is 'not so truly dangerous in its fortresses nor in its territories as in its spirit and its principles' (1887d, II, p. 347).

Religious tradition helps us to understand why the Evil Spirit can so easily influence the Sons of Light. This is so because everybody has got the devil inside him: 'Our vices are the same as theirs, neither more nor less' (Burke, 1887d, IV, p. 90). Or, again:

> By flattering us that we are not subject to the same vices and follies, it includes a confidence that we shall not suffer the same evils by a contact with the infamous gang of robbers who have thus robbed and butchered our neighbors before our faces. [1887d, IV, p. 90]

In the final analysis, this implies that the defender must become similar to the enemy—that is, the good must become the evil—as suggested by the religious mythologies (cf. Aho, 1981):

. . . to destroy that enemy . . . the force opposed to it should be made to bear some analogy and resemblance to the force and spirit which that system exerts; that war ought to be made against it in its vulnerable parts. [Burke, 1887d, II, p. 377]

In consequence, the law of neighbourhood justifies anybody interfering in the developments in France (Burke, 1887d, I, p. 324). Furthermore, Burke finds similar justifications for his positions and activity in the role of a 'voice crying in the wilderness'. He perceives himself as a prophet speaking to his nation and urging it to act (1887d, III, pp. 507–8). Burke wishes to warn his fellows of the devil creeping into the hearts of the Sons of Light.

It is fundamental, in the light of the dualistic traditions, that the problems were caused by internal developments in France, by the Regicide Directory itself. No continental power in Europe was the enemy of France (Burke, 1887d, I, p. 236). It was the Regicide Directory alone which had, in Burke's opinion, committed a serious sin, and was the sinful, the wicked, by its very nature.

Burke's fury can be explained by this perception. The Regicide Directory, 'the republic of regicide', and 'the republic of assassins' represent the sins committed by the revolutionaries in France. They are guilty of murdering their king, the father. But the most fundamental sin is their 'atheism by establishment' (Burke, 1887d, I, pp. 238, 246, 309–10). Burke speaks of persons who do not love religion but hate it (1887d, III, p. 362); about the rebels against God who 'perfectly abhor the Author of their being'. They hate Him 'with all their heart, with all their mind, with all their soul, and with all their strength'. They are not able to revenge themselves on God; therefore they have a 'delight in vicariously defacing, degrading, torturing, and tearing in pieces His image in man' (Burke, 1887d, III, pp. 362–3). The Regicide Directory has a predominant object which it pursues with a fanatical fury; it is the utter extirpation of religion (Burke, 1887d, II, p. 361).

In short, 'this pretended republic is founded in crimes, and exists by wrong and robbery'. And wrong and robbery are at war with mankind: 'It violates the rights upon which not only the community of France, but those on which all communities are founded' (Burke, 1887d, I, pp. 325–6).

It is interesting to note that Burke often uses words like 'Christendom', 'mankind' and 'Europe'. Religion unites mankind and Europe, and it is this unity which is important for Burke. According to Burke the European system of states is based on religion. There have been long and bloody wars in Europe, but the nations in Europe are less separated than other communities at peace because of 'the similitude throughout Europe of religion'. Also laws and manners 'are all the same', that is, they are reflections of common religion. In other words, people in Europe are originally—and the states derivatively—children of the same God; the polity and economy of every country in Europe has been derived from the same sources' (Burke, 1887d, I, pp. 318–9). A united Europe can only be based on shared religious values (1887d, IV, p. 80). The Regicide Directory is responsible for a violent breach of the community of Europe (1887d, I, p. 320). Therefore it is, for Burke, 'the common enemy of the quiet of Europe' (1887d, III, p. 475).

France—under the Regicide Directory—is, as suggested earlier, in Burke's opinion an expanding power. Now we know that expansion is atheistic, pursued by the Sons of Darkness who have an inherent drive to expansion: 'the social nature of man impels him to propagate his principles, as much as physical impulses urge him to propagate his kind' (Burke, 1887d, II, p. 361). The revolution did not aim at accommodating France to the old structure of the European states, but at producing a new one:

> The Revolution was made, not to make France free, but to make her formidable,—not to make her a neighbour, but a mistress,—not to make her more observant of laws, but to put her in a condition to impose them. [Burke, 1887d, II, p. 360]

Indeed, France had been 'new-modelled' for expansion (Burke, 1887d, II, pp. 360–1). The Regicide Directory makes France extremely powerful in a new expansionist policy:

> France differs essentially from all those governments which . . . are confused with the multitude and with the complexity of their pursuits. What now stands as government in France is struck out at a heat. The design is wicked, immoral, impious, oppressive: but it is spirited and daring; it is systematic; it is simple in its principle; it has unity and consistency in perfection. . . . To them the will, the wish, the want, the liberty, the toil, the blood of individuals, is as nothing. Individuality is left out of their scheme of government. The state is all in all. Everything is referred to the production of force; afterwards, everything is trusted to the use of it. It is military in its principle, in its maxims, in its spirit, and in all its movements. The state has dominion and conquest for its sole objects,—dominion over minds by proselytism, over bodies by arms. [1887d, II, p. 375]

The destruction of religion, especially, 'was to supply them with means of conquest, first at home, and then abroad' (Burke, 1887d, II, p. 363). And again reflecting a more modern jargon of geopolitics, Burke maintained that 'the leaders of that sect secured the centre of Europe; and that secured, they knew, whatever might be the event of battles and sieges, their cause was victorious (1887d, II, pp. 345–6).

Discussion

In conclusion: Burke maintained that France was and ever must be in conflict with other systems (Burke, 1887d, II, p. 378). Therefore he never thought England could make peace with the Regicide Directory:

> . . . it was not for the sake of an object we pursued in rivalry with each other, but with the system itself that we were at war. As I understood the matter, we were at war, not with its conduct, but with its existence,—convinced that its existence and its hostility were the same. [1887d, II, p. 343]

In consequence it was, according to Burke, impossible to come to any arrangement with the enemy without abandoning the interest of mankind (Burke, 1887d, II, p. 244). There was no longer 'a common political war with an old recognized member of the commonwealth of Christian Europe', neither was the dispute 'turned upon a mere matter of territorial or commercial controversy, which a peace might settle' (Burke, 1887d, IV, p. 17). The war had become a holy war, a religious battle, a war 'against example' and for the 'property, honour, virtue, and religion of England, of Germany, and of all nations' (1887d, I, p. 331). The war was religious. There were other objects, including 'every other interest of society', but religion was 'the principal and leading feature' (Burke, 1887g, p. 449). Therefore, the war was just in the religious sense:

> If to prevent Louis the Fourteenth from imposing his religion was just, a war to prevent the murderers of Louis the Sixteenth from imposing their irreligion upon us is just: a war to prevent the operation of a system which makes life without dignity and death without hope is a just war. [Burke, 1887d, I, p. 305]

Furthermore, Burke suggested that the war against the Regicide power was a positive phenomenon. It had, at least, suspended the operation of evil and given a reprieve to the Christian world. There were no compromises available in making 'France' safe: it had to be destroyed, or it would destroy all Europe (Burke, 1887d, II, pp. 344, 377). According to Burke, it was up to Pitt's government to preserve

Christian Europe, and this could not be the fruits of a negotiated peace and the coexistence of diametrically opposed world views. England's divine mission required victory (Kramnick, 1977, p. 37).

It is easy to understand the consequences of Burke's arguments. Burke consistently denied the existence in this case of objective conflicts, and therefore of any peaceful solutions. It was not possible to resolve the conflict between good and evil by negotiations; there were no objective interests to negotiate. England and France represented two different political systems, and the difference was religious in the fundamental sense. 'The Catholic King' could not embrace 'the most Unchristian Republic' (Burke, 1887d, IV, pp. 81–2).

Burke was the first to formulate ideas of relations between different political systems in the modern sense. Indeed, he had an important role in the transmission of the dualistic traditions to modern political thinking. Burke's political significance lies in the fact that these traditions emerged again after the Soviet revolution, particularly during and after World War II, in the process leading to the Cold War. It is no coincidence that Reinhold Niebuhr, who consciously sought to contribute to this process, entitled one of his works *The Children of Light and the Children of Darkness* (1944); for him 'The Enemy' still lived in Germany, and only partly in the Soviet Union, but his task, too, was to warn those stupid and idealistic people who take democracy and peace for granted, without considering the danger of the Sons of Darkness.

President Reagan was calling upon the same tradition in his utterances on the state of Satan. Towards the end of his presidency, however, he showed clear signs of change. After the Reykjavik summit meeting (1986) and the INF agreement (1987) he went to the Moscow summit meeting (1988). Then he spoke of 'the recognition and resolution of fundamental differences with our adversaries'. According to him, the US and the Soviet Union were 'beginning to take down the barriers of the post-war era'. Reagan envisaged that the two powers were entering a new era in history. And ultimately, he was ready to say: 'I pray that the hand of the Lord will be on the Soviet people.' Burke was never capable of a similar move; nor have been the other representatives of dualistic thinking. The future will show whether this change really represented a true challenge to the dualistic legacy.

Notes

1. The concept of international theory comes from Martin Wight. 'International theory' is a tradition of speculation about relations between

states, a tradition imagined as the twin of speculation about the state to which the name 'political theory' is appropriated (Wight, 1966, p. 17).

2. Burke's works cover at least four areas outside England: Ireland, India, the American colonies and France. Ireland (see Mahoney, 1960, esp. pp. 16–19), India, America and France did not turn out in a successive order; they were partly overlapping cases. For example, during the 1790s Burke was attacking both Warren Hastings and the French revolutionists. But this only strengthens the differences between the two Burkes: there were two Burkes at the same time—during the 1790s the conservative was born but the radical was still going strong.
3. Kramnick (1977, p. 10) claims that no adequate alternative to a psychological explanation exists to account for the frenzied passion and obsessiveness of Burke's attack on Warren Hastings or the Jacobins, or the fascination with America. However, I am going to suggest here just such an alternative, which overcomes the psychological explanation of Burke's role in the Cold War discourse. All this can be well explained in psychological terms (Kramnick, 1977, pp. 8 and 132). Psychology, however, merely gives 'more scientific' wording to the facts I am dealing with here. The psychological explanation, furthermore, ignores the dualistic tradition, neither can we know if there was some need for the suppressed homosexuality of Burke in the Cold War discourse.
4 In writing this short paper on Burke's dualism, I have had no reason to go carefully through the enormous amount of material on India. I have simply availed myself of Marshall (1981), in addition to selected texts by Burke.
5. This solution is rather similar to the modern attempt to influence and restrict the behaviour of transnational corporations through an international code.
6. This precedes the ideas of the New International Economic Order of the 1970s.
7. But it is equally possible to accept Wight's (1966) classification of realists (Machiavellians), rationalists (Grotian), and revolutionists (Kantians), where Burke is placed in the middle group.
8. For example, when Burke was devising defences for party activity, he saw it as a device to be deployed in times of danger to the constitution: 'when bad men combine the good must associate'. That is, good men (i.e. the Rockingham Whigs) had to have power (Mahoney, 1960, pp. 45–6).

Bibliography

Aho, J.A., 1981. *Religious Mythology and the Art of War*. London: Aldwych Press.

Airas, P. 1978. *Die geschichtlichen Wertungen, Krieg und Friede von Friedrich dem Grossen bis Engels*. Rovanniemi: Societas Historica Finlandiae Septentrionalis.

Burke, E., 1887a. *A Letter to the Marquis of Rockingham with Addresses to the King and the British Colonists in North America, January 1777*, in Burke, 1887j.

Burke, E., 1887b. *A Letter to Sir Charles Bingham, Bart. on the Irish Absentee Tax 30 October 1773*, in Burke, 1887j.

Burke, E., 1887c. *Speech on Moving Resolutions for Conciliation with the Colonies, 22 March 1775*, in Burke, 1887j.

Burke, E., 1887d. I–IV. *Three Letters on the Proposals for Peace with the Regicide Directory of France, 1796–7*, and *Fourth Letter on the Proposals for Peace with the Regicide Directory of France, 1795–7*, in Burke, 1887j.

Burke, E., 1887e. *A Letter to Charles James Fox, on the American War, 8 October, 1877*, in Burke, 1887j.

Burke, E., 1887f. *A Letter to Sheriffs of the City of Bristol, on the Affairs of America, 1777*, in Burke, 1887j.

Burke, E., 1887g. *Remarks on the Policy of the Allies with Respect to France, October 1793*, in Burke, 1887j.

Burke, E., 1887h. *Speech on American Taxation, 19 April 1774*, in Burke, 1887j.

Burke, E., 1887i. *Thoughts on French Affairs*, in Burke, 1887j.

Burke, E., 1887j. *The Works of Edmund Burke*. London: John C. Nimmo.

Burke, E., 1981a. *Speech on Fox's India Bill, 1 December 1783*, in Burke, 1981c.

Burke, E., 1981b. *Ninth Report of Select Committee, 25 June 1783*, in Burke, 1981c.

Burke, E., 1981c. *The Writings and Speeches of Edmund Burke*, vol. V. Oxford: Clarendon Press.

Dalby, S., 1988. 'Geopolitical Discourse: The Soviet Union as Other', *Alternatives*, vol. 13, no. 4.

Donelan, M., ed., 1978. *The Reason of States*. London: Allen & Unwin.

Greenleaf, W.H., 1975. 'Burke and State Necessity: The Case of Warren Hastings', in R. Schnur, ed., *Staatsräson*. Duncker & Humblot.

Kramnick, I., 1977. *The Rage of Edmund Burke*. New York: Basic Books.

Macpherson, C.B., 1980. *Burke*. Oxford: Oxford University Press.

Mahoney, T. H.D., 1960. *Edmund Burke and Ireland*. Cambridge, Mass.: Harvard University Press.

Marshall, P.J., 1981. 'Introduction', in Burke, 1981.

Miller, D., 1987. *The Blackwell Encyclopedia of Political Thought*. Oxford: Blackwell.

Nathanson, C.E., 1988. 'The Social Construction of the Soviet Threat', *Alternatives*, vol. 13, no. 4.

Niebuhr, R., 1944. *The Children of Light and the Children of Darkness*. New York: Scribner.

Parkin, C., 1956. *The Moral Basis of Burke's Political Thought*. Cambridge: Cambridge University Press.

Said, E., 1979. *Orientalism*. New York: Vintage.

Wight, M., 1966. 'Why is there no International Theory?', in H. Butterfield and M. Wight, eds., *Diplomatic Investigations*. London: Allen & Unwin.

5 Carl Schmitt's Concept of the State and the 'Enemy'[1]

Alexander Demandt

> There is not any thing amongst civil affairs more subject to error than the right valuation and true judgement concerning the power and forces of an estate.
> Francis Bacon

Since Thucydides at the latest historians have been concerned predominantly with political events. In the broadest sense events are 'political' when what is involved is the control of coexistence, that is, of power. In the narrowest sense we call events 'political' when the state is represented as either subject or object of the action.

There are dozens of definitions to enlighten us as to what the state is, and that of Carl Schmitt is perhaps as open to attack as any; it has however the advantage of not being easily forgotten. Schmitt uses the *ius belli* (the right to declare war) to differentiate between the state and other forms of community. The state imposes a state of emergency in domestic affairs, distinguishes between friends and enemies in foreign affairs, and declares war at its own discretion. A state which is not free to declare war on every other state cannot declare it on any. Such a state is not sovereign, not free. Schmitt defines the state by its domestic and foreign enemies. Statehood and enmity are mutually dependent. Thus a change in the form of a state may be expected to imply a change in the concept of an enemy and vice versa.

Schmitt was a philosopher of the state whose knowledge of world history was unparalleled. Only when one is aware of this, is it possible to understand his political philosophy. In the strict sense, there are as many forms of state as there are states. Taking the argument with a pinch of salt, however, we can juxtapose two basic models between which Schmitt's philosophy of the state oscillates: the *polis* (a state-like community, generally a town) and the *imperium* (empire). The *polis* is proud of its external freedom and defends it against its neighbours. In this conflict it acquires and improves its borders, its form, its being. The *polis* exists as a plurality. Within are the parties, without live friends and enemies.

The *imperium*, on the other hand, places peace above freedom. It demands priority or even exclusive authority among states and knows only provisional borders. Its domestic enemies are rebels against whom civil wars must be fought, its external enemies are barbarians who must be pacified with colonial wars and then civilized.

The constitutional history of Antiquity proceeds from *polis* to *imperium*. The Greek cities had worn each other down in endless wars. The yearning for universal peace, for the *koine eirene*, evoked the king, and he brought the end of freedom. In the period from Issos, 333 BC, to Actium, 31 BC, it was a question of what the world order would look like. Alexander and the Hellenistic dynasties failed, Rome came out the victor. Rome thrived by merit of its ability to protect itself and its friends. The 'eternal connection between protection and obedience' emphasized by Thucydides (I. 8), Pascal (1904, p. 310), Hobbes (1839, p.186) and Schmitt (1963, p. 53) brought ever more people within the sphere of *imperium* and ever wider territories under Roman jurisdiction.

Boundless power gave rise to boundless presumption. While the Romans claimed to wage only 'just wars' (Cicero, III. 34ff), they placed their interests on a par with those of mankind, a claim which Schmitt (1963, p. 50ff) unmasks as fundamentally imperialistic ideology. Virgil (*Aeneid*, I. 279) described the Empire under Augustus as one of predestined world power with neither temporal nor territorial borders as *imperium sine fine*. Eusebius (Drake, 1976) pronounced Constantine God's representative on earth, ruler of all mankind, of the faithful and of those still to be converted. Constantine's state had no longer any concept of enemy. The Teutons were considered (Seeck, 1976, p. 251) as a developing race, who forced their way into the Empire in search of food and land, in order to be civilized and Christianized. Barbarian plunderers were made Roman generals, and from AD 382 were entitled to live on their own terms on imperial territory. Philosophers like Themistius preached philanthropy to the emperors, the Church Fathers impressed upon their flock that the real enemy was neither Alarich nor Geiserich, but Satan and his henchmen, that is, believers in different creeds. Dissenters lost one right after another, under Justinian even civil rights (*Cod. Just.* I. 11,10). The law declared them *hostes publici*, enemies of the state.

The *imperium* disintegrated when it could no longer afford protection to its citizens. The *magistri militum* of late Antiquity, combining the offices of Roman generals and Teuton kings, took over this role. Nevertheless, the idea of the Empire survived: in the Roman Pope, in the Byzantine Emperor, in the German Emperor. After the waning of these three universal powers about 1500, a pluralistic form of states emerged once again in the modern European era. Roman conceptions and ideas of state, adopted by the Catholic Church, assisted at the birth of the modern state, allowing of the impression—one which Schmitt also partially shared—that 'states' first came into existence in modern times. The basic terms since used in politics (previously theological) are of political origin, their secularization is a resecularization.

The emergence of the national states was followed by the division of the globe. That is the *nomos* (law) of the earth. The wars this entailed once more awakened a longing for peace. In the material terms of world trade, in the ideal terms of the Enlightenment, territorial systems were discussed. In 1795 Kant (1920, vol. V, p. 657ff) drafted a universal amphictyony, a world state. The French Revolution furnished the democratic ideals of a state concept intensified on the model of Antiquity. These were further evolved in the United States and in Russia. Since Tocqueville's day two world powers can be seen to have emerged in the West and in the East, which have threatened to absorb Europe. Donoso Cortes thought—thus Schmitt (1950a, p. 48ff) —that the unification of Germany would interrupt this process and should therefore not be permitted. Germany functioned as *catechon*, a force to hold up the Antichrist (2. Thess. 2: 6ff).

The rise of the world powers in the modern era created a constellation comparable with the transition from the Greek *polis* world to the Roman *cosmopolis*. This parallel has been drawn so often that Schmitt (1950a, p. 102) calls it 'the essence of intellectual history in the last century'. Following Spengler, Schmitt extended the analogy to the present and deemed the days of Actium to be of greater relevance to us than any other moment in world history (1950a, p. 94). Once again the *pluriversum* (system of common shape) seemed to be turned into a *universum* (a system of different elements). At Actium the question was still limited to whether a world state of Western (Augustus) or Eastern type (Antonius) would emerge. That was for Spengler and Schmitt the beginning of the end.

At first Schmitt accepted this development. In 1937 he wrote that it was 'right and meaningful' that an 'already existing, unchangeable, real and total enmity should lead to the ordeal of total war' (1940b, p. 239). At the end of this war, he (1950b, p. 14) lamented that an intensification of statehood led to the total state, which resulted in an aggravation of enmity. The connection between people's state, people's enemy and people's war put an end to the 'restricted' war resembling a courtly duel, and bestowed upon us total war with total opposition, the partisans (Schmitt, 1975). With the intensifications of war and thus of resistance, the parties demoralize each other. Such was the external aspect of the expanding universal system.

Even more than this Schmitt (1940c,p. 295) was alarmed at the depoliticization and neutralization advancing within the universal system, and the elimination of the diversity of states as the superpowers encroached from East and West, 'regardless of territorial rights, in their universalizing process'. This would lead to a spiritual void'. Behind this he suspected, in 1936, was the 'Jewish spectre', which Mommsen in 1856 had described as the 'ferment of cosmopolitanism and national decomposition'. This expression was passed on, via von Treitschke and Lagarde, to Hitler (Mommsen, 1909, p. 550; Hitler, 1933, p. 743).

Mommsen saw Rome's transition from a national state to a world empire as the beginning of the end. The universal empire with its levelling of culture, its economic and social problems, its politically unmotivated citizens, seemed to him inviable, the old notion that great empires enervate and destroy the forces of the natives which they have subdued (Bacon, 1806, p. 264). Mommsen and Schmitt recalled the national stand against the concept of world empire during the wars of independence from 1812 to 1815. At that time Germany turned against Napoleon as he spread the universal ideas of the French Revolution on the point of his bayonet. The French wanted to become the new Romans, the Germans the new Greeks. What the Germans lacked in the shaping force of politics, they thought they could make up in the realm of culture.

The fight against the universal powers became Germany's vocation: Arminius and Luther had been the forerunners. Dostoyevsky described Protestantism in this sense in 1877 as 'the' German principle. After Napoleon's downfall, England seemed to play Rome's role, and there was no dearth of authors who compared the British Empire with the Roman, who viewed the *Pax Britannica* (peace granted by Britain) as a new *Pax Romana* (peace granted by Rome), and chose Rome's civilizing and regulating political system as an example. Even Winston Churchill (see Wells, 1972, p. viii) cited Virgil's '*parcere subjectis et debellare superbos*' (Virgil, *Aeneid*, VI. 853, 'to spare the humble and wear down the proud'). Once again the universal powers threatened to swallow the national states.

In the eyes of many eminent Germans, the purpose of the world wars was to thwart this. In the World War I, Max Weber, Friedrich Naumann and Eduard Meyer were of this opinion; in World War II, Konrad Lorenz and Carl Schmitt. They envisaged between the two blocs a strong Central Europe under German leadership. Bearing in mind, however, how Rome had ended, they ruled out a multiracial empire. On this point Schmitt (1940d, p. 304) agreed with Hitler.

Schmitt saw the more dangerous enemy in the West (1940b, p. 296ff). The liberal-democratically garnished dollar imperialism with its universal right of intervention appeared to him threatening in that it gave itself out to be unpolitical (Schmitt, 1940e, p. 162). Later he also turned against the Socialist International with its missionary expansionist aspirations, but Bolshevism elicited from him—as it did from Spengler and Eduard Meyer—more respect than did Americanism. Behind this was perhaps the insight that socialism as an idea was too weak in the long run to subsist without Schmitt's highly valued principle of nationalism, while, for business reasons alone, liberalism and capitalism could turn the world into a market and level all national boundaries.

For Schmitt, Western and Eastern doctrines of salvation were nothing more than masks covering designs for power. A war waged in the name of humanity, progress, justice, was always particularly inhuman; 'righteous' wars were self-righteous wars, where the enemy was to be destroyed not only militarily but also morally. This applied especially when the war was declared to be the 'final' war, the war to end all wars. The opponent could then be classified as world enemy 'number one' against whom all means were permissable (Schmitt, 1975, p. 94)—the gas chamber or the atom bomb.

Schmitt argued in eschatological spirit. He saw himself surrounded by prophets of destruction and preachers of salvation. As in the early days of Christianity, the end of the Old World was expected, accompanied by the dawning of the 'New World' and the 'New Man' (Schmitt, 1975, p. 80). This is exactly what Scmitt thought. As early as 1941 he declared that the age of statehood was elapsing under the pressure of liberalism and socialism. In opposition to this, he assumed the role of *catechon* (i.e. a force to hold up the Antichrist, see 2 Thess. 2: 6ff). He repeatedly quoted—though fundamentally anti-Roman yet now in the Roman tradition—Virgil's avowal from the fourth Eclogue: *magnus ab integro saeclorum nascitur ordo*, 'the great succession of the centuries is born afresh' (Schmitt, 1940f, p. 132; 1940d, p. 312).

World War II reduced sovereignty even further. The original pluralism became a dualism, surrounded by a remainder of mock states in the Third World. The universal state advances in small steps. In so far as it contends to be the secular Kingdom of Heaven on earth, Schmitt's concern is justifiable. This would be followed by a Last Judgement and a descent into hell for the damned. A last kingdom on earth would thus be a state without freedom (Kant, 1920, vol. VI, p. 436ff), indeed the most totalitarian of all totalitarian states, because only human angels would have access to it. In the world state there are only civil wars, in which the losing side has no more room to retreat. There is no longer any exile, minorities are placed in reservations. The police have nuclear warheads.

In a pluralistic state system, on the other hand, the opposition in a given state must not be so pressured that they open the gates to the enemy without. The mere possiblity of an external enemy forces us to spare the adversary within our walls. He for his part, however, must also exercises restraint if he will prevent the situation from becoming beneficial to an alien force. Within this balance is the humanitarian effect of a 'cherished' enmity between two sovereign states on which Schmitt places his hopes. The fact of enmity as such cannot be altered, only its forms can be shaped.

Schmitt advocated the idea of political autonomy and the autonomy of the political. The state is entrusted with the task of retaining and shaping the peace by force and law. How this is carried out is at its own discretion. The Enlightenment understood the state as an educational establishment for humanity; Romanticism saw in it a framework of a people, the soil in which culture is rooted; socialism understood it as an instrument for economic interests. In all these cases the *ius belli* would be senseless. To sacrifice human beings for economic advantage is for Schmitt (1963, p. 49) cruel and lunatic, and this applies even more in the case of 'humanitarian' objectives.

For Schmitt the state appears, as Hegel interprets it, as the highest realization of intellect. In it the collective will is institutionalized. No decision from pure facts or pure morality alone; normative values always play a role. The sequence of such decisions yields the historical identity of the state, the 'only essential mode of existence'. Politics is a battle for the essence of existence. Not 'to be', but 'how to be', that is the question.

Schmitt's unwitting associate Konrad Lorenz (1973, p. 252ff; Demandt, 1985, pp. 4–14) affords a biological justification for pluralism of states. He sees states in analogy to biological species; their cultural identity appears to him accessible only by delimitation from other kinds of collective individuals, so that civilized states have a natural right to oppose any opening of all borders, any world-wide levelling. For Schmitt, as for Lorenz, the civilized state offers its single member the form of his collective identity, and this is only achievable in a pluralist system of states defined by borders, never in a universal world society which respects no borders. Hammer and anvil create the form. The melting pot destroys it.

Schmitt's doctrine of states has its roots in his anthropolgy. He reckons with the incarnate evil in humanity (1963, p. 60ff). In Lorenz's case it is aggression that preserves the species. Schmitt cites on the one hand 'all true political theories', especially those of Machiavelli and Hobbes. In a world of wolves we need the pack, the wolf leader, the leviathan. On the other hand, he relies on the dogma of original sin. Here he reaches beyond the humanist heritage into Christian doctrine. The word 'evil' is not translatable into any of the classical languages. The Latin *malus* and the Greek *kakos* originally meant 'bad'. The Greeks and the Romans knew no devil. Only with the appearance of the 'Evil One' came 'evil'.

If any reproached him with political mythology, Schmitt would counter with a charge of political Romanticism, which subsists in the denial of original sin. Out of such enthusiasm would grow anarchy, the natural state of war by all against all. For Schmitt, no form of state is too inferior to avert civil war.

This view he shares with the Catholic dogma, with de Maistre: 'tout gouvernement est bon, lorsqu'il est établi' (any government is good as long as it has undisputed power). Pascal (1904, p. 330) supplies the reason for this: the greatest and most important matter in the world, the king's authority, is based on the weakness and folly of the people. What is based solely on sound reasoning, is insufficient. In the Christian theory of the state, authority wields the sword borrowed from God to penalize evil and repel enemies. Paul claims this for the heathen emperor, Nero; Eusebius verifies it for the Christian emperor, Constantine; Eusebius legitimates the Roman Empire from the Bible; this Erik Peterson in 1935 (1951. p. 45ff) called 'political theology'. Augustine again annulled the ideological marriage between state and Church upon discovering that heretic emperors created domestic problems and orthodox emperors were incapable of solving foreign problems. Peterson agreed with Augustine.

Schmitt (1970) raised an objection, however, on behalf of Eusebius and political theology, for the sake not of religion but of the state, which had its own value and without a theological basis did not seem durable. Schmitt underlined, firstly, the structural affinity between theological and legal thought, both of which are concerned with the interpretation and application of enacted laws. Secondly, he recalled the respect demanded by theologians and lawyers for Order, which protects us from anarchy. Thirdly, he acknowledges the basis of law and authority, the evil in mankind. 'The human being is born to be a rebel', says Ivan Karamazov, therefore we need authorities which control our fear. Otherworldy fear is supervised by the Church, fear of this world is looked after by the state. Schmitt places himself in the succession of Grand Inquisitors who intend to burn the returned Jesus because he relieves mankind of the fear which alone holds the herd together. Christian people—as the Inquisitor remarks—call for a shepherd. For the sheep are in reality wolves who fear their own kind.

Schmitt appealed repeatedly to the doctrine of the state conveyed in the fable of Aesop, which transfers the natural differences between the animal species to the cultural sphere of humans. This theory is deceptive: either we are all lambs or we are all wolves. Then, however, the rulers are also wolves. Schmitt perceived Hitler's wolfish character too late. Hitler had ended and won the national civil war in 1933, but had lost the international civil war in 1945. He wanted to take on the world enemy but was himself declared the world enemy. 'The reluctant precipitators' were not the forces on the wings, as Schmitt (1942) imagined, but those in the centre. They followed Spengler's (1933, p. 165) exhortation, threw the dice in 'the monstrous game', and lost. The 'reserve infantrist' Schmitt (as he described himself in a letter to Ernst Jünger in 1944) belongs to the defeated party.

The world enemy calls for the world state. Integration grows, borders are in the way, differences between external and internal are obscured. Friend and foe, countryman and alien, war and peace differ from each other only in degrees. International 'violators' are no longer castigated by war, but by warlike police action, as though they were robbers. Police measures are not usually concluded by peace treaties. After World War I such a farce was still being played at Versailles, after World War II there was not even that. The Nuremberg war crimes trials simulated the world state.

This development goes further. Violators of the inner order, in as far as they are powerful enough, are accepted as negotiating partners of the state authority; they are no longer considered mere law breakers, as if they were subjects of international law. Given the requirement of the traditional idea of the state this contrast is paradoxical. If for the moment we waive this, we acknowledge the common basis of the partners, which can of course be differently interpreted. Advocates of the traditional theory of sovereignty will in both cases bring in a verdict of moral laxity such as will virtually encourage the internal or external user of force to continue. Champions of the modern idea of the world state, in contrast, will in both cases extol the humane demeanour, which 'avoids the unnecessary spilling of blood'. Pessimists there against optimists here.

As in the days of Constantine the 'New Man' has no longer any concept of enemy. Remnants of enmity are still to be found in three forms. Political enmity in the old style exists behind the East–West conflict, but this seems to be abating. It is too expensive. The superpowers no longer hope to gain from a world war and are content with cock-fights in the Third World. They fasten blades on to the fighting-cocks' heels and let them loose in a free-for-all. If Idi Amin, Ghadaffi, and Khomeini only had weapons made in their own workshops, they would be the last representatives of Schmitt's beloved state pluralism. It would have a future if the number of states producing the atom bombs were to increase.

New-style political hostility is embodied in international terrorism. These are the world's domestic partisans. In spite of Schmitt's warning, we would imprison anarchists and terrorists as normal criminals if we had the courage or could apprehend them.

A third front runs neither through space not through the system, but through history. This enemy stands behind us. To this category belong men like Carl Schmitt, whose image of state and mankind are directly opposed to our own. This difference is not political, but philosophical. It involves the *Weltanschauung* or philosophy of life, belief, political theology. In contrast to Schmitt we sacrifice our identity to integration and—like to the Greeks in the Roman Empire—place peace above liberty, because we want to keep what we have, and are content with what is permitted us. When Schmitt (1963, p. 76) claimed that there is no equivalent to political independence, 'be the bribe never so high', we are all corrupt, or else Schmitt was dazzled.

As we come to terms with Schmitt's view we acquire our own inner form. Unlike Schmitt, we believe that mankind can be humanized. Unlike Schmitt, we reject theological reasoning for anthropological and political theories. Unlike Schmitt, we waive sovereignty and insistence on the notion of enemy and say with Francis Bacon (1806, p. 12): 'Men create oppositions which are not'. We do not believe that with the departure of an external enemy, an even worse domestic one comes. For a safeguard to our cultural tradition we look to the inner pluralism of a liberal world community, which for Schmitt (1940c, p. 296) was an Anglo-American propagandist lie, a dangerous illusion. For all that we can lay claim to Herder's *Völkergarten* and Kant's *Völkerbund*, an intellectual inheritance from which Schmitt is far removed. Schmitt always warned against blurring enmities. He greets his 'real opponents'[2] and that deserves a greeting in return.

Notes

1. This chapter grew out of a contribution to the Carl Schmitt Colloquium, which took place at the Wissenschaftskolleg in Berlin, organized by Bernd Rüthers, 15–16 June 1987. I have profited from the suggestions made by

E. Flaig, H. Quaritsch, R. Söhnen and my brother Ecke Demandt. The original version of this chapter was published under the title 'Staatsform und Feindbild bei Carl Schmitt', in *Der Staat*, no. 27, 1988, pp. 23–32.

2. Schmitt (1940a), Preface, p. 5.

Bibliography

Bacon, Francis, 1806. *Essays. Moral, Economical and Political.* London: Jones (first published 1612).

Demandt, Alexander, 1985. 'Biologische Dekadenztheorien', *Saeculum*, vol. 36.

Drake, H.A., 1976. *In Praise of Constantine.* Berkeley, Calif.: University of California Press.

Hitler, Adolf, 1933. *Mein Kampf.* Munich: Eher.

Hobbes, Thomas, 1939. *Leviathan*, in W. Molesworth, ed., *The English Works of Thomas Hobbes of Malmesbury*, vol. III.

Kant, Immanuel, 1920. *Sämtliche Werke in sechs Bänden*, 6 vols., Ed. Felix Gross. Leipzig: Insel.

Lorenz, Konrad, 1973. *Die Rückseite des Spiegels, Versuch einer Naturgeschichte menschlichen Erkennens.* Munich: Piper.

Mommsen, Theodor, 1909. *Römische Geschichte*, Vol. III. Berlin: Weidmann.

Pascal, Blaise, 1904. *Pensées*, 3 vols. ed. Léon Brunschvicg. Paris: Hachette.

Peterson, Erik, 1951. *Der Monotheismus als politisches Problem. Ein Beitrag zur Geschichte der politischen Theologie im Imperium Romanum*, in *Theologische Traktate.* Munich: Kösel (first published 1935).

Schmitt, Carl, 1940a. *Positionen und Begriffe im Kampf mit Weimar–Genf–Versailles 1923–1939.* Berlin: Duncker & Humblot.

Schmitt, Carl, 1940b. *Totaler Feind, totaler Krieg, totaler Staat* (1937) in Schmitt, 1940a.

Schmitt, Carl, 1940c. *Grossraum gegen Universalismus* (1939), in Schmitt, 1940a.

Schmitt, Carl, 1940d. *Der Reichsbegriff im Völkerrecht* (1939), in Schmitt, 1940a.

Schmitt, Carl, 1940e. *Völkerrechtliche Formen des modernen Imperialismus* (1932), in Schmitt, 1940a.

Schmitt, Carl, 1940f. *Das Zeitalter der Neutralisierungen und Entpolitisierungen* (1929), in Schmitt, 1940a.

Schmitt, Carl, 1942. 'Beschleuniger wider Willen oder: Die Problematik der westlichen Hemisphäre', *Das Reich*, 19 April 1942.

Schmitt, Carl, 1950a. *Donoso Cortés in Berlin* (1949), in *Donoso Cortés in gesamteuropäishcher Interpretation. Vier Aufsätze.* Cologne: Greven.

Schmitt, Carl, 1950b. *Ex captivitate salus. Erfahrungen der Zeit 1945/47.* Cologne: Greven.

Schmitt, Carl, 1963. *Der Begriff des Politischen. Text von 1932 mit einem*

Vorwort und drei Corollarien. Berlin: Duncker & Humblot.
Schmitt, Carl, 1970. *Politische Theologie*, vol. II. Berlin: Duncker & Humblot.
Schmitt, Carl, 1975. *Theorie des Partisanen. Zwischenbemerkung zum Begirff des Politischen*. Berlin: Duncker & Humblot.
Seeck, Otto, ed., 1976. *Notitia Dignitatum*. Frankfurt: Minerva (first published in 1962).
Spengler, Oswald, 1933. *Jahre der Entscheidung*. Munich: Beck.
Wells, C.M., 1972. *The German Policy of Augustus*. Oxford: Clarendon Press.

6 Philosophical History and the Third World: Hegel on Africa and Asia

Shiraz Dossa

In contemporary, mainstream academia, serious analyses of the plight of the Third World are by no means conspicuous. The general run of studies slides, uncritically, on the surface of things. Far too many scholars seem unaware of the global power structure and of the philosophical assumptions that empower Third World studies. Hegel's influence in shaping the commanding ideology and the disposition of students of the Third World in the West has been massive, though generally unrecognized. To understand the thrust and the details of the Western perspective on the Third World, it is necessary to have some sense of the Hegelian background and philosophy. In this chapter I shall argue that the Enlightenment ethic and the Hegelian theory of history lie at the core of the Western understanding and misunderstanding of the Third World. I shall argue further that an informed, humane understanding of the Third World and of the world we all share, is beyond the reach of the Hegelian worldview. To achieve a just global vision and practice, it is vital to transcend the lure of Hegelianism.

Fabricating the single 'enlightened' world

To sensibilities less jaded than is usual in these self-obsessed times, the lowly stature of the Third World in the prevailing Western monologue on success and failure may seem surprising. Though specific to the politically triumphant neo-conservatives, this judgement is tacitly and widely conceded in general conversation and argument in the liberal West. But the fact is that this status is not really an anomaly, it has been the norm, more or less, since the beginning of the sixteenth century when Western technology, naval supremacy and superior firepower transformed, in the space of 200 years, the human race 'into a single society of literally world-wide range' (Toynbee, 1958, p. 69).

By force of arms and sheer gall the newly discovered continents of Africa, Asia and America were taken over, their peoples subjugated, their resources harnessed to the needs and the demands of the conquerors. From the outset the unified world was Western in its enabling ethos, and the new subjects were automatically assigned the marginal position and functions befitting the weak and the visibly different.

Backed by unusually powerful technical expertise and new scientific knowledge, conquest conferred on the victors the privilege of rulership and the right to adjudicate bounds of the categories of the human, the ethical, the good, the beautiful—it gave them the authority, legitimated by conquest, to depict and define reality, to decide the values of this fabricated single world. As Arnold Toynbee (1958, p. 80) observes, the denizens of the conquered regions were obliged to 'familiarize themselves with Western history if they [were] to learn how to take their bearings in a new world-wide society of which we Westerners [had] made them members by main force'.

Taking their bearings in face of 'Europe's assault on the world' was equally a matter of learning the new ideas and new ways that had made the West their master.[1] The new learning placed the tanned and pigmented nations at the intellectual and moral margins of the white man's world. Western politics in collaboration with Western epistemology created a worldview and outlines of conduct that confirmed the subordinate position of the darker nations, their values and practices.

Notwithstanding the generally arrogant attitude towards the natives, the new world picture was not uniformly marked by prejudice: it was after all the product of the European Enlightenment and its sense of rationality and tolerance. From Voltaire through Descartes to Kant, this distinctly modern ethic seemed to valorize reason in one way or another, and it tended to encourage a view of all human beings as fundamentally similar and thus entitled to equal rights.

But its very rationalism contained seeds of intolerance. To the extent that people were rational they were all presumed, indeed expected, to prize what the Enlightenment postulated as universal values: autonomy, liberty, efficiency, science, disciplined effort, individualism and so on. As human beings they were all also assumed to have identical needs and desires no matter where they happened to find themselves in this world.[2]

In an obvious sense this was a liberating, human doctrine, and tolerably clear, as long as the argument remained at the level of basic human needs. Beyond this point the dangers were equally and ironically clear in the parallel notion of universality. But other cultures, nations, peoples did not necessarily share the values central to the Western Englightenment; they usually placed a premium on the values of community, responsibility, duty, mandatory obligations to kin and village, and so forth. They deemed these values superior on the basis of an understanding of humanity that was traditional and intrinsically anti-individualistic. To the champions of the Age of Reason these attachments smacked of an unenlightened medieval, unacceptably constricting, mentality that was both inhumane and irrational.

If this aggressive universalism of the modern West fashioned the highly visible others under its jurisdiction into the 'Other', it did the same to a number of nations in Europe much earlier. Less visible than their counterparts in the regions outside the West, these nations were nevertheless distant from the heartland of the Enlightenment, and they understood themselves as different, and entitled to assert that difference. To the brokers of universal reason this line of defence made little sense. Beneath the accretions of culture, so they argued, human beings were naturally and fundamentally the same, hence the relevance of a universally applicable set of values (Geertz, 1983, pp. 34, 51).

Riding the new version of reason, the Enlightenment reduced the European dissidents to outsiders within Europe, transforming them into internal others. Anti-semitism was not the only source of dispossession and displacement in the West: the Englightenment contributed its own measure of tyrannical rule that was as lethal potentially as anti-semitism proved to be in practice at a particular point in history. In the long-drawn-out process of industrialization and modernization in Europe, thousands suffered and died, and millions were made superfluous under the regime of modern rationality: mastery of nature and of people was an integral part of the new ethic (Rubenstein, 1983, pp. 1–33; cf. Grant, 1969; Polanyi, 1957).

Radically new, fluently brash and confident, the universalism of the eighteenth-century rationalists was bound to be challenged, and so it was. Initiated by the intellectual sympathizers of the disaffected in the European family of nations, the challenge produced the Counter-Enlightenment associated with the names and the prestige of writers like Hamman and especially Herder. Neither despised or decried reason as such; but both cared deeply about national cultures, particular values, special idioms and gestures, and about all those nuances and shades of sentiment that distinguished human beings and peoples (Berlin, 1981, pp. 1–24).

Theirs was an anthropological revolt fuelled by the commanding conviction (one of them) that the Enlightenment had badly misread human nature. As Clifford Geertz (1983, p. 59) has succinctly noted in another context, the modern Western conception of humanity

as a bounded, unique, more or less integrated motivational and cognitive universe, a dynamic centre of awareness, emotion, judgement, and action organised into a distinctive whole and set contrastively both against other such wholes and against its social and natural background, is, however incorrigible it may seem to us, a rather peculiar idea within the context of the world's cultures.

This image seemed very peculiar to many Europeans before it was rejected, eventually, by many in the Third World as a misrepresentation of mankind, and especially non-Western mankind. Flying usually under the banners of Romanticism, the disruptive particularism of the Counter-Englightenment was never too far behind the advancing universalism of the Age of Reason.

Postmodernism and the Third World

To this day the commanding *Weltanschauung* of the West is sustained by the assertive values of the Enlightenment that brought the modern, unified world into being. For all its self-doubts, modernity is the ideology of the contemporary world in one form or another. Postmodernism, in an ironic twist, in nearly all its styles, has revived the particularism of the Counter-Enlightenment, not apparently to restore legitimacy to national cultures worldwide, but to celebrate Western (in fact WASP) ethnocentricism with a vengeance. In the writings of its leading luminaries like Richard Rorty, postmodernism is, with respect to Western values, essentially an exercise in 'moral narcissism' (Geertz, 1986, p. 109; Rorty, 1986, pp. 525–9; Bloom, 1987, pp. 36, 78–9, *passim*).

Postmodernism is in crucial ways a throwback to the old arrogance, to the facile faith in the superiority of the Enlightenment and the West—minus the claim of universalism which is now, in keeping with the new temper, a covert undercurrent. But its pride in the efficacy of Western rationalism is fully intact, as it was during the Western conquest of other worlds.

Postmodernist debates are critically important because they reveal the extent to which the Enlightenment was implicated in justifying colonization of distant lands and nations (Geertz, 1986, p. 109, *passim*; cf. Toynbee, 1958, Ch. 5). They force us to confront the slippery fact that the Third World was fabricated in the back-rooms of imperial

Europe, that it is the carnal issue of Western empires that collapsed in the aftermath of the two world wars (actually European tribal wars). Postmodernism's continuing allegiance, in the end, to the old values of the Enlightenment, provides a stark illustration of the real, sustained judgement of the modern West on the Third World. That judgement has been in the main politically and morally negative.

Time and many changes have done little to alter that gross assessment, because the Third World was intellectually apprehended and appropriated as weak, chaotic and primitive: it was assimilated into the European consciousness and practice as a cluster of inferior, exotic cultures right from the start. That sense of its quintessential second-rate status has consistently shadowed the Third World in its life in the corridors of the Western mind; it has never been permanently replaced by a more adequate, intelligent view. Neither Enlightenment modernism, nor the qualified, ostensibly fairer reconsiderations of postmodern thinkers, has shaken this basic conviction.

That this view is still very powerful has a great deal to do with the hold of the 'pre-da Gaman' outlook on the minds of the mainstream thinkers in the West. By depicting the contemporary Western attitude in these terms, Arnold Toynbee has unravelled a consequential paradox in the Western self-image. Despite their protestations of rationality and commitment to progress, the heirs and the heroes of the Enlightenment have collectively refused to revise their essential judgement on the Third World—a judgement conceived and fixed in the sixteenth century. Toynbee (1958, pp. 80–81) tellingly notes that

> The West today is still looking at history from *the old parochial self-centred standpoint* which the other living societies have by now been compelled to transcend. *Yet, sooner or later, the West, in her turn, is bound to receive the re-education which the other civilizations have obtained from the unification of the world by Western action.* [Emphasis added]

To judge by the writings of some of the leading figures in the postmodern school, their re-education has apparently not yet begun. They seem, on the contrary, to have bypassed the outpouring of supportive Third World sentiments that characterized the 1960s and the early 1970s, and jumped straight from the Western-centred universalism of the Enlightenment to unashamed praise of things and values Western, in a way that dismissively scants the cultures and ways of the Third World.

Saying that Western universalism and rationalism have no mandate to rule the world, that the West should abandon the Englightenment ambition to impose its good values on others, as Rorty does, is necessary. But it accomplishes nothing if it manages to elide the Western political and nuclear power that suffuses this world of ours. To leave the Third and other worlds to their devices, to permit them to decide their own destines, after conquering, colonizing and neo-colonizing them, after forcing them into the 'worldwide' society and market, and after initiating and deepening their dependence on the Western world, is to perpetuate their poverty and misery.

Rorty and like-minded postmodernists legitimize the international status quo, they play the deadly politics of Reaganism by pretending not to be political, and their undeclared politics sanction the dependency and the recurring debt crises that plague the Third World (Frank *et al.*, 1972; George, 1988; Chomsky 1987, 1988; Rorty, 1983, pp. 583–9). For these postmodernists, the Third World never really mattered and it does not matter now when the Western world's sense of self-assurance, America's in particular, has been wounded by increasing resistance to its hegemony in the Third World, and by Japan's stunning rise to the summit of global economic power.

Neo-conservatism's electoral successes in Western liberal democracies in the past decade is hardly an accident: it signals a retrenchment, a political turn inwards, an infatuation with things Western, in face of worldwide opposition to Western global power; and it is not surprising that Rortian postmodernists are not at all unhappy with the neo-conservative agenda for the Third World which is at best indifferent, and as a rule interventionist in the interests of the West. US F16s bombing civilians in Tripoli, or US-trained and supplied death squads in Central America may be unpalatable to postmodernists, but not apparently the policies of the World Bank and the IMF's draconian austerity and economic privatization measures that produce impoverishment and instability in Third World nations.

From its original absorption into Western empires in the eighteenth and nineteenth centuries to its arrival on the world stage in the twentieth century, the Third World has suffered a steady diet of cultural insult, economic exploitation and political domination. For a brief period, though, it was an enchanted place in the consciousness of the students and the avant-garde in the West, a place of hope, humanity and brotherhood, but this spell disappeared as the 'real world' of economics and power resumed control in the West.[3]

Discovery, conquest, domination and degradation are thus terms that roughly but fairly describe the realities of the Third World. Now the interesting question in this context is why the negative view of the Third World has retained its strength intact through three centuries. Hegel and Hegelian philosophy contain a substantial part of the answer, but this is not commonly understood because the intellectual sources of contemporary politics and ethics rarely, if ever, figure in academic analyses of the Third World.

Political theory, currently, in the Anglo-Saxon West has in general been both preoccupied with empiricism and individualism and naively unhistorical, with the consequence that general ideas and philosophical assumptions are neither discussed nor appreciated as vital to understanding academic culture in particular, and the culture of Western civilization in general (e.g. Wolin, 1969, pp. 1062–82). Hegel's contribution to modernity is outstanding: he not only articulated the enabling themes of modernism, he also set the terms of theoretical debate in politics, philosophy and ethics for posterity. In Ernst Cassirer's words 'no other philosophical system has exerted such a strong and enduring influence upon political life as the metaphysics of Hegel' (1946, p. 248).

In the form of his philosophy of history, this Hegelian metaphysics has not only been at the core of Western self-understanding and self-interpretation as a culture, it has immeasurably influenced and in a way fixed the Western view of the Third World. Hegelian philosophy has authorized a metaphysics of the Third World, a cluster of foundational assumptions that has become the canonical point of departure for its study by Western and many Third World scholars. Few of them suspect or are inclined to suspect that the philosophical rationale for much of conventional modernization and development theories is buried in the writings of a clutch of political thinkers in the Western tradition. Hegel is one member of this junta, very much a founding father not only of the Western idea of the West, but also of the Western notion of *what the Third World is and what, in a critical sense, it ought to be*. Hegel's impact on theorizing about the Third World has been huge, and largely unrecognized because political theory is usually not part of the training of Third World specialists.

Inventing the philosophy of history

Two values in particular distinguished the Englightenment: scientific rationalism and a universalist ambition. Hegel was heir to both and he constructed his theoretical edifice on this dual base. But Hegel learned as well from the Romanticism of Herder to think in terms of national units and cultures; he combined reason, culture and universalism in his thinking to come up with a unique product: a philosophy of history. To Voltaire, who invented the term, it denoted a secular interpretation of history, in contrast to the standard theological view of history. Kant, building on Voltaire, firmly invested the ideas of progress and meaning in the definition of the philosophy of history, which in his judgement did not make sense without them (Lowith, 1949, p. 1, introduction; Walsh, 1960, pp. 119–27).

Hegel accepted the Kantian view, but he took the concrete, actual history of nations, and the thesis of progress, far more seriously than Kant who was, like many Enlightenment thinkers, quite unhistorical in his approach (Walsh, 1969, pp. 134–5). In Hegel's philosophy history is not a marginal affair: it is central to his novel interpretation of the link between theory and practice.

Political theory prior to Hobbes had resolutely committed itself to spelling out a vision of life as it ought to be. Whatever the theorist had to say about community, needs, interests and purposes, was said within the context of the overriding notion of the just society or the good life as it was envisioned by him. Political theory was assertively normative, it was part of the mandate of the theorist to imagine the best, to dare to be utopian, to go out on a limb and sketch the ideal.

In the nature of things human and political, practice never matched the theory, the distance between the ideal and the real was never fully bridged. To the extent that it was the vessel of political imagination and idealism, an intellectual building that housed the critical standards of communal judgement, political theory remained faithful to its primary task. No political theorist could be expected to do more in his capacity as a theorist: if he chose to tutor an Alexander, as Aristotle did, that was his privilege as a citizen, not his duty as a theorist.

Hegel of course knew all this. He was one of the great modern admirers of the achievements of ancient Greece, surpassed only, one supposes, by Nietzsche and Heidegger. But Hegel lived in the age of Napoleon, and ancient political theory was too distant a vision for his turbulent present. Hegel consciously abjured political theory and replaced it with a philosophy of history that recast the relationship between theory and practice, between the ideal and the real. Political theory in the classical sense was killed off by Hegel (it had been mortally wounded by Hobbes when he decided that the business of political theory was to justify tyranny, as he did in his *Leviathan*): the mandate to think of politics and citizenship as it ought to be was revoked.[4]

For Hegel (1967, pp. 11–12) it is not the purpose of philosophy or political philosophy

> to construct a state as it ought to be. The instruction which it may contain cannot consist in teaching the state what it ought to be; . . . To comprehend what is, this is the task of philosophy, because what is, is reason.

In one radical stroke Hegel clears the deck for dialectical reason and history. His philosophical history supplants political theory and elevates history to a rank it had never enjoyed in the tradition of political thought.

But Hegel does not jettison idealism: his Reason is still reason but it is now inseparable from History, from its real, actual shape in the historical world. His philosophy can only understand, his political philosophy can only describe. Neither can fulfil what Plato and Aristotle had supposed were their essential responsibility: the right and the obligation to prescribe, to paint the best city in words, in the mind.

To Hegel history is universal history, it is the stage on which Reason reveals itself in the conduct of nations and in their values. History is both progressive and meaningful, *history* is purposive. To know History as such is to know that it is nothing more than the march of Reason in this world. Reason lurches forward not in the guise of individuals but of nations. Not all nations are favoured, in fact very few qualify and even in batch of the chosen each is ranked in terms of a list of critical attributes ranging from the degree of spiritual self-consciousness to its commitment to freedom for all in the nation (Hegel, 1956, introduction, pp. 8–79).

As Hegel depicts it there is a necessary logic to the progress of Reason towards freedom, and this logic has reached its highest stage in the Western world. Freedom has been most fully realized in the West because Reason has achieved its most rational expression among the Central European peoples. Nothing that has happened elsewhere comes close to the magnificent display of Reason in the European and especially the Prussian setting in which Hegel lived. History in this special sense had come to its end in the West, though it had begun incompetently, chaotically, unselfconsciously in the East.

Hegel's claim that the zenith of the real world is the West highlights two points critical to his philosophical history. The first is that the Western world represents the peak of rationality in the annals of human history. In this sense the West is the most real of all the historical worlds because it conforms to the highest demands of Reason: this is the meaning of his notorious thesis that the *real is the rational*. Hegel took pains to distinguish the real or reality from the merely existing, and he was incensed by the common suggestion that he had conflated them (Cassirer, 1946, pp. 261–2).[5]

Nevertheless the intrinsic trend of his philosophical history, his deep sympathy for 'the power of tradition' and the 'ethical order' of custom (Cassirer, 1946, pp. 251–2, 269), and his rejection of the enterprise of political theory, leave little doubt as to his essential conservativism and his sympathy for the status quo. In the real world of his readers the actual was readily confused with the rational, and with his personal blessing: it was Hegel (1956, p. 36) who had said that 'the real world is as it ought to be'.

Philosophical history's second crucial feature was the claim that the triumph of the West was not merely secular, it was the will of the Almighty. As Hegel put it bluntly: 'This *Good*, this *Reason*, in its most concrete form, is God. God governs the world; the actual working of his government—the carrying out of his plan—is the History of the world.'

The unmatched strength of freedom and rationality in the West was seemingly ordained by God. But He obviously is not the God of non-Christian nations: they are relegated to the fringes of History and of Reason.

Reason and God in Hegel's understanding were not just squarely on the side of the West, they were very much European phenomena with universal responsibilities. As John Plamenatz has pointed out, Hegel's 'bias' was blatantly European, he was convinced that Europeans were superior and justified in ruling other nations. His *Philosophy of History* 'sets up the standard of one part of mankind *to judge all mankind*' (Plamenatz, 1963, pp. 204–5, emphasis added). In this grand design of European Reason these nations have neither rights nor duties, in fact Hegel (1967, pp. 218–19) characterizes them as 'barbarian' nations.

If the rational is both actual and real in the Hegelian sense, then it follows that history is not simply a haphazard collection of actions and events but the expression of a purposeful Spirit. In this sense it is History and concretely embodies, not just reflects, the rational design of Reason. History then is the arena of the Spirit, it is the ground on which reason develops, on which it clothes itself in material form. History is the space in which Reason comes into its own but it does so nation by nation, culture by culture; it obeys the principle of development from its beginnings to its highest accomplishment in the West.

For Hegel the crucial point is that world History is a progressive development from germ to maturity by way of selected nations and cultures. The idea of development is the seminal link in the Hegelian thesis on the march of Reason towards freedom and towards self-consciousness of this progress (Hegel, 1956, pp. 53–79, *passim*). Reason's reality is vouched for in the bosom of the concrete, visible record of national and cultural action. Non-Western nations, even those that figure sympathetically in Hegel's analysis, serve as a prelude, as stepping-stones (to be precise, as stepped-on nations) to the final incarnation of Reason's unsurpassable genius in the Central European West—the Protestant West.

Reason and the non-Europeans

For Hegel, Africa is unarguably no part of History or even history in the ordinary sense: it is well beyond the pale of what he calls human history. Reason has no places within which to accommodate the humanness of Africans because it does not see them as human at all. For Africa and Africans, Hegel could summon no sympathy or respect. His discussion of them is saturated with unconscionable contempt and derision.

Hegel confidently charges Africans with a basic lack of rationality, accuses them of possessing no morality and no inclination to value politics or things of the intellect. To Hegel, Africans exemplify the prehistory of humanity which for him is summed up in their utter lack of rational consciousness of ideas and concerns that transcend mankind and nature: 'The Negroes indulge . . . that perfect *contempt* for humanity, which in its bearing on Justice and Morality is the fundamental characteristic of the race. . . . Among the Negroes moral sentiments are quite weak, and more strictly speaking, non-existent' (Hegel, 1956, pp. 91–9).

Hegel's knowledge of Africa was anecdotal, comprising snippets of travellers' information, strictly second-hand and essentially unreliable. It was neither philosophical nor historical knowledge in Hegel's own understanding of these terms, yet he felt he could from such 'knowledge' judge and dismiss Africa with facility. The historian W.H. Walsh, while conceding that Hegel's 'picture of native Africans could scarcely be blacker' (an incredibly insensitive choice of words in the context), asserts that Hegel 'was not any kind of racist'. Walsh does not discuss the phenomenon.

In Hegel's day this sort of rank prejudice against Blacks was more or less normal, and it was plainly racist in so far as racism is the dehumanization of other cultures, groups or races as intrinsically inferior on a scale devised by members of one culture. Walsh's (1971, pp. 186, 192) claim, though true, that Hegel's judgement was not '*simple* prejudice' but a 'rational' assessment, does not make it any less racist: the notion of rationality is itself to a considerable extent culture bound. The surprising thing about this is that another scholar was sufficiently incensed by Walsh's timid censure of Hegel to take him to task. Duncan Forbes (1975, p. xxii, fn. 7) had this to say: 'It is . . . fashionable to display one's broadmindedness by criticizing Hegel for being Europo-centric or Western-orientated. The latest example is W.H. Walsh. . . . But isn't Hegel's perspective broadly the right one?'

Forbes to the contrary, the supposition that in 1975 it was fashionable to be generous about the Third World, to doubt the essential superiority of the West, is as absurd as the notion that European scholars were prepared to espouse cultural and ethical relativism *en masse*. For all his sensitivity, Walsh's broadmindedness was severely limited. By that time, in fact by the end of the 1960s, the Third World had slipped back into its old slot as the colonized 'bush society' (V.S. Naipaul) in the minds of most Western scholars. Failure to develop in the path carved for it by innumerable Western scholars was the main reason for the Third World's redefinition as an intractable case of irrationality and backwardness.

Hegel's influence on the judgement of experts on Africa and Africans was visible in both their language and their attitude. Like Hegel, they claimed, without recognizing their debt to him, that Africa was beyond and indeed incapable of genuine development.[6] For Asia as a whole, on the other hand, Hegel could muster a kind of respect as long as he confined his judgement to certain facets of its culture and mind. But in terms of Reason and the dialectic of consciousness, the Asian region of India, Persia and Egypt did not elicit his full approval or acceptance.

For Hegel the point was not simply that Reason's highest range was the privilege of the West, it was also his European feeling that Asia was by nature not fitted for universal achievements. Flirting with History at best, Asia was nevertheless capable of producing conduct and values that at least amounted to events and actions Hegel called history. Africa never had a chance, but parts of Asia did leave their mark in the vicinity of his exalted Reason (Hegel, 1956, pp. 18–9, 54–6, 61–2, 73–4, 103–16).[7]

In the Asian realm, India struck Hegel as both fascinating and horrifying, less because it had done horrible things than because it was the spiritless emblem of jaded refinement. India had a 'soft, yielding and relaxed' beauty that was really ersatz: it was antithetical to the progress of freedom and consciousness. India was altogether too close to 'Nature', it was quintessentially 'the region of phantasy and sensibility', the '*Land of Desire* . . . in General History'. To Hegel (1956, pp. 139–42, 144, 154, 157) the horror of the Indian civilization was that it had no political deeds, 'no foreign conquests' to its credit: India was the land of 'dumb, deedless expansion', it had not done anything recondite or memorable in internal or international politics.

Aristotle had depicted Asia as the negating Other, the fate that awaited the West if it did not understand its difference from the East. The West's identity was rooted in this radical differentiation, spelled out in the speculations of ancient Greek philosophers and in the practice of the Athenian *polis*: the watchwords of this revolution were reason, politics, glory, excellence. In the Greek mind there was a necessary link between the life of politics, reason and freedom (Dossa, 1987, pp. 343–58).

Hegel's view of the non-West, in its essentials, was nearly identical though more elaborate and incisive: he had after all learned at the feet of the ancient Greeks. His view of Asia, in particular India, was however dissimilar in a consequential way: Hegel apprehended and painted Asia as the seductive, devouring Other. Not obviously threatening or politically dangerous, and not challenging in intellectual and moral terms, Asia was for Hegel still dangerous precisely because it was so alluring to the senses, so unreservedly natural in its temper and demeanour.

In Hegel's analysis the notion that Asia generally, and India especially, is the region of irrational, unmastered evil is never too far from the surface, and never too far behind his frequent claims 'that it is the necessary fate . . . [of Asians] to be subjected to Europeans' (Hegel, 1956, pp. 158–60, 166–7). For Hegel the European area is not saintly or *sans* moral blemish, it is rather the case that the unethical and evil in the West are part of the controlled design of God, of the universal agenda that underlies his philosophy of history. Human wrongs and evil in the West serve larger purposes, they are meaningful because they are legitimated ultimately by Hegelian teleology, more accurately by Hegelian eschatology.

Asian evil by contrast, untutored and unmanaged by Reason, is purposelessly evil and without meaning in its own terms, and in terms of the global responsibilities of Reason. India certainly frightened Hegel; he did not share the great enthusiasm of his compatriots like Friedrich von Schlegel for the high culture and values of ancient India. Hegel was not, it needs to be stressed, even marginally interested in the nature and the character of modern Asia when he was composing his *Philosophy of History*. For him modernity was synonymous with and the spiritual preserve of the West; his backward-looking historical philosophy was premised on the essential equivalence of modernity and Westernism.

If India had succumbed to the claims of Nature, ancient Persia, mistress of a political empire, had struggled valiantly to liberate itself intellectually and in practice from it. Zoroastrianism, with its potent principles of light and darkness, of good and evil, suggested to Hegel that Persians had understood, more or less, the primacy of Reason and consciousness, that they were trying to distance themselves from the hold of Nature. In ancient Persia, unlike China and India which 'remain stationary, and perpetuate a natural, vegetative existence even to the present time', Hegel sensed the beginnings of the development of universal history in accordance with the dictates of Reason.

They were the first 'Historical People', and interestingly they were also of Caucasian stock, though confined to the Oriental world, and

Hegel found them personally congenial because of 'their European dispositions, human virtues and human passions'. But despite its obvious advantages, ancient Persia had by no means understood or accepted the doctrine of freedom and free politics, it had not advanced to that level of consciousness demanded by Reason, it was still Asian in substance and practice. As Hegel (1956, pp. 173–6, 188, 192, 198) saw it, ancient Persia's historical significance lay in its having crossed the border of Nature and in having redeemed the Asians by literally seeing and espousing, though with limited success, the principle of light and consciousness.

To Hegel, ancient Persia was not the obvious Oriental Other, it was a half-way house to the real Orient, a mixed offspring with a rather clear stake in and attachment to Oriental principles. But ancient Egypt, the 'Land of Marvels', though immersed in the ways of the East, represents a startling movement in the Orient: it was the ancient Egyptians who were the first in this world to recognize that 'Spirit is immortal', that it is antithetical to Nature. But despite this awareness, Egypt was unable to 'liberate' itself from Nature, its Spirit was 'sunk in Nature'.

Neither the extent of its consciousness of Spirit nor its historical record were of sufficiently high calibre to move Egypt into the house of Hegelian Reason without qualification. Thus Egypt represents a confusing mixture of spiritual sophistication and natural primitiveness: 'It is that African imprisonment of ideas combined with the infinite impulse of the spirit to realize itself objectively, which we find here. But Spirit has still, as it were, an iron band around its forehead' (Hegel, 1956, pp. 198–9, 207; cf. 198–222).

In fact Hegel (1956, p. 204) is surprised that Egypt has come as far as it has on the ladder of universal Reason 'in the vicinity of African stupidity'. He is nevertheless magnanimous, in his mind at least, in recognizing ancient Egypt's marginal achievement in the march of universal consciousness.

In Hegel's portrait, Egypt comes aross as the intermittent outsider, the ambiguous Other in his architecture of Reason: it lacks the seductive evil of India but it is tainted by its African origin and Oriental temper. Like ancient Persia, Egypt was in the dialectical throes of spiritual self-discovery, in articulating for itself a passage to Hegelian Reason. In this sense ancient Egypt traces a path closest to the real beginning of History that took place in ancient Greece: it 'never rises to the Universal and Higher', it never achieves the requisite self-understanding and self-consciousness but it marks the 'transition' to the Western world. That is the reason Hegel (1956, pp. 219–20) is solicitous of ancient Egypt and unprepared to condemn it outright as the diabolical Oriental Other.

Transcending Hegelianism

Social science theorizing on the Third World of Africa and Asia, since Hegel, has become much more systematic, even scientific, elaborate and methodologically advanced, and indeed plural in its approaches (Wiarda, 1981, pp. 163–97). But its essential suppositions, in the mainstream, have remained Hegelian in ways that are both obvious and distressing. Hegelian-style knowledge of the Third World is intrinsically and ethnocentrically arrogant, generally false and necessarily destructive inasmuch as the kind of understanding it produces is predisposed to view this world as basically irrelevant in the post-Enlightenment universe of modernity.

To the ongoing dynamic of modernity, the Third World has little, if anything, to contribute in this Hegelian scenario: by the will of God or fortune this world has had its memorable moments in the past and Reason has now bypassed it. The power, will and knowledge to create and advance civilization is now the universal responsibility of the modern West. In fact the situation is truly depressing since the end of History is in sight and the Third World, as a whole, has not reached the point at which it can participate fully in, contribute to, or seriously challenge, Western modernism.

Hegel's philosophical history sanctions theories of development and modernization that condemn the Third World to a Western plan that has no room within it for the cultural uniqueness and the human diversity that distinguish this world. In every fundamental way the Third World will be permanently lacking because it can never reproduce the precise substance of the norms of politics, freedom, morality, justice and the peculiar individualist dispositions that separate the modern West from the rest of the world. For all the derangement and disruption caused by conquest and colonization, Third World identities are still rooted in native attachments: land, culture, religion. Hegelian epistemology has little inclination to sympathize with Third World allegiances.

By its very nature modernity is an unending project, a series of transformations that generate new ones (e.g. Bell, 1980, pp. 275–302; Schabert, 1986, pp. 9–34). For the Third World to catch up is well-nigh impossible within terms set by the modern project itself. Yet the Hegelian logic that underlies the development paradigm can recognize the Third World as worthy of attention only if it achieves substantial modernity (Walzer, 1980, pp. 189–200). To see the Third World even in this negative sense is to see it through the eyes of a relaxed, soft Hegelian view of history.

But the commanding ideas buttressing conventional Western theories of development are Hegelian in the hard sense. For the Third

World generally, Hegel did not feel intellectual affinity or cultural empathy. In step with Hegel, theorists of modernization are as impatient, in the end, as Hegel was with the traditional patterns of social and moral life in the Third World, notwithstanding their protestations to the contrary. This Hegelian approach is problematic in itself as the basis of an epistemology of distant, unfamiliar societies, as the basis of an anthropological map of the nature of the Third World. But these theorists' ignorance of the history and meaning of the Hegelian and other philosophical assumptions that constitute the structure of their discipline, that permeate their social and moral life, lessen further the relevance of their thesis on modernization.

No less destructive are the ideological–fundamentalist positions that this hard-headed Hegelianism legitimizes in the form of the foreign policies of the West, and of the United States in particular. Hegelianism is no longer, assuming it ever was, an abstract enterprise of interest only to spectral intellects. By transforming classical metaphysics into a philosophy of history, by insisting that the rational is the real in this world, Hegel intended to liberate pure philosophy from its ancestral obscurity, and to rescue history from its 'unbearable lightness of being' (Milan Kundera).

Hegelianism in one form or another is *de rigueur* these days in the academic study and in the conduct of international relations, and in social policies for the underprivileged in many Western nations. Liberal development theories have usually espoused a soft Hegelianism, tempered by a measure of cultural tolerance, but the assumption that the West is superior has never been doubted by liberals. By contrast, the neo-conservatives represent a vulgar, blatant, right-wing version of hard Hegelianism whose real agenda, revealed in the writings of 'thinkers' like Jeane Kirkpatrick and Henry Kissinger, is the re-placing of the Third World on the fringes of History, on the margins of humanity.

Hegelianism of this kind is by no means business as usual for the Third World, though that is bad enough. This tough new approach is an attempt to *mentally construct, and in practice reconstruct the Third World* (by policies that support and finance ruthless despots like Mobutu in Zaire, Noriega in Panama, Marcos in the Philippines, the Shah in Iran and so forth) *as the place of evil it was imagined to be in the heyday of imperialism in the nineteenth century*. Now it is imagined by most Westerners to be beyond the outer reaches of enlightenment, an inhospitable world obeying its own irrational rhythms. The intellectual logic of this hard Hegelianism is clear: the Third World of Asia and Africa is not relevant to world history or world culture in the modern cosmology, and to all intents and purposes it does not really matter what the West does in it and to it.

But it does matter a great deal that this world can cause (so it is believed) great damage to the West, to Civilization—period. It is thus necessary to keep it at bay, to control its teeming millions, to tame its elemental danger. By representing it as collectively and intrinsically evil, hard Hegelianism justified the *Third-Worldization* of the Third World, legitimized its transformation into a playground of indiscriminate evil, and sanctioned its recolonization. *Indiana Jones* and a plethora of similar films, much in vogue in the West since the late 1970s, visually encapsulate the essential, nightmarish, hard Hegelian vision of the Third World, and its place in the modern universal order that is retailed in the (mainstream) academic world in much less strident tones and sentences (Robinson, 1984, pp. 83–92).

To Hegelians of this stripe, the desecration and degradation of the Third World is not a moral issue, since how else should one treat natives with evil proclivities, and why should one feel guilty when one is carrying out the historical and rational mandate of Reason? In the hard Hegelian interpretation, the Third World, the world of Others, is beyond good and evil.

For a number of years now, the arrogant, ethnocentric, Hegelian universalism has been under siege in the citadels of learning in the Third World and by Third World intellectuals living in the West, and it is under attack by an increasing array of penetrating and insightful Western scholars in the Western world. Frantz Fanon, Aime Cesaire, Edward Said, Ali Mazrui, Ashis Nandy and Gayatri Spivak easily come to mind as outstanding Third World critics of mindless Hegelianism.

In the latter category, the work of philosopher Jacques Derrida, Richard Falk, Noam Chomsky, R.B.J. Walker, and many others, has served to deconstruct and dismantle the dominant, hegemonic discourses of the West, especially those on the Third World, and on minorities and women in the West.[8] What is indisputably clear is that the postmodern world that is becoming a reality all around us will, in fundamental respects, have to be a post-Hegelian world in the interests of minimal harmony, to say nothing of the pressing claims of international peace, justice and plain decency. Neither the West nor the Third World can afford the Hegelian logic of us and them, insiders and outsiders, ourselves and Others, if this global village we share together is to remain a place fit for all human beings.

Notes

1. This apt phrase is the subtitle of one of the chapters in Roberts (1983, pp. 587–607).
2. For example see the erudite essays of Isaiah Berlin (1981) on this subject, in particular his piece, 'The Counter-Enlightenment'.
3. For a critical and insightful analysis of the sudden rise and fall of the Third World in the consciousness of the West (the essay's focus is France but its conclusions are applicable to the West generally), see Garnier and Lew (1984, pp. 299–323).
4. For a notably insightful analysis of the meaning and consequence of Hobbes' and Hegel's assault on political theory, see Hannah Arendt's essay 'The Concept of History' (1968) in her *Between Past and Future*, especially pp. 68, 76 and 86. Arendt is one of this century's outstanding *political* theorists who is partly responsible for the revival of political theory in our time. For a critical interpretation of the central themes, accomplishments and limitations of her thought, see Dossa (1989).
5. For Hegel's own language and expression, see Hegel, 1967, pp. 10–13, and 1956 p. 36.
6. For example see the critical and informed analysis of various development theories in Randall and Theobold (1985); and in Gendzier (1985). Hegel is not mentioned or discussed in either of these works but his ideas and assumptions are very much part of the general analysis.
7. For a recent vulgar Hegelian view of Asians and Asian politics, see Pye (1985).
8. For a comprehensive and instructive discussion of the main thrust and substance of contemporary Western critiques of Hegelian universalism and prospects for the future, see Walker (1988; 1984).

Bibliography

Arendt, H., 1968. *Between Past and Future*. New York: Viking.

Bell, D. 1980. *The Winding Passage*. New York: Basic Books.

Berlin, I., 1981. *Against the Current*. Oxford: Oxford University Press.

Bloom, A., 1987. *The Closing of the American Mind*. New York: Simon & Schuster.

Cassirer, E., 1946. *The Myth of the State*. New Haven, Conn.: Yale University Press.

Chomsky, N., 1987. *On Power and Ideology*. Montreal: Black Rose.

Chomsky, N., 1988. *The Culture of Terrorism*. Montreal: Black Rose.

Dossa, S., 1987. 'Political Philosophy and Orientalism', *Alternatives*, vol. 12, no. 3.

Dossa, S., 1989. *The Public Realm and the Public Self*. Waterloo, Ontario: Wilfrid Laurier University Press.

Forbes, D., 1975. 'Introduction', in *Hegel's Lectures on Philosophy of World*. Cambridge: Cambridge University Press.

Frank, A.G.; J. Cockcroft & D. Johnson, 1972. *Dependence and Underdevelopment*. New York: Anchor Books.
Garnier, J-P. and Lew, R., 1984. 'From the Wretched of the Earth to the Defence of the West: An Essay on Left Disenchantment in France', in Milibrand, R. and J. Savile, eds, *Socialist Register*. London: Merlin Press.
Geertz, C., 1973. *The Interpretation of Cultures*. New York: Basic Books.
Geertz, C., 1983. *Local Knowledge*. New York: Basic Books.
Geertz, C., 1986. 'The Uses of Diversity', *Michigan Quarterly Review*, vol. 25, no. 1.
Gendzier, I., 1985. *Managing Political Change*. Boulder, Col.: Westview.
George, S., 1988. *A Fate Worse Than Debt*. London: Penguin Books.
Grant, G., 1969. *Technology and Empire*. Toronto: Anansi.
Hegel, G.W.F., 1956. *Philosophy of History*. New York: Dover Publications
Hegel, G.W.F., 1967. *Philosophy of Right*. London: Oxford University Press.
Lowith, K., 1949. *Meaning in History*. Chicago: University of Chicago Press.
Plamenatz, J., 1963. *Man and Society*. London: Longmans.
Polanyi, K., 1957. *The Great Transformation*. Boston: Beacon Press.
Pye, L., 1985. *Asian Power and Politics*. Cambridge, Mass.: Harvard University Press.
Randall, V., & R. Theobold, 1985. *Political Change and Underdevelopment*. London: Macmillan.
Roberts, J.M., 1983. *History of the World*. London: Penguin Books.
Robinson, C., 1984. 'Indiana Jones, the Third World and American Foreign Policy', *Race and Class*, vol. 26, no. 2.
Rorty, R., 1983. 'Postmodernist Bourgeois Liberalism', *The Journal of Philosophy*, vol. 80, no. 10.
Rorty, R., 1986. 'Rejoinder to Geertz', *Michigan Quarterly Review*, vol. 25, no. 1.
Rubenstein, R.L., 1983. *The Age of Triage*. Boston: Beacon Press.
Schabert, T., 1986. 'Modernity and History', I and II, in A. Moulakis, ed., *The Promise of History*. Berlin: Walter de Gruyter.
Toynbee, A., 1958. *Civilization on Trial & The World and the West*. New York: Meridian Books.
Walker, R.B.J., 1984. *Culture, Ideology and World Order*. Boulder, Col.: Westview.
Walker, R.B.J., 1988. *One World, Many Worlds: Struggle for a Just Peace*. Boulder, Col.: Lynne Rienner.
Walsh, W.H., 1960. *Philosophy of History*. New York: Harper & Row.
Walsh, W.H., 1971. 'Principle and Prejudice in Hegel's Philosophy of History', in Z.A. Pelczynski, ed., *Hegel's Political Philosophy*. Cambridge: Cambridge University Press.
Walzer, M., 1980. *Radical Principles*. New York: Basic Books.
Wiarda, H.J., 1981. 'The Ethnocentrism of Social Science Implications for Research and Policy', *The Review of Politics*, vol. 43, no. 2.
Wolin, S., 1969. 'Political Theory as a Vocation', *American Political Science Review*, vol. 63, no. 4.

7 Savagery and Neo-Savagery: An African Perspective on Peace

M.A. Mohamed Salih

'Savage' is generally defined as a simple and primeval mode of behaviour. In contrast, 'civilized' societies are said to be characterized by complexity in social, economic and political institutions and intricate advances in technology. The history of mankind has, therefore, been seen as a development from 'savagery' to 'civilization' or from simple to complex systems of social and political organization. Moreover, the civilized societies have a formidable command of military technology, whereas the so-called 'savage' societies are disadvantaged and have fewer alternatives in their relationship with 'civilized' societies. In this relationship, 'savage' wisdom is whispered or else fades into the silence of the agony of suppression. Diamond (1974, p. 2) rightly argues that,

> The original crimes of civilizations, conquest and political repression, were committed in silence and that is still their intention, if not always their result. For most of the victims, through most of human history, could not and cannot read and write.

The dominance of the 'civilized' over the 'savage' normally produces contradictory modes of behaviour: assimilation instead of rebellion and subdued silence rather than loud protest. The evidence available reveals that the psychology of dominance does not always prevent the oppressed from adopting the values of the oppressor. In fact, oppression sometimes militates against the internalization of the values of the dominant partner in a relationship—whether in domestic or international relations. Hence, many 'semi-Westernized' or rather 'Europeanized' Africans have exhibited an urge to achieve economic prosperity and military superiority similar to European 'civilization'. Furthermore, many Africans have for good or bad perceived European values and scientific heritage as the only passage to 'development'. It seems that Africans are either not aware of or not concerned with the negative aspects of 'civilization' which have earned Europe considerable psychological discomfort and fear of accidental nuclear war or nuclear fall-out. At the time when some European scholars are preoccupied with concepts such as 'Europeanizing peace', Africa has suffered, since colonial times, from the 'Europeanization of war'. For example, the integration of European values and modern weaponry systems into the making of war in Africa has devastated the continent and created a vicious circle of military, economic and political crises. None the less, many Africans still deceive themselves by taking pride in their Europeanized military values and institutions and by seeking more weapons from the neo-colonial Europeans. It is unfortunate that Africa has assembled unnecessary weapons at the expense of 'development' and amidst considerable poverty. It is also most unfortunate that some Africans do believe that such developments are part of the process of being 'civilized'.

In their fear of being called 'primitive' or 'savage' and their desire to be 'civilized', many Africans are trying the best they can to imitate Europe and look up to it in order to 'develop' their societies. In doing so, they do not seem to appreciate that the 'savage' is fortunately impecunious in developing any abominable arms and arsenals of destruction such as nuclear, chemical or biological weapons. As a matter of fact, some of the products which involve high technology represent a ghastly form of savagery which may endanger the very survival of the human race. Therefore, I redefine the development of products such as nuclear weapons and call them neo-savagery, since they signal a dangerous course and an unpredictable amount of fear.

In this chapter I argue that an African perspective on peace and development should not be a replica of the European perspective and should instead advocate a different approach. The quest for an alternative African approach to peace emanates from the fact that Africa does not possess a nuclear capability and that Africans should not relish today's prosperity by rendering themselves captives to a new deity disguised in the semblance of science. Nor should Africans follow the example of European history which is characterized by the lust for dominating others and subjecting them to their colonial and imperial interests.

A negation of Europeanism

An African perspective on peace, therefore, is a negation of Europeanism. It has been spelt out clearly by Hansen in his widely read volume on *Africa: Perspectives on Peace and Development*. Hansen (1987, pp. 1–2) argues that an African perspective on peace differs from the European perspective because,

> for us the perspective on the peace problematic which we can defend and justify is that which makes it possible for the majority of the people in this planet to enjoy physical security, a modicum of material prosperity, the satisfaction of the basic needs of human existence, emotional well being, political efficacy and psychic harmony.

It is a perspective which expands the narrow sense of security for Africa into that of the whole planet earth. In connection with this humanistic perspective, Nnoli (1987, pp. 215–32) proposes a plan of action capable of realizing peace, development and regional security in Africa based on four pillars. First, eliminating direct and structural violence which is externally sustained by advanced capitalist powers. Second, eliminating economic and political repression. Third, eliminating military intervention by the superpowers in African affairs. Fourth, combating South African aggression. Although I agree with this proposition, I believe that it represents a minimum condition for realizing peace and development in Africa. Even though such minimal conditions are prerequisites to peace, Hansen (1987, p. 4) argues that they will leave the social and material conditions which cause tension intact. In other words, one cannot propose one plan for peace and another for development. They are two faces of the same coin.

It is obvious that many African scholars have fashioned their discussions about peace and development in reaction to Europeanism which in a sense could not recognize the basic differences between the African and the European perspective. The European perspective is based on economic, political, technological and military dominance while the African perspective is based on the management of bare survival. These African scholars have also failed to recognize that the prevailing European values in international relations do not hold any promise for the realization of such a wish. This position can be explained in many ways. For example, Aluko (1982, p. 198) argues that, 'Africa is a weak continent with very little or no bargaining power with the superpowers. In most cases, the African states are bound to take more or less diktats from the industrial powers.'

A more revealing statement about Africa's relationship with Europe and how both sides view their importance to each other is made by Adisa and Agbaje (1986, p. 129) who assert that,

> two decades after the European flags went down, Europe's influence is still pervasive in the continent via the multinationals, paratroopers, the jeans and

Coca Cola culture, the Commonwealth and the Franco-African summits. Africans would like to believe that the presence underlines the strategic importance of their continent to Europe, a tendency which Europeans, in turn, are inclined to ridicule.

These two statements point out that an African perspective on peace can never be realized through a European perspective because the two differ in pursuit, priorities, values and cultural background. An African perspective on peace, therefore, can be realized only if Africans have taken pride in their social, political and economic systems and developed from within their own distinctive character. The failure of the European models to bring about prosperity in Africa is also a clear indication that a European peace perspective based on military deterrence is unthinkable. The so-called simple, 'savage' or 'primitive' way of living carries some high human virtues that the 'civilized' should reckon with. Africans should start their search for their own perspective on peace and development and in so doing they should start from the paradoxical situation that there are more chances of survival in the 'savage' way of life than that of the 'civilized'. It is not surprising that the earlier quotation from Hansen (1987, pp. 1–2) perceives an African perspective on peace and development as a global one.

The present universal fear of a nuclear war is certainly a creation of the European civilization, not of the 'savage'. If concepts such as 'savage' are reconsidered, they definitely deserve a gentler connotation than what the historical tradition has told us so far. Again, an African perspective on peace and development cannot be defended by military supremacy, but with the high human values which the so-called 'savage' possesses.

The many faces of the savage

In this section I introduce several works of some of the European writers who reflected on the problem of savagery and civilization in human societies. The main objective is to identify some of the enemy images which persisted in European values in relation to some non-European societies in general and Africa in particular. Although the relationship between Europe and Africa dates back centuries before the advent of colonialism, this section concentrates more on the colonial and post-colonial encounters.

The colonial powers disguised their economic and political interests in Africa under the pretext of bringing civilization to its 'primitive' people and cultures. The 'savage' or 'primitive' is often described by some colonial anthropologists, among other European writers, as non-literate, non-domesticated, wild, uncultivated, naked and ferocious in temper. It was under such negative attributes that European colonialism assumed that one of its prime objectives was to bring civilization to such 'savage' societies. In other words to bring Africans out of savagery to the state of civilization by means of making them refined in culture and social development. A justification of the colonial domination over Africa is reported by Howe (1968, p. 585) who made the point that,

> It [Africa] possessed no maps. With eighteen thousand miles of coast, it produced no oceangoing ships, no navies or navigators. It sent no trade missions or emissaries around the world, of which it knew and contrived to know nearly nothing; each tribe was ignorant of almost all African Lands except its own, and those of its neighbours and present and past enemies. A female continent, Black Africa, was to be discovered, penetrated and dominated by others. There were few exceptions to this image of passivity.

This description, which presents Africa as a savage or primitive continent, has at least three serious implications:

1. The concept of being savage is associated with being passive and having little interest in the outside world. The lack of military power such as navies to subdue others is considered a prime difference between the 'savage' and the 'civilized'. Savage here denotes passivity and the lack of desire to conquer others beyond the neighbouring societies, immediate enemies and competitors.
2. As such, the 'savage' is similar to the female in that he has to be penetrated and dominated by others who command navies, ocean going ships and trade interests in the outside world.
3. Because the European civilization controls navies, external trade and ocean-going ships, these are considered sufficient factors to justify colonialism and its desire to penetrate Africa and integrate it into the European world.

Colonial anthropologists are particularly dubious in their accounts of Africa. Schapera (1967, p. 34) describes the Old Bantu culture like this,

> Bantu life in the past was at times no doubt savage and harsh. The horrors of witchcraft and ritual practices, infanticide, the constraining fear of the spirits, the cramping insistence on the hierarchy of age and tribal seniority, the occasional tyranny of a chief, and the possible destruction of life and property through ruthless warfare or irresistible famine did not always make for happiness.

When Schapera argues in the same passage that 'to the average native, as long as things went well, life was far from unpleasant', he could easily be regarded as a sympathizer of the African traditional way of life. But Schapera, in fact simultaneously supported the South African policy of establishing tribal reserves in order to separate the privileged Whites from the deprived Blacks. In his second article in the same book, with the title 'Present-day Life in the Native Reserves' Schapera (1967, p. 61) argues that,

> It is difficult to summarize briefly the full effect of contact with the Europeans upon BaKxatla [a native reserve]. Admittedly European civilization has given them greater security of life and property than they formerly enjoyed, it has improved their material standards of life, it has also given them, the benefits of Christianity and education.

The same argument was voiced by Botha, ex-President of South Africa and many other racists groups inside and outside South Africa. This means that the 'savage' is not only passive (see Howe, 1968, p. 585, quoted earlier) but also warlike, idle, embedded in mythical, repulsive and horrifying ritual practices as we were told in the first quotation from Schapera (1967, p. 34). European civilization is glorified even if it means apartheid. It is likewise justified by the colonial anthropologists like Schapera who earned their living from the very misery of the 'savage'. It is obvious that Schapera and so many other scholars of his type have not questioned the inhumane practices brought by some elements of European civilization in Africa. Schapera's (1967, p. 61) quotation implies that the Bantu who live under apartheid enjoy the fruits of civilization in the form of Christianity and education. By inference, Schapera's views about the 'savage' can be interpreted as follows,

1. The Bantu are civilized through penetration and domination under apartheid. Hence political repression is conceived as the only way to free the 'savage' from passivity through domination, colonialism or neo-colonialism for that matter.
2. The Bantu under apartheid are now developed, refined and possess higher cultural values, something which they lacked before colonialism and the arrival of the Afrikaners.
3. The civilized Bantu lead a more fulfilling life because they are no longer hanging on to the horrors of witchcraft and rituals. Instead, a civilized Bantu is an educated Christian who belongs to one church denomination or another.

Schapera's work among the native tribes of South Africa not only justifies colonialism, but also finds room for defending racism and apartheid as a legitimate way of extending civilization to the 'savage'. His findings serve the interests of the while tribe of South Africa both psychologically and materially in the struggle over values and material resources.

In general there is a false assumption that the Africans are leading a gratifying life today as they come closer to the world of the civilized. Some Westernized Africans do have the impression that they have freed themselves from the image of being 'savage', as propagated by early European writers, by accepting European values. In contrast, the classic image of the 'savage' is still persistent in the average European mind. This is most visible in the political programmes of the mushrooming national fronts, neo-Fascist, neo-Nazi groups, and even some of the nationalist political parties and their attitudes towards non-European refugees, migrants, gypsies and Blacks. These political organizations have consciously or unconsciously projected an unjustified enemy image on to a lame continent like Africa, which is often described by Europeans themselves as weak and fragile in the face of their military and economic power.

The Savage disguised and involved

With the wake of Pan-Africanism and independence during the 1960s, some cynically disguised uses of the term 'savage' began to emerge in the literature. It is particularly during this period that the term 'savage' has been concealed and alternative terms, mainly borrowed from political economy, brought to use. Such patronizing terms as the 'Third World' and 'underdeveloped' with their economic rather than biological evolutionary connotations have dominated the academic and literary scene. However, it is implicit in these terms that 'savage' denotes low culture since culture itself is measured merely in terms of economic and technical developments. As such the phrase 'Third World' may imply a 'third-grade' culture while 'underdeveloped' may be interpreted as 'primitive' or 'savage'. Hence, these seemingly polite terms carry some negative attributes derived from their plausible cultural meanings within the confines of modern economic living.

Many anthropological and philosophical works which seem to represent a crusade to retrieve the word 'savage' from some of the negative descriptions bestowed upon it by early European writers, have failed to free themselves from these old enemy images. Such an attempt was made by Lévi-Strauss (1981) in *The Savage Mind* and in a more disguised and cynical form by Sartre's *Critique of Dialectical Reason* (1976).

Both Sartre and Lévi-Strauss attempt to draw structural parallels between the European (the civilized) and the non-European (the savage) mind. Their endeavour to understand the human mind is of great interest and relevance to any discussion about peace. This is mainly because issues related to peace cannot be discussed in statistical or technical terms by counting and reducing the numbers of nuclear arsenals possessed by the superpowers. Peace research should concentrate more on understanding how the human mind develops, acts and reacts to situations and what values it holds important in its pursuit of peace or conflict. It is such values, whether local, regional or international, which shape international relations and justify or condemn the use of force against others. An enemy image which is consciously, unconsciously or symbolically perceived might justify hatred and prejudice as well as the need to eliminate the threat imposed by such an assumed enemy. Both Lévi-Strauss and Sartre, in their criticism of the savage mind, have unconsciously highlighted some of the most positive aspects of the mental process that govern the 'savage' way of life. They have, in fact, consciously or unconsciously revealed a fabulous criticism of the 'civilized' rather than the 'savage' mind.

Sartre's chapters on the 'savage' in *Critique of Dialectical Reason* were, in the first place, prompted by Lévi-Strauss' *Elementary Structure of Kinship* (1948) and in response to Lévi-Strauss' argument that the social structure of the 'savage' is capable of organizing and maintaining itself, that is, it is not characterized by anarchy as some early European writers had proposed. When Lévi-Strauss argues that elaborations in the 'savage' internal reality and understanding of his cosmology represent a thought, Sartre (1976, p. 505) counters this argument by stating that, 'the savage construction is not a thought. It is a piece of manual work controlled by unexpressed synthetic knowledge.' In other words, the savage does not possess any philosophical or intellectual ability to develop and exercise his intellect as an ultimate criterion of synthetic knowledge.

Here again the 'civilized' mind is described as possessing the ingredients of dialectical reasoning while that of the 'savage' stops at the edge of a concrete analysis of its social structure and organization. Sartre has, therefore, criticized the 'savage' life because it is centred on collectivity and totalization as an antithesis to existentialism and individualism. The question is whether individualism promotes the European sense of identity with its expanding 'civilization' and 'neo-savagery', or whether the 'savage' pleas for collectivity and totalization promotes its 'passivity'.

Sartre's (1976) criticism of Lévi-Strauss led the latter to reconsider some of his own work by arguing that both the 'savage' and the 'civilized' possess scientific thought. However, the distinction between the two is that 'savage' thought is close to intuition while civilized thought has been removed far from intuition. According to Lévi-Strauss—if the 'savage' is illiterate and has no written history—any claims of a distinction between an analytical and a dialectical reason should cease to exist. This led Lévi-Strauss to stress that the 'savage' life is encompassed in nature and subsumed to it and that is why the elementary structure of human kinship, religion and totemism are nothing but an elaboration of various forms and types of mankind/nature and mankind/culture relationships. Lévi-Strauss (1981, p. 40) states that in the 'savage' world,

> each animal or plant corresponds to natural element, itself dependent on rites whose extreme complexity is well known. . . . Trees are named after the basic sorts of characteristics: their supposed sex, their medical properties and their visual or tactual appearance.

For Lévi-Strauss, such properties possess the basic features of scientific classification, and they are not manual work controlled by synthetic knowledge, as Sartre argues. The totalization process is, therefore, expressed by the fact that the relationship between humanity and nature is deeper than the daily usage of plants and animal species as food or medicine. For example, totemism is one such expression of the relationship between nature and culture which combines some elements of the social structure and the formation of social groupings. Hence it may be inferred that the intimate relationship between humanity and nature originates in a 'savage' instinct that human being share.

In brief, existentialism and structuralism reflect contemporary dualistic thought and they both emphasize the contradictions in social values rather than what is common in human societies. The essence of such patterns of thought is felt more when they are judged against reality: the passivity of the 'savage' *vis-à-vis* the dynamism of the 'civilized'; the ferocious and uncontrolled temper of the 'primitive' *vis-à-vis* the refined and domesticated behaviour of the 'civilized'. But the end result contradicts itself when the 'savage' is described as irrational and warlike, and the 'civilized' as a peace-loving, docile human being. Once the real nature of the 'savage' is unmasked, what is left behind the mystique of the enemy images are orderly, organized and self-organizing human values.

It is unjust to describe all European writings about the 'savage' as negative. Some European writers have attempted to unveil some of the positive characteristics of the 'savage' way of life. Most noticeable among them is Diamond (1974, p. 173) who argues that,

Our illness springs from the very centre of civilization, not from too much knowledge, but from too little wisdom. What primitives possess—the immediate and ramifying sense of the person, and I have tried to show that that entails an existential humanity—we have largely lost. We cannot abandon the primitive; we can only outgrow it by letting it grow within us.

Horkheimer (1947) proposes a similar critique of European civilization by highlighting the fact that the eradication of the mimetic impulses (i.e. symptoms of disease) in Europe will not eventually lead to the solution of the hysterical conditions created by civilization. According to Horkheimer (1947, p. 116) the renunciation of such mimetic impulses,

does not promise to lead to the fulfilment of man's potentialities, this impulse will always lie in wait, ready to break out as a destructive force. That is, if there is no other norm than the status quo, if all the hopes of happiness that reason can offer is that which preserves the existing as it is and even increases its pressure, the mimetic impulse is never really overcome. Men revert to it in a regressive and distorted form.

It is also premature to assume that the 'savage' tranquillity with nature is a sufficient reason to believe that the 'savage' did not fight wars. None the less, none of the primitive wars were of the scale of World Wars I or II, and were evidently not nearing the dismal proportion likely to result from a nuclear holocaust. In Mead's words,

So simple people and civilized peoples, mild peoples and violent peoples, will all go to war if they have the invention, just as those peoples who have the custom of duelling will have duels and peoples who have the pattern of vendetta will indulge in vendetta. And conversely, peoples who do not know duelling will not fight duels, even though their wives are seduced and their daughters ravished; they may not fight duels. [Quoted in Cox, 1981, p. 198]

It follows that peoples who do not know nuclear weapons will not fight with nuclear weapons, nor will their vendetta involve nuclear weapons. As to the prospect of civilizing the 'savage' there is a choice between 'developing' him into the realm of 'neo-savagery' and self-destruction or letting him continue in the ignorance of not knowing how to overkill the world.

The paradox of the 1960s which marked the independence of many African countries is that it was during the same period that the 'savage' was disguised by incorporating some of the cultural values of the 'civilized'. Africa's long experiences of the slave trade and colonialism had produced malformed economic, political and social structures.

The independent African states were unable either to maintain themselves or to become successful replicas of the European systems. Furthermore, post-colonial Africa is ravaged by brutal ethnic conflicts, secessionist movements, inter-state wars and an unprecedented violation of human rights which can be eclipsed only by the inhumane practices of the slave trade and the Nazi genocide of the Jews.

Many arms and weapon systems which have been developed by the 'civilized' have found their way to Africa today and have unfortunately inflicted greater suffering on the poorest and most vulnerable to natural and man-made disasters. This theme reveals that the development process from the stage of being 'savage' to that of being 'civilized' means the integration of the 'savage' into violent value systems defined by the 'civilized'. These may also mean the purchase of some of the destructive products of civilization such as modern arms. These weapon sales to Africa and other parts of the 'Third World' have maintained employment and the flow of resources from the 'savage' to the 'civilized'. As if 40 years of peace in Europe had also marked the removal of wars from Europe to Africa. This, on the other hand, reveals that European values in relation to the 'savage' have persisted even though some believe that the essence and nature of the relationship between the two have changed.

Europe and the resuscitation of savagery

The present European 'civilization' is developing some elements of neo-savagery which set the world on a dangerous course. Moreover, unlike savagery which is in harmony with nature, neo-savagery marks not only a move away from nature, but the ability to annihilate the human race altogether. This argument is based on four postulates.

First, the recent literature has disguised the use of the term 'savage' while new forms of savagery began to emerge within the confines of the present civilization.

Second, neo-savagery is by no means more refined than savagery. The realization of the concept of the noble savage is no longer possible in neo-savagery. In the most likely event of a nuclear war, present civilization will be reduced to mutilated forms which are neither 'savage' nor neo-savage. Neo-savagery would by then envy the humanistic nature of the early forms of savagery.

Third, the resurrection of various forms of 'neo-savagery' throughout human history indicates that a living civilization develops the conditions for its own destruction. There are signs that the present civilization is no exception. It is, unfortunately, lacking in any impetus to rid itself of the fear of its own dangerous creations—in the form of nuclear weapons and industrial pollution.

Fourth, European civilization, which pretends that it has a humanistic nature, continues to be silent about the fate of tribal societies which live outside the nuclear age, but cannot escape exploitation by the superpowers or the aftermath of a worldwide pollution or nuclear fall-out. It may be understood that Europeans have risked their survival in return for the material comfort which they enjoy, but why should the 'savage', too, bear that same risk?

In tracing the development of civilization Diamond (1974, p. 1) reminds us that 'civilization originates in conquest abroad and repression at home'. However, the picture looks no different when we relate this to the development of civilization in terms of the development of arms. One can simply distinguish the following stages in the development of different weapons systems:

1. The earliest stage was characterized by the use of physical power, sticks, bows and arrows or weapons made of stone.
2. Civilization and states began to emerge, with the use of weapons made of bronze and iron such as knives, swords, spears and the like.
3. The use of rifles, cannons and other forms of artillery gave way to colonialism which is considered a more sophisticated level of civilization.
4. At the highest level of civilization mankind has mastered the production of tanks, fighter planes, nuclear missiles, chemical and biological weapons.

So we see that to define the highest level of civilization in such terms is to reduce civilization to is ability for self-destruction. I believe that it is this concern with world peace which prompted some European scholars to question the very essence of the European identity (Chernus, 1986; Finger, Chapter 11 in this volume; Harle, Chapter 1 in this volume). An African might perceive the new peace groups as rebellious movements or an expression of discontent with European reality. Moreover, they reveal a need to get rid of the war machine that has gone astray and become stronger than the European's desire for peace. These peace movements also represent a criticism of neo-savagery, its creation of the instruments of self-destruction and its barbaric attack on humanity, its cultural, ethical and moral heritage.

The fact that the 'civilized' have tampered with nature, polluted it by the disposal of toxic waste and industrial pollution, indicates that there is no apparent reason to believe that the reconstruction of the original forms of nature or going back to the stage of 'savagery' is possible. The present worldwide ecological crisis has demonstrated that the days of the 'noble savage' have gone, and for ever. What remains is the inaccurately perceived dichotomy or dualism between the 'savage' and the 'neo-savage'.

One important aspect of the present universal outcry for peace, the proliferation of various peace movements and their resistance to 'neo-savagery', is the link between feminism and its fight for ecology and against nuclear power and weapons. This linkage is equally important as women struggle to share power resources with men. It expresses a basic strive by matriarchy to gain her legitimate position prescribed by nature, denied by patriarchy and aborted by the dominant culture of the neo-savage. It is now well know that patriarchy has, through the years, extended its influence beyond its natural domain. The creation of nuclear weapons is only one example of how patriarchy has outgrown itself. Therefore, I suggest that Howe's (1968, p. 585) admission that Africa is a female continent to be penetrated and dominated is of great significance in the feminists' fight for a society in harmony with nature. It seems as if 'nature; is always subjected to domination and subjugation by the culture of 'civilization'. European women's pressure groups for ecology and against genocide are a clear sign of an emerging gap between the material comfort provided by European civilization and the horrors and fears that it conceals.

Decades after the confrontation between Africa and Europe some basic differences in their valuation of humanity still persists. Europeans still cling to the enemy image which amounts to a direct and indirect support of South Africa. The longing for plunder and profit at any expense have not died out and the values that support these policies are still alive in the European mind. It was Europe which supported South Africa's building up of a nuclear capability and it is Europe which opens its markets to South African products and the fellow white tribe of South Africa. What Europeans could not learn from their own recent history and the Nazi experience is that no political regime which is based on racial pride can ever be content with anything less than dominating the whole world. However, European values in international relations have always shown us, Africans, that their own prosperity is more important than the prevalence of apartheid in South Africa or political oppression in other parts of the world. One observes with great interest that the very 'underdevelopment of Africa' means that it is one of the main continents with severely under-utilized strategic natural resources. The question is, would this be a sufficient excuse for subjugating and dominating the 'savage' in the future, and in this case would racist South Africa trigger off a world war or would it continue to be the European middleman in Africa? The European/African dialogue requires more than modelling Africa after the image of Europe, the building of confidence, shared human values and the elimination of the enemy images which have persisted through the years.

In conclusion

Despite the increasing contacts between cultures and societies the world over, it seems that Europe is not yet ready to reconsider some of the concepts which were developed by early European writers. One such concept which still persists, albeit in disguised forms, in the European values in international relations is the concept of 'savage'. Such concepts and their associated enemy images could be detrimental to world peace and the peaceful coexistence of human societies. This brief note transcends the historical tradition which attributes savagery to African and other economically and technologically 'underdeveloped' societies by arguing that the creation of nuclear weapons and increasing industrial pollution represents a new form of savagery. It is my conviction that these forms of 'neo-savagery' are incapable of maintaining the basic psychological security even if they were to succeed in creating economic affluence and procuring an European collective and national security.

However, confining peace efforts to international conferences and speeches by the leaders of the superpowers would not achieve more than reducing the overkill to a world holocaust. This is mainly because European collective and national security could easily be perceived by creating symbolic enemy images (such as blacks, refugees, migrants, Coloured or Russians, etc.) rather than by promoting confidence and trust. The real search for peace, I believe, lies in the dismissal of prejudicial concepts such as 'savage' and 'neo-savage' and the elimination of the sources of suspicion between cultures and societies.

Africa should not adopt European dualism and enemy images (see Harle, Chapter 1 in this volume) in retaliation for European mimetic impulses. An African perspective on peace is better based on humanistic values with the recognition that the material development gap between Europe and Africa has so far been reduced to the fact that both the 'savage' and the 'neo-savage' are in less control over their destiny. Africa is still under increasing economic and political constraints mostly exerted upon it by Europe. There is an unparalleled scale of poverty, famine and devastating civil wars. Europe, on the other hand, is less in control of its own products such as nuclear weapons and environmental pollution and cannot fully grasp the future trends of its so-called 'civilization'. Nevertheless, there is the unfortunate predicament that savagery may develop into neo-savagery, but 'neo-savagery' can never turn into 'noble savagery'. Africans, therefore, need not remain discontent with the blessings of mother nature, but with any conventions of 'savagery' used by Europeans against them.

Bibliography

Abraham, W.E., 1976. *The Mind of Africa*. London: Weidenfeld & Nicholson.

Adisa, J. & A. Agbaje, 1986. 'Africa and its Strategic Relationship with Western Europe', in I. M. Shaw *et al.*, eds., *Africa and the International Political System*. Washington, DC: University Press of America.

Alexandrowicz, C.H., 1973. *The European/African Confrontation*. Leiden: A.E. Sijthoff.

Aluko, O., 1982. 'Africa and the Great Powers; in T. Shaw and S. Ojo, eds., *Africa and the International Political System*. Lanham, New York: University Press of America.

Arkhurst, F.S., 1972. *Arms and African Development*. New York: Praeger.

Buzan, B., 1983. *People, States and Fear*. Brighton: Wheatsheaf.

Carney, D., 1972. 'Notes on Disarmament and African Development', in F.S. Arkhurst, ed., *Arms and African Development*. New York: Praeger.

Chernus, Ira, 1986. *Dr. Strangegod: On the Symbolic Meaning of Nuclear Weapons*. Boulder, Col.: University of South Carolina Press.

Cox, J., 1981. *Overkill, the Story of Modern Weapons*. Harmondsworth: Penguin Books.

Diamond, S., ed., 1964. *Primitive Views of the World*. New York: Columbia University Press.

Diamond, S., 1974. *In Search of the Primitive: A critique of Civilization*. Newburnswick, NJ: Transaction Books.

Hansen, E. ed., 1987. *Africa: Perspectives on Peace and Development*. London: Zed Books.

Horkheimer, M., 1946. 'Eclipse of Reason', in M. Jay, ed., *The Dialectical Imagination*. London: Heinemann.

Howe, R.W., 1968. 'Man and Myth in Political Africa', *Foreign Affairs*, vol. 46, no. 4.

Lévi-Strauss, C., 1948. *Elementary Structure of Kinship*. London: Weidenfeld & Nicholson.

Lévi-Strauss, C., 1963. *Totemism*. Boston: Beacon Press.

Lévi-Strauss, C., 1981. *The Savage Mind*. London: Weidenfeld & Nicholson.

Marcuse, H., 1948. 'Existentialism–a Critique of Sartre', *Philosophy and Phenomenological Research*, vol. 8. no. 3.

Mazrui, A.A., 1970. 'Current Socio-political Trends', in F.S. Arkhurst, ed., *Africa in the Seventies and the Eighties*. New York: Praeger.

Mazrui, A.A., 1972. 'Regional Development and Regional Disarmament: Some African Perspectives', in F.S. Arkhurst, ed., *Arms and African Development*. New York: Praeger.

Nettleship, M.A., *et al.*, 1975. *War and Its Causes*. The Hague and Paris: Mouton.

Nnoli, O., 1987. 'Realizing Peace, Development and Regional Security in Africa: A Plan for Action', in E. Hansen, ed., *African Perspective on Peace and Development*. London: Zed.

Ogot, B.A., 1972. *War and Society in Africa*. London: Frank Cass.

Sahlin, M.D., 1973. 'Evolution: Specific and General', in M.D. Sahlin & E.R. Service, eds., *Evolution and Culture*. Michigan: University of Michigan Press.

Samuel, M.A., 1980. *Africa and the West*. Boulder, Col.: Westview.

Sartre, J.P., 1976. *Critique of Dialectical Reason: Theory of Practical Ensembles*. London: NLB Publishers.

Schapera, I., ed., 1967. *Western Civilization and the Natives of South Africa*. London: Routledge & Kegan Paul.

Wright, S., 1987. 'Africa in World Politics: Changing Perspective', in S. Wright & J.N. Brownfoot, eds., *Africa in World Politics*. London: Macmillan.

8 The German Question from the Conservative Point of View, the Nuclear–Cosmic Age and Karl Jaspers

Jouko Jokisalo

The German question has experienced a renaissance in West Germany since the end of the 1970s. There are a variety of motives behind this new interest. One of the decisive factors is of a political nature and has to do with peace and armament (NATO's double-track decision, the deployment of medium-range missiles, the upswing of the peace movement and the INF treaty). Among other reasons are the European integration process, the problem connected with generation change, the move towards conservatism in West Germany and political processes in the socialist countries, particularly the Soviet Union.

The aim of this chapter is to analyse conservative points of view in this debate on the interrelation of German reunification and security policy. The analysis concentrates on four conceptions put forward in discussion of German policy in the 1980s by Kurt Feldmeyer, Bernhard Friedman, Bernard Willms, and Michael Stürmer.

The last section compares these different conceptions with the views of Karl Jaspers. In *Die Atombombe und die Zukunft des Menschen* (The Atom Bomb and the Future of Mankind) (1958) Jaspers takes as his starting-point the requirements of the nuclear age. On the eve of the grand coalition and the new *Ostpolitik* Jaspers wrote a book called *Wohin treibt die Bundesrepublik?* (1966), in which he thought out afresh the interdependence of the nuclear age and the German question. By comparing Jaspers with the other perspectives an attempt is made to see how the conservative conceptions of the 1980s have viewed the impending threat of nuclear destruction in relation to the German question.

Feldmeyer and the time factor

Kurt Feldmeyer, correspondent on the *Frankfurter Allgemeine Zeitung* from Bonn, sees that there is a serious weakness in the idea of the 'European peace order'. In his opinion, the situation in Europe based on the status quo cannot be described as peace but as a state of 'no war'. In order to establish lasting peace in Europe, the political sources of tension should be eliminated. The factors involved derive from the unsolved German question. A 'solution to the German question' in the form of reunification of the two German states would be 'the key to political understanding, to *détente* in the full sense of the word' (Feldmeyer, 1984, p. 283) and one of the indispensable prerequisites for peace.

According to Feldmeyer, this entails the necessity to 'go into the division in great detail so as to understand its preconditions and its internal power structure and to be able to recognize the chances of overcoming them in the course of political events' (1984, p. 280).

On the one hand, Feldmeyer regards the reunification policy as a policy of peace on a European scale; its aim would be stability and order. On the other, he admits that such a policy is inherently dangerous, because 'reunification that would increase the possibility of war between the superpowers would in fact be unjustifiable' (1984, p. 200). Hence Feldmeyer calls for an operative policy, the aim of which would be a solution to the German question without increasing the threat of war.

The central category of such a policy is, according to Feldmeyer, the time factor. He criticizes the reunification policy of the ruling parties in West Germany. Despite the urgency of reunification defined in the preamble to the constitution, the parties consider the solution of the German question 'a task for future generations' (Feldmeyer, 1984, p. 279). 'It is relatively simple', he says, 'to declare one's belief in the unity of Germany and to state on what conditions one is ready to approve of it, but otherwise it cannot be considered one of the current problems of our time' (1983, p. 66).

Firstly, this approach gives the impression that the time factor is infinite, and secondly, it leads to a political passiveness which is not in keeping with peace policy and reunification. If the time factor is given an essential role in overcoming the division, the consequences are exactly the opposite. Time is, above all, an 'incentive for action' and urges it 'when the chances to reach the aim on one's own seem modest'. According to Feldmeyer, such an attitude brings the political flexibility which makes it possible to react to 'surprising changes'. This is necessary, because there is no knowing how long the division will last and 'whether the division of Germany will lead to a new unity'. If the division lasts long enough, 'new identities' may conceivably emerge 'which could destroy the prerequisites for unification' (Feldmeyer, 1984, p. 279).

Feldmeyer sees a danger, above all, in an increasing acceptance of the division. There are those who wish

> that the common national consciousness would fade away in both German states, that people in Bonn and Leipzig would no longer see themselves as equally Germans who are part of the same people and therefore belong together; instead, they wish for the development of new identities: West Germans here—East Germans there [1983, p. 67].

Such attitudes constitute great 'danger for the continuation of our will to stick to the aim of unity and self-determination' (Feldmeyer, 1983, p. 67). Feldmeyer himself admits 'that German identity cannot permanently bear the reality of a continuous division' (1984, p. 280). The process of drifting apart experienced by the people in both states cannot simply be put down to subjective impressions; rather, empirical results show very clearly that consciousness of identity among West Germans refers to the Federal Republic of Germany and not to a fictive 'united Germany' (cf. Hess, 1986, p. 9).

Feldmeyer does not consider this development the greatest danger because, according to him, 'the identity of Germans' in West Germany is 'not at risk'. The matter of jeopardized identity relates, above all, to the foreign population in West Germany, because 'the German question can also be solved in that the population of West Germany ceases to be German'. He paints a horrifying racist picture of the development of a new 'mixture of peoples' in West Germany and the disappearance of identity. Thereafter East Germany could rightly describe itself as the only German state. Thus policy on foreigners should be a part of German domestic policy and its aim ought to be 'to see to it that the substance of the people is preserved'. Feldmeyer calls for 'political courage to oppose attacks like "xenophobia" in order to guarantee the preconditions for the restoration of national security' (1984, pp. 285–6).

According to Feldmeyer, the reason for the emergence of two German states can only be seen in the politics of the superpowers. The division is nothing but 'a product of a power projection of the two superpowers in an area where neither of them is at home' (1984, p. 281; cf. 1983, p. 67). The state of division is merely an order given by foreigners and it 'can only last as long as the two world powers are determined to and able to project their power on Central Europe'

(Feldmeyer, 1984, p. 281). The division is a result of a hegemonic conflict between the two superpowers.

Feldmeyer describes the presence of the Soviet Union as 'suppression' in the East and, for the West, a threat. As far as the presence of the USA is concerned, he sees in it 'a hope of escaping Moscow's control, in other words the hope that the Soviet Union will some day give up the position it has seized'. The greatest obstacle to reunification is the Soviet Union's striving for hegemony. 'Interest in the restoration of German unity involves the question *whether and under what circumstances Moscow could regard itself as obliged to reassess its interests*' (Feldmeyer, 1984, p. 281; emphasis added). Feldmeyer will not countenance a voluntary renunciation of the socialist order in Eastern Europe; his answer is power politics.

A 'reassessment' could only be brought about if the balance of power clearly developed 'to the disadvantage of Moscow'. The prerequisites for a realization of power politics with aims like the reunification of Germany and 'the reorganization of the situation in Europe' are a crisis in the socialist countries, NATO's unity and resistance and, above all, NATO's armament policy. Feldmeyer proclaims NATO's decision of *Nachrüstung* (reaction armament) to be a 'turning-point'. According to him, this development could mean that the Soviet Union 'no longer considers' Eastern Europe 'a victory but rather a burden'. In such a case the Soviet Union would conceivably be ready for a 'reorganization of Europe' and for a solution to the German question (Feldmeyer, 1984, pp. 281–3, cf. p. 68ff., 284).

The operative German policy relevant to West Germany or NATO aspiring to the reunification or reorganization of Europe is based on the conception of military power and speculates on erosion in the socialist countries. It does not pave the way for a constructive policy aiming at *détente* in Europe and allowing for European co-operation based on coexistence and joint operation. Feldmeyer's political conception would not mean fewer arms; rather, it would accelerate the arms race.

Feldmeyer's overall conception is of a 'neutralized Germany as a sovereign nuclear power' which has a certain 'fascination from the German point of view' (cf. 1984, p. 283ff.). Thus his ultimate aim is not to establish stability and peace; rather he is concerned with West Germany's power claim directed East as well as West. Components of this claim include reunification and the use of nuclear weapons. Feldmeyer's proposal for the solution of the German question is counterproductive and a danger to peace.

Friedman and reunification as a security concept

Bernhard Friedmann, a representative of the CDU (Christian Democratic Union), has linked reunification and security policy with the revival of the arms control process in the case of medium-range nuclear weapons. He points out that 'the new détente and arms control process should include not only the aim of better security and peace in Europe from West Germany's point of view but also the intention of restoring the unity of Germany' (1987, p. 10; cf. p. 17).

Friedmann starts from two premises: firstly, he states that the existence of nuclear warheads and foreign troops in both German states is an 'expression of a profoundly abnormal and unsettled situation'. There is no stable peace in Europe. It is clear that 'Germany' has become 'the centre of Europe's potential theatre of war'. This fact makes for a common interest for both German states: they will have to 'carry the main burden in the case of war', a situation whose culmination would be a 'destructive catastrophe' resulting in 'reunification in a mass grave'. Secondly, the preservation of peace is, according to Friedmann, closely connected with the German question. There is thus an 'interrelation between the German question and security policy' and moreover a 'connection between the German question and armament and disarmament policy'. These conclusions entail of necessity a close correlation between disarmament and reunification, the precondition of which is an active German policy (1987, pp. 31, 33, 63, 68).

Friedmann's main criticism of the *Ostpolitik* of the social liberal coalition is that it seeks to preserve peace through the recognition and normalization of the division. He criticizes the 'element of insecurity and endangerment of peace' that is seen 'in the changes concerning the current status of the division' (1987, p. 29). This would also mean a policy which detaches disarmament and security from reunification.

Friedmann also criticizes the passiveness of Kohl's government in the matter of reunification. Although Chancellor Kohl has often clearly declared his belief in reunification policy, he has always used wording that has reassured 'all opponents of the reunification': 'the German question is open, "but its solution is not at the moment on the agenda of world history" '. One of the objectives in the new discussion of German policy should be the promotion of an operative policy 'aiming not only at alleviating of the consequences of the division but also at their overcoming'; this policy must be brought irrevocably into day-to-day politics (Friedmann, 1987, pp. 19, 21; cf. 52ff., 115, 144). Friedmann also points to the failure of the Federal government to 'inform its own people of the consequential actions of the allies in the reunification question and to promote an invincible will for reunification corresponding to the allies' attitude (1987, p. 28).

Friedmann further maintains that the German question has been insufficiently emphasized by the Federal government during the discussion. He states with insistence: 'We must *ourselves* want reunification—we cannot expect them to serve us with it one day on a silver tray from the agenda of world politics'. This statement evinces suspicion as to the actual preparedness of NATO allies to support reunification. Friedmann also threatens NATO allies directly, if moral support for West Germany is only verbal and not real. Were the allies to betray the Germans, the Germans would have to be prepared for 'reactions of disappointment of unpredictable extent'. He goes on: 'In the long term this would be a considerable and unbearable risk factor in the political development of Europe' (1987, pp. 21, 103, cf. p. 115). Such statements addressed to West European neighbouring countries are typical of those expressed by West German politicians. *The Federal Government State of the Nation Review* presented by the Chancellor Kohl in the Bundestag on 27 February 1985 stated with regard to reunification:

> We need friends more than anything else. All neighbouring countries *must* realize—I emphasize: all neighbouring countries—that lasting peace will exist in Europe only if Germans are given the opportunity . . . to determine for themselves their way in history. [Quoted in Kühnl, 1986, p. 36ff; emphasis added]

On the other hand, quite different voices are to be heard among Conservatives. Bruno Heck, one of the leading politicians of the CDU, has stated: 'We are not wrong to assume that our allies—in spite of article 7 of the German Treaty—considered the German question a burden rather than a duty as early as 1961' (1984, p. 323.)

The summit meeting between Reagan and Gorbachev in Reykjavik and discussion of the zero option were the crucial factors inducing Friedmann to reassess the interrelation of security policy and German policy. His starting-points were fear of a possible rapprochement between the USA and the Soviet Union and the detachment of United Nations interests from those of Western Europe. In Friedmann's opinion, the new course for the future development of East-West relations was set by the USA and the Soviet Union 'without taking our views into account and against our German interests' (1987, p. 14; cf. pp. 35, 57, 75).

The core of Friedmann's critique of the zero option—and that expressed by the CDU/CSU (Christian Socialist Union) in general—is that the dismantling of medium-range nuclear arms in Europe has a destabilizing effect. According to Friedmann, medium-range weapons had, on the one hand, had 'a central function' in NATO's deterrence potential (1987, p. 59, cf. pp. 69ff.). On the other, Friedmann considers the stationing of medium-range weapons 'for us Germans . . . a quite crucial event' which meant 'a transfer of weightings and emphases of nuclear deterrence in Europe from the level of nuclear combat and short-range weapons to the level of medium-range weapons introduced in the course of *Nachrüstung* (Friedmann, 1987, p. 69). On the whole, his opinion is that 'the nuclear risk for us Germans could be reduced' by stationing nuclear weapons in West Europe. According to Friedmann, it was clear that medium-range missiles were indispensable to NATO and that they were stationed completely irrespective of the Soviet SS-20s. He states: '*Nachrüstung* was not only necessary to balance the SS-20 potential' (1987, pp. 69, 71).

However, Friedmann not only rejects the zero option and sees in it a danger for the security of Europe, because 'the elimination of medium-range weapons deprives the West of this major deterrent against the invasive and offensive capability and the superiority of the Warsaw Pact'; he also clearly questions the *détente* effect of disarmament. 'The question of security and peace in Europe cannot be solved by disarmament alone'. Arms are only a symptom of existing tensions. The reason for these tensions is 'the contrast between the political system', and the assumption that this problem could be solved merely by disarmament is 'an illusion' (Friedmann, 1987, pp. 74, 82–3).

Friedmann sees the core of the interrelation between security policy and German policy to lie quite simply in the fact that 'a situation of peace in Europe' requires 'restoration of the right of self-determination and unity of the German nation on the basis of a peace treaty for Germany and within the framework of European peace'. This would in fact mean for disarmament a negative role in Europe similar to that of the zero option. The reunification of Germany alone would be a real 'contribution to an active policy of peace'. It would be a way 'to get rid of the arms race'. Friedmann does not accept the idea that the German question could only be 'solved in connection with a united and integrated Europe' (Friedmann, 1987, pp. 83, 147–8). Here he disagrees with the West German constitution on foreign affairs, because its content is 'a policy of orientation towards the West' (Hacke, 1985, p. 4). Friedmann questions this priority. He demands that 'the Fatherland of Germans' must 'first emerge as a united state'. If events occur in some other order, there could be a danger of 'postponing the reunification of Germans until the never-never' (Friedmann, 1987, p. 44). Supporters of reunification criticize Friedmann for this idea in particular. In their opinion, his theses seem to have reached 'the limits of German centricity, if indeed they have not gone beyond them'. Friedmann's theses work 'counterproductively in the national sense' (Rosenbauer & März, 1988, p. 368).

As to the territory of the envisaged united Germany, Friedmann emphasizes 'that reunification defined as a security concept can only include West and East Germany'. However, he conceives of more far-reaching changes to the territorial status quo in Europe. In his plans the so-called 'Eastern areas' extend as far as the 1937 frontiers. 'If there is to be a large united Europe, then there will also be a possibility of solving the problems connected with the former Eastern areas' (Friedmann, 1987, pp. 139, 148).

The interrelation of disarmament and reunification as propagated by Friedmann is not a security concept to 'replace weapons' (1987, p. 143); rather, it is a connection which forces to armament, obstructs disarmament and requires, instead of co-operation, territorial changes in Europe—threatening towards the East but also towards the West. It is no wonder that Mrs Hensel, spokeswoman for the Greens in the Bundestag, put Friedmann's proposals in a category with other suggestions governed, to a great extent, by 'anti-Americanism'.

Bernard Willms and the national imperative

Bernard Willms, Professor of Political Science in Bochum, is one of the most influential representatives of the so-called neo-nationalism. He is part of an ideological and political trend in West Germany which prevailing opinion sees as serious but which is treated with a certain reservation (cf. Kühnl, 1986, p. 26ff.; Hess, 1986, p. 12). Willms is, however, a very popular political philosopher among the extreme right-wing circle (Leggewie, 1987, p. 102). His writings are for him not only theoretical considerations: he regards them as 'instructions for political action' (Willms, 1986, p. 10).

Willms starts from the assumption that 'the new quality of destruction techniques and therefore the new meaning of peace' change 'the fundamental conditions of human existence'. In the nuclear age there also exist such things as 'the necessity for political self-assertion', which comprises the concentration of politics on war as an emergency as well as 'the determination of friend and foe'. According to Willms, political self-assertion presupposes 'a struggle for identity' and 'a policy of restoration of national unity' which is 'the national imperative' of the German people. All this requires a 'renewal of national consciousness' (1984, pp. 88, 102, 104).

Willms sees the post-war period in Europe as characterized 'by the Allies' policy of permanent stabilization of defeats . . . and by the division of Germany'. The identity and national consciousness of Germans were stolen by the Allies when they compelled West Germany to cope with the past. 'The discussion of war crimes' is 'a continuation of the war by other means' which prevents 'the restoration of a stable political self-consciousness' (Willms, 1986, pp. 15–16; cf. p. 97).

For Willms the first step towards the rise of the German nation entails a 'revision of historiography in the sense of national argument' with the aim of 'reconstructing the national identity' (1982, p. 133). The precondition for this would be the liquidation of the anti-Fascist consciousness. 'The moralization and criminalization of German history' must be resolutely stopped. Concentrating on guilt means 'submission'. According to Willms, anti-Fascism is 'one of the most serious dangers to the German identity' and as 'disturbing for the identity as collective self-hatred'. His conclusion is: 'Whoever preaches on guilt or keeps open the wound caused by Hitler does not fight for but against identity' (Willms, 1986, pp. 42, 97–8).

The preconditions for identity are 'the renationalization of the German people' and 'restoration of the unity' (1986, pp. 49–50) of Germans. For 'the development of an individual's identity' is possible only in a nation whose creation is simultaneously a 'task' and a 'fate' (Willms, 1984, pp. 85, 88).

The restoration of national unity means not only the reunification of the two German states; Willms also considers Austria a part of the imaginary German national state. He proclaims this aim to be 'an imperative imbedded in the idea of the German national state, its *raison d'état*' (Willms, 1986, p. 49, cf. p. 41). In this, he stands doubly in contradiction with the officially recognized *raison d'état* (*Staatsräson*)[1] of West Germany. Firstly, dissociation from Fascism and its crimes as well as recognition of guilt for the war were and still are an integral part of the official image of West Germany. These 'were the price West Germany had to pay' in order to win a place among the 'free nations' of the 'Western value community' (Kühnl, 1987, p. 204; cf. Willms, 1986, p. 49). Willms sees in this an attempt by the Allies 'to beat the Germans as a nation so that Germany would be ruled out of European politics as an independent entity capable of acting' (1986, p. 16). He also looks at the division of Germany from this angle. The aim of the West, including the USA, has also been 'to oppress Germany and deprive it of power' (Willms, 1984, p. 98). This means, he maintains, that 'measured by the objective of the restoration of the nation . . . Germany has no friends'. He continues: 'Political "friendship" . . . can be reached temporarily in the West and the East only on condition of the division'. His conclusion is this: 'The restoration of Germany must start from Germany itself' (1986, pp. 39, 51, cf. 64f.). Willms finally advocates a solo effort by West Germany and thus ends up in total contradiction of the official policy of orientation towards the West.

He also repudiates parliamentary democracy of a liberal character as a basis for the common Western value community. In his opinion an unconditional move of West Germany towards the political culture of the West means the denial of German independence and the rejection of national primacy. Willms places supporters of the Western orientation in the category of Germany's internal enemies. 'Everyone giving preference to any political interest other than that of Germany, i.e. its restoration, is Germany's internal enemy' (Willms, 1986, p. 67). According to Willms, these people are objectively in a 'situation of a civil war' (1982, p. 106). He describes the peace movement in particular as a 'movement of fear' which means a 'weakening of the nation' and a 'strengthening of its enemies' (1986, p. 107). Moreover, he regards 'radical democrats' and 'anti-Fascists' as major enemies, and he also considers them among 'idiots useful to the Soviet Union'. The fight against these enemies requires a restriction of German democracy, because democracy becomes 'apprehensive' and 'scared' when 'the inner enemies ought to be determinedly eliminated' (Willms, 1984, pp. 90, 92ff.; cf. 1982, p. 267).

According to Willms, the major external enemy of West Germany is the Soviet Union. He also levels criticism at the USA as victor in 1945 and supporter of the division (cf. Willms, 1984, p. 98; 1982, p. 255ff.).

Willms thinks that the peoples of Europe and the German nation have a common interest in the fight against the superpowers: 'The confrontation of the superpowers in Europe not only prevents the unity of Germany but also hinders the restrengthening of the whole of Europe and constitutes an unparalleled threat to peace' (1986, p. 78). In his view, the firm grip of the superpowers will mean 'slow death for the whole of Europe'. To avoid this the first necessary step is 'the restoration of Germany'. Europe cannot have a politically independent role without this (Willms, 1986, pp. 38, 78ff.). A strong Germany is 'the prerequisite for the self-assertion of Europe' and 'for the first time in history the national interests of Germany are similar to those of Europe' (Willms, 1982, p. 321).

Willms openly admits that his conception is 'revisionist'. 'Its aim is to restore Germany, i.e. to revise Jalta and the division' (1982, p. 313). He does not accept the results of the defeat of 1945 but still insists on a (militarily supported) key role in Europe. His demands are not only at odds with the requirements of the nuclear age and the interests of the peoples of Europe; they also contradict the *raison d'état* of the Federal Republic of Germany.

Stürmer, the *raison d'état* and the German question

The central concept of Michael Stürmer, who is a historian and one of the advisers of the Federal Chancellor, is *raison d'état* (*Staatsräson*). The West German *raison d'état* and its applications do not result, according to Stürmer, 'from the national duty' (1986, p. 253); rather, 'integration into the West' (Stürmer, 1983a, p. 220) has been the vital law of West Germany since its establishment in 1949. In Stürmer's view, it was something of an achievement for Chancellor Adenauer to make 'Germans partners of the West'. The result is that the political culture, economic system and security policy of West Germany were and are 'connected to the West only'. The relationship with the West is, according to Stürmer, vital to West Germany: West Germany's membership in the Atlantic and the West European communities is a precondition for its existence. He stresses, however, that the dependence is not unilateral; West Germany is also indispensable to the West. The reason is that West Germany forms the 'core in the European defence structure of the Atlantic system'. According to Stürmer, the system devised to stem Soviet expansionist tendencies is not efficient without West Germany; therefore the allied partners are dependent on West Germany (1988, pp. 12, 72, 83, 87, 173).

This pre-eminence of the orientation towards the West has its consequences. In the first place, it requires that the hegemony of the USA be recognized; the USA has, according to Stürmer, a global leading role (1988a, p. 120). However, German people should not only be 'followers', they should be recognized as 'allied partners' (1983a, p. 87). He demands 'that the past should be bygone'. The situation cannot be 'good Germans in the alliance and bad Germans as a model of moral depravity' (Stürmer, 1988a, p. 31).

Stürmer is ready to accept West Germany's relinquishment of nuclear weapons in the future. The abandonment of this demand is, in his view, 'one of the means of holding on to the American presence in Europe' (1988a, p. 120; cf. pp. 87, 134ff.). Stürmer also deals with the problems of association and dissociation. Dissociation means for him 'being rid of the American nuclear shade'. He is looking for a way 'to relate in the long term the commitment of North Americans to Europe'. He is not convinced that the securing of the former US commitment in Europe through new nuclear weapons and new warfare options is the most important means of achieving this. The denuclearization of Central Europe would better serve dissociation and it would be an invitation 'to future capitulations'. According to Stürmer, security thinking based on deterrence, which includes elements of totalitarian theory, does not meet the requirements of the nuclear age. He supports the Strategic Defence Initiative (SDI), for instance, and complains that Germans do not have the courage 'to think in terms of emergency'. His most severe criticism is directed towards the peace movement. He rejects the vision of the 'Common House of Europe' as a Trojan Horse: the proposal would only disguise the Soviet struggle for hegemony (1988a, pp. 112, 120, 122, 147, 193, cf. pp. 69, 87, 105ff., 134ff., 181, 298).

Second, the precedence of the Western orientation means a denial of all solo efforts by West Germany and of the restoration of the national state with the borders of 1937. 'The age of national states is over' (Stürmer, 1988a, p. 173). According to Stürmer, the two German states are among 'the most stable elements in an unstable world' (1983a, p. 86; cf. 1983b, p. 64). Stürmer contradicts every variant of operative German policy. German policy must be 'pragmatic' (1988a, p. 12) and the politicians of West Germany must start 'from the reality of the division' (1988b). He warns against any illusionary reunification policy which could lead to the brink of a third world war. The German question has enormous explosive force because it is 'one of the central questions of the world' (Stürmer, 1983b, p. 101) and 'one of the big yes–no . . . questions of recent history' (1986a, p. 314). Therefore public discussion of reunification on a large scale could endanger the security status of West Germany (Stürmer, 1983b, p. 103).

Third, West Germany's *raison d'état*, based on ties with the West, requires that the German question be seen as a European problem. Considering it as a 'national question' provokes, according to Stürmer, 'answers that are anti-Western, anti-European and anti-historical'. His basic axiom is: 'The German question was never Germans' property' (1984, pp. 290, 293). It must be considered within a European framework. Reunification policy is possible under the conditions of Western orientation only as 'it is understood in the Atlantic and European alliance structure'. Stürmer sets out from the assumption that the division of Germany is not solely a result of the Cold War but also a product of the security interests of the European peoples. 'For the existence of this state is based on the interest of the victors of 1945 neither to *leave* Germany on *its own* nor with the opponent' (Stürmer, 1988a, pp. 75, 173; emphasis added).

This approach opposes the solo effort of West Germany suggested by the Right Wing. Furthermore, it reflects a hope that reunification could be accomplished in the future with the help of the united forces of Western Europe.

In spite of several realistic elements in his conception, Stürmer becomes entangled in the dilemma of German post-war conservatism. On the one hand, he regards the unconditional relation of West Germany to the West as crucial to the existence of the West German state. This question implies the exclusion of all possibilities of German going it alone and makes unity for Germany impossible within the framework of a national state. On the other, Stürmer sticks to his theory of a united Germany. He also pleads for 'a national policy which would simultaneously abandon the idea of a national state' (Fülberth, 1987, p. 26). Stürmer does not offer any solution to this contradiction. He states that German policy means 'overcoming the division'. He emphasizes in the same article that the desire 'to overcome the division' belongs 'to the intellectual foundations of West Germany'. Stürmer underlines the fact that 'Germans cannot contravene the decrees of the Constitution concerning reunification without causing damage to their souls and to the republic' (1988a, pp. 182–3, 190). What should in fact be the aim of German policy? Should it be confederacy, a policy of coexistence of the two German states or a policy of revision with the help of the economic and military potential of Western Europe? Stürmer offers no answer to this question.

Stürmer approaches the nationalist tendencies of West Germany by sticking to deterrence based on the totalitarian theory; he rejects, however, the conception of security partnership, balance of power and disarmament.

Jaspers, the German question and the conservative answers of the 1980s

The nuclear age mercilessly confronts mankind with the problem of survival in the sense of preventing a nuclear war. The fundamental starting-point for every consideration of security policy must be the new quality of threat embodied in the modern weapons of mass destruction. The atom bomb 'brings mankind face to face with the possibility of totally destroying itself' (Jaspers, 1958, p. 17; cf. pp. 20, 30, 37, 49, 95): Karl Jaspers described the new fact as early as 1958. It is not sufficiently reflected in the texts analysed above. To take an example, Stürmer writes that 'strength and courage are needed in order to keep both key questions of Europe together: the German question and nuclear security'. He further specifies: 'Whoever considers war the opposite of peace or is spellbound at the prospect of a nuclear holocaust does not see the core of the problem'. The other three thinkers similarly ignore the fact that peace is a priority of human life. Those who think of categories like 'emergencies' and power politics in the nuclear age cannot but think in terms of violence and they refuse to regard peace and a non-violent world as the priority above all considerations. They stick to the doctrine of nuclear deterrence and to the mutual threat of destruction inherent in this. 'Deterrence remains the basis of West European security and of the stability of world politics, and it is efficient only in nuclear form', Stürmer explains (1988a, pp. 113, 141, 190ff., 193,; cf. p. 147). In 1984 Feldmeyer still regarded the power politics based on nuclear superiority as a possible key to the solution of the German question.

As early as 1958 Karl Jaspers propounded some remarkable approaches which might well constitute to overcoming the fixation on nuclear deterrence. In his view mankind stands on a bridge between a nuclear war leading to destruction and a world without violence. 'But today we are in a state of complete transition: either the destruction of mankind . . . or the process of a changing man' (which is founded in a new world order), Jaspers states. According to him, mankind is living in a 'period of transition between history hitherto—a history of wars—and a future which will bring either a complete end or a state of world peace'. Jaspers goes on to draw conclusions which, to a great extent, correspond with the requirements of the nuclear age. First he points out that armament can no longer bring security in the nuclear age: 'Military armament has lost its value in the age of these bombs'. This basic truth about the nuclear age is brought out by none of the four other German writers. Second, intimidation by nuclear weapons is, according to Jaspers, 'an illusion'. He thus questions the basis of deterrence policy. He criticizes the logic which sets out from the assumption that nuclear powers will never dare to use their weapons. The presumption that a total threat produces total rescue is wrong. 'Fear alone is no sufficient and reliable means in the long term' (Jaspers, 1958, pp. 37, 54, 88, 95).

This logic is quite different from that of Stürmer, who writes: 'Experience of many centuries shows that conventional balance does not prevent a war. Experience of the past four decades, however shows, that the existence of nuclear weapons does'. He continues to proclaim: '*West European defence without nuclear weapons would, as far as anyone can judge, make war more likely* . . .' (Stürmer, 1988a, p. 147); emphasis added). For Stürmer the fear instilled by nuclear deterrence is and remains the most secure means of preventing a war. The friend-enemy thinking of Willms meets the requirements and necessity of the present day even less adequately than Stürmer's deterrence doctrine.

Willms' starting-point makes the aspiration to power and superiority between social opponents indispensable in the military field in particular. Then the deployment of military instruments of power is kept open as an option in a clash between different systems. This, however, makes it impossible for peace to become the most important value.

For Jaspers, the establishment of world peace is the only solution in the survival of mankind. Humankind's strategy and action must be directed towards this. 'The destruction of mankind cannot be prevented without global peace', he states. To this end, every action must be considered with respect to the aim of global peace (Jaspers, 1958, pp. 39, 88; 1966, p. 224). Secondly, we must get rid of the atom bomb. Thirdly, peace should be established on justice. The elimination of the nuclear danger requires a transition 'into a community of states which is based on the right of treaties'. Fourthly, a state of co-operation must be established (Jaspers, 1958, pp. 37–8, 47).

Jaspers' strategy of global peace is thus in contradiction with the concepts of Stürmer and the others.

The limitations of Jaspers' ideas lie in their totalitarianism. His book (1958) is one of the best examples to sustain the view that the totalitarian doctrine stands in the way of peace (Eppler, 1988, p. 67). Jaspers proposes two alternatives: the Bomb or total power. This leads to a situation where approaches supported by peace research are rendered void. Jaspers finishes up in a blind alley. 'The tension between self-assertion and the interests of the human race . . . is insurmountable', he writes. His remarks are partly diametrically opposed. Ultimately he throws up his arms in face of the problem and explains that it is 'rationally insoluble' (1958, pp. 110, 222). This limitation prevents him from penetrating to insight that security must be seen as common security.

The totalitarian theory which equates the Soviet Union with Nazi Germany is also the ideological basis for Stürmer and Willms. Stürmer warns against rejecting the totalitarian doctrine: 'If this doctrine is forgotten, a new generation will take advantage of the inalienable human rights in their search for misfortune' (1988a, p. 83ff.). But here one can, however, point out that while the totalitarian doctrine can contribute methodologically to research into the form and method of power, it cannot help to examine the purpose and content of power. This doctrine has catastrophic consequences if applied to international relations. It leads to a maximization of the struggle between systems and obstructs or delays the establishment of a stable peace. No solution to the East-West problem is possible 'without overcoming the deep ideological confrontation causing the current division of the world'

(Schachnasarow, 1989, p. 495). The application of a totalitarian doctrine in international relations brings the problems of rivalry to the fore. This has an unfortunate influence on the suggested solutions to German reunification.

Jaspers had freed himself from the totalitarian doctrine in 1966 to the extent that he found the way out of the blind alley. In the nuclear age 'the results of previous political history have produced something final in the establishment of state borders'. For Jaspers there is only one alternative: 'Either the will to new violence or to reconciliation on the basis of reality'. Violence would mean a world war, a nuclear war, the destruction of mankind. Jaspers' conclusion is this: 'Whoever wants peace must recognize the facts which cannot be changed without violence'. He does not accept the 'claim according to which failure to reunify Germany would constitute a danger to peace' (Jaspers, 1966, pp. 233–5ff., 244).

According to Jaspers, 'the idea of a reunited powerful Germany is a nightmare' to the East and to France. It is 'a worry' for all European states. Therefore the support of the West for the demand for reunification is only 'formal'. Jaspers' conclusion is that West Germany must one day give up 'if it does not want to be totally isolated and regarded as a dangerous disturber of the peace' (1966, pp. 236, 244).

From Jaspers' point of view, the conceptions of Friedmann, Feldmeyer and Willms are still embroiled in the old views which, according to him, 'endanger peace'. The answers introduced by conservative thinkers in the 1980s have not yet shown the way out of the blind alley of the German question. Stürmer's denial of a national state is largely in accord with Jaspers' opinion. The difference between the two is, however, that Stürmer clings to the idea of nuclear deterrence and will not dissociate himself from the rhetoric concerning a united Germany. He thus fails to reach Jaspers' conclusion according to which

> West Germany is bogged down in an incredible fantasy world which it bases on demands for rights. It is hopelessly stuck in a blind alley and will come out of it only if it changes its ways, remembers its real situation and constructs its policy on a supporting and non-fictive base' (Jaspers, 1966, p. 257).

Notes

1. The category comes from Friedrich Meinecke, who defined the term as follows in his book *Die Idee der Staatsräson* (The Doctrine of *Raison d'Etat*, 1924): 'The *raison d'état* forms the maxim of the state's actions . . . They

tell the statesman what he has to do in order to keep the state strong and healthy'. This means that a state should 'understand itself and its environment and create its maxims of action on the basis of this understanding' (Meinecke, 1963, p. 1).

Bibliography

Eppler, E., 1988. *Wie Feuer und Wasser, Sind Ost und West friedensfähig?* Reinbek bei Hamburg: Rowohlt Taschenbuch.

Feldmeyer, K., 1983. 'Anmerkungen zur Deutschlandpolitik—worüber die Parteien schweigen?' in K. Lamers, ed., *Suche nach Deutschland. Nationale Identität und die Deutschlandpolitik*. Bonn: Europa Union.

Feldmeyer, K., 1984. 'Die deutsche Frage und der Faktor der Zeit', *Deutschland Archiv*, no. 3.

Feldmeyer, K., 1987. 'Deutschland im Gespräch', *Frankfurter Allgemeine Zeitung*, 21 May.

Friedmann, B., 1987. *Einheit statt Raketen: Thesen zur Wiedervereinigung als Sicherheitskonzept*. Herford: Busse & Seewald.

Fülberth, G., 1987. '"Mitte" und "Westen". Über die Grenzen einer Kritik, die auf Imperialismus-Theorie verzichtet', *Das Argument*, no. 161.

Grewe, W., 1988. 'Appeasement und Entspannung. Zur Substanz zweier politischer Schlagworte', *Politische Studien*, vol. 39, no. 302.

Hacke, C., 1987. 'Von Adenauer zu Kohl: Zur Ost- und Deutschlandpolitik der Bundesrepublik 1949–1985', *Das Parlament*, no. 51–2.

Heck, B., 1984. 'Europa und die deutsche Frage', in K. Weigelt *et al.*, eds., *Heimat und Nation. Zur Geschichte und Identität der Deutschen*. Mainz: Haase and Kohler.

Hess, J.C., 1986. 'Westdeutsche Suche nach nationaler Identität', *Neue politische Literatur, Beiheft*, no. 3.

Jaspers, K., 1958. *Die Atombombe und die Zukunft des Menschen*. Munich: Piper & Co.

Jaspers, K., 1966. *Wohin treibt die Bundesrepublik?* Munich: Piper & Co.

Kühnl, R., 1986. *Nation, Nationalismus, Nationale Frage*. Cologne: Pahl-Rugenstein.

Kühnl, R., 1987. 'Ein Kampf um das Geschichtsbild. Voraussetzungen—Verlauf—Bilanz', in R. Kühnl, ed., *Vergangenheit, die nicht vergeht. Die 'Historiker-Debatte'. Darstellung, Dokumentation, Kritik*. Cologne: Pahl-Rugenstein.

Leggewie, C., 1987. *Der Geist steht rechts*. Berlin: Rotbuch.

Mehlich, S., 1988. 'BRD-Konservatismus: Vom Abschreckungsdenken zur Akzeptanz gegenseitiger Sicherheit?', *IPW-Berichte*, vol. 17, no. 2.

Meinecke, F., 1963. *Die Idee der Staatsräson in der neueren Geschichte*. Munich: Oldenbourg.

Reusch, J., 1988. *Neue Sichherheit im Nuklearzeitalter*. Cologne: Pahl-Rugenstein.

Rosenbauer & Märtz, P., 1988. 'Deutsche Frage und Europa. Überlegungen und Perspektiven', *Politischen Studien*, vol. 39, no. 300.

Schachnasorow, G., 1989. 'Der "Gegensatz der Systeme" als fixe Idee', *Blätter für deutsche und internationale Politik*, no. 4.

Schmidt, M. & W. Schwartz, 1988. 'Das gemeinsame Haus Europa—Realitäten, Herausforderung, Perspektiven' (I & II), *IPW-Berichte*, vol. 17, nos. 9 & 10.

Stürmer, M., 1983a. 'Kein Eigentum der Deutschen: die deutsche Frage', in W. Weidenfeld, ed., *Die Identität der Deutschen*. Munich: Carl Hanser.

Stürmer, M., 1983b. 'Wem gehört die deutsche Geschichte?', *Dokumentation*, no. 9.

Stürmer, M., 1984. 'Die deutsche Frage als europäisches Problem. Ein Sonderweg deutscher Geschichte?', in K. Weigelt, ed., *Heimat und Nation*. Mainz: Haase & Kohler.

Stürmer, M., 1986a. *Dissonanzen des Forschritts*. Munich: Piper & Co.

Stürmer, M., 1986b. 'Der lange Schatten der Tyrannen. Westbindung und Geschichtsbild in Deutschland', in *Von Geschichte umgeben. Joachim Fest zum Sechzigsten*. Berlin: Siedler.

Stürmer, M., 1987. 'Mitten in Europa. Die deutsche Frage in Geschichte und Gegenwart', in O. Franz *et al.* eds., *Europas Mitte*. Göttingen: Muster-Schmidt.

Stürmer, M., 1988a. *Deutshce Fragen oder die Suche nach der Staatsräson*. Munich: Piper & Co.

Stürmer, M., 1988b. 'Solange Europas Mitte umstritten bleibt', *Frankfurter Allgemeine Zeitung*, 16 June.

Sutor, B., 1967. 'Existenzphilosophie und Politik. Zur Sturktur politischen Denkens bei Karl Jaspers', *Das Parlament*, no. B/16.

Willms, B., 1982. *Die deutsche Nation*. Cologne: Hohenheim.

Willms, B., 1984. 'Überlegungen zur Zukunft der deutschen Nation', in *Nation und Selbstbestimmung in Politik und Recht, Abhandlungen des Göttinger Arbeitskreises, Bd. 6*. Berlin: Duncker & Humboldt.

Willms, B., 1986. *Identität und Widerstand*. Tübingen: Hohenrain.

9 Violence—An Israeli Perspective[1]

Gershon Weiler

Thomas Hobbes remains to this day the greatest philosopher of security and consequently he is not only a philosopher of peace but also of violence and war. He rests his whole conception of how people ought to live with each other on a 'general rule of Reason' and its statement appears at the very beginning of Hobbes' exposition of his political theory, at the opening of Chapter XIV of *Leviathan*:

> *That every man, ought to endeavour Peace, as farre as he has hope of obtaining it; and when he cannot obtain it, that he may seek, and use, all helps, and advantages of Warre.* The first branch of which Rule, containeth the first, and Fundamentall Law of Nature; which is *to seek Peace, and follow it.* The Second, the summe of the Right of Nature; which is, *By all means we can, to defend ourselves.* [Hobbes, 1958, p. 100]

The natural right of war is, then, part of the general rule of reason. Under circumstances of insecurity, resorting to war is the most rational thing one can possibly do. War, for Hobbes, as he expounds this in Chapter XIII, is not battle or 'actual fighting' but 'the known disposition thereto, during all the time there is no assurance to the contrary. All other time is PEACE' (1958, p. 96).

Clearly, these definitions are in need of some correction. Hobbes sees war as the condition of radical insecurity for the individual. It seems to me better to say that such a condition of insecurity is more properly labelled as condition of permanently potential violence, such that it may erupt at any time, without any structured system of warning. Indeed, the whole description of the state of nature in Hobbes fits much better a situation of unstructured violence than that of war. For war, whatever else may be true of it, is always a highly organized and structured affair, presupposing a system of direction and command, something which comes into being, in Hobbes, only with the establishment of sovereignty. Individuals may be violent towards each other but they cannot be said to engage in warfare when they are violent merely at an individual level. In seekng a better grasp of the relation obtaining between war and violence, it is natural to turn to Carl von Clausewitz. On the very first page of *On War*, where he defines war, we find the following:

> *War therefore is an act of violence intended to compel our opponent to fulfil our will.* . . . Violence, that is to say, physical force (for there is no moral force without the conception of States and Law), is therefore the *means*; the compulsory submission of the enemy to our will is the ultimate *object*. [Clausewitz, 1982, p. 101]

Clausewitz later explains that '*War is always a serious means for a serious object*' (1982, p. 118). Wars are fought for political ends, or, to quote Clausewitz once more (p. 119): 'Policy, therefore, is interwoven with the whole action of War, and must exercise a continuous influence upon it, as far as the nature of the forces liberated by it will permit.'

Now, if we consider these conceptual statements from an Israeli perspective, we find ourselves in something of a quandary. While it would be wrong to say that the *dicta* of Hobbes and Clausewitz are beside the point, yet we cannot help feeling that, seen from this perspective, they are not exactly to the point either. The precise understanding of this odd circumstance is the first step which needs to be taken if we seek to understand the unique nature of Israel's permanent coexistence with violence and the special perspective of Israelis, which outsiders often find objectionable and, at any rate, difficult to share.

Let us go back to Clausewitz. What he is telling us is both simple and reasonable: violence is an *ingredient* of war and wars are fought between states for political objectives. 'Submission of the enemy to our will' presupposes the *being* of the enemy, the fact that he exists and the further assumption that he will continue to exist even after he submitted 'to our will'. For, obviously, if this latter assumption were denied, then submission could have no rational element in it; submission would then be strictly equivalent to mere physical incapacity to defend oneself. This is more like accepting extermination than submission to the enemy. In other words, wars are typically fought for the sake of extracting something from the enemy which cannot be obtained by other means. This is part of the normal traffic of states which can be related to each other in only two ways, through diplomacy and war. This, as said, presupposes a certain conservatism on behalf of those who are engaged in these inter-state practices. Even Kant (1927) regards existing states as rightfully entitled to continue to exist. This conservative principle is fully recognized at present too. Although the non-state right of self-determination is given honourable mention in Articles 1 (2) and 55 of the United Nations Charter, these references must be read in the general context of overriding conservative principles, notably the supremely important Article 51 of the Charter which *recognizes* the inherent right of states to self-defence, and the UN Declaration of Friendly Relations between States (1970) which prohibits the use of force against the territorial integrity of member nations.

The Israeli discomfort with the political aspects of war in Clausewitz, as it applies to the Israeli situation, has its roots in the fact that the Arab hostility to Israel is very far from being a special case of hostility between states. The Arabs do not say to Israel, do this or that and *then* we shall leave you alone as a state, but they say something which sounds, to Israeli ears at least, like threats of extermination. This may well sound somewhat paranoid, yet it is this perception which gives the Israeli perspective on violence its special character. It is the purpose of this chapter to make this perspective, even if not shared, at least comprehensible.

The first ingredient of the situation we must take note of is the self-understanding of the parties to the conflict. Clausewitz speaks of the state, yet it is a fact that the state, as a political entity different from both rulers and ruled, is a relatively new phenomenon. There have long been empires of all kinds but the state, which is the subject-agent of inter-state relations in the meaning of international law and international relations in general, is a relatively new phenomenon. It can be dated to a development which began not earlier than the fifteenth century and which was not completed before the eighteenth (Shennan, 1974). Now, it is a hard fact that this development did not occur in non-European cultures and it is not only the Arab–Israeli conflict which bears witness to the strains which the international system is subjected to on account of the extension of membership in the international community to states which do not share the cultural heritage of European states. Most significant among these culturally out-of-step states are the Arab states. On the one hand they *are* states within the meaning of international usage while, on the other hand, they see themselves as *qualitatively* different.

For Arabs, the most basic fact of existence is religion, Islam; fundamentally, Arabs see themselves as members of the *Ummat al-Islam*, the community or nation of Islam. By comparison to this most fundamental of all ties of belonging, citizenship in states, like Egypt or Syria, fades into insignificance. In Arabic there are two words for nationality: *qúamiya* refers to membership of the universal Arab nation, while *wataniya* indicates citizenship of particular states (e.g. Iraq). Moreover, the conception which is basic to the Arab view of the outside world is decidedly Manicheistic, if this mixture of religions be forgiven. Those who belong to the *Umma* constitute the *Dar al-Islam*, the House of Islam, while the whole outside world is defined as the *Dar al-Hirb*, as the House of War. Between these two 'houses' no peace is possible, only truce, depending on the contingencies of power relations. To illustrate this: some years ago, the Libyan ruler, Col. Ghadaffi, made a visit to Paris. In the course of that event he appeared at a press conference and there he stated that the Arabs are regaining the power they had lost to the European powers some centuries ago; the time has come to rectify the results of the defeat at Poitiers. The reference was to the battle of 732, in which Charles Martel defeated, between Poitiers and Tours, on the so called 'pavement of the martyrs', the Moslems advancing towards Paris and into the heart of Europe. Those present could scarcely believe their ears, so they asked that the statement be repeated. It was. The war for Europe, such was the message, is not yet over.

The point is important enough to be laboured a little more. There is a real problem about the genuineness of any settlement made with Arabs. If after the lapse of more than 1000 years the legitimacy of a situation then created is still in question, then there is good ground for real fear that, at the first opportunity, the House of War will be under attack again. Israel's peace treaty with Egypt has been holding well enough since it was signed, on the White House Lawn, on 26 March 1979. Yet it would be difficult to dispute the widely shared belief that the continued existence of this agreement strictly depends on, and is contemporaneous with, Egypt's interest in remaining in the good books of the United States. This is not to belittle the enormous significance of Israel's peace with Egypt, but rather to put it into the context of a historical perspective which, with all inevitable uncertainties, takes in the future too.

I would like to cast a glance here at a lesson learnt by Israel from her experiences in Lebanon. As is well known, that war gave rise to one of the most bitter controversies in Israel and I shall ignore it here. But it is perhaps less known that that war had a rather more lasting effect, as a by-product, on the thinking of the Israeli public regarding possibilities of peace with Arab neighbours. This came about through the circumstance that the war gave large numbers of Israelis, both national service men and reservists, a first-hand opportunity to observe how 'well' functions a state, 'secular and democratic' in an Arab context, which has non-Muslim populations. More than that, not only Christians and Muslims, but also varieties of Muslims and even Muslims of the same sect are ready to kill each other in their pursuit of domination as, for example, at the time of this writing contending groups of Shi'a

Muslims are lustily butchering each other. These experiences had the effect of greatly reducing the readiness of Israelis to believe in the possibility of peaceful coexistence with Arabs.

These 'contemporary' considerations are readily supported, in the context of the Israeli perspective, by the evidence of history. This is not the place to survey the *wars* of Israel. It is sufficient to remind ourselves of the fact that Arab violence precedes the establishment of the Israeli state and is contemporaneous with the Jewish settlement in Palestine. The form of *violence* changes with time, and ranges from individual terror to organized communal uprising, as in 1936–9 against the British and recently as *intifada* against Israeli rule, to wars and warlike acts (such as closing of the sea routes to Israeli shipping in 1956) initiated by Arab *states*. All this has the effect of persuading Israelis that Arabs do not fight them for a *political* objective with which Israel should be able to live, but for the sake of discontinuing the existence of Israel as a state, and the Israeli population there as a national entity. Thus considered, violence exercised by Arabs is not perceived as a Clausewitzian *ingredient* of war, but rather as an objective in itself, the purpose of which is to eliminate what is different. And Israel, it has to be admitted, *is* different.

It might be thought that nothing said so far goes beyond what one would say of ideological conflicts. In a sense, this is a reasonable enough comment on the Arab–Israeli conflict. All the same, this classification does not fit the situation too well. In a very wide conception of ideology anything, of course, could be included. Yet, in its normal connotation, ideological objectives denote matters relating to principles of government, natures of regimes and such like and these, as suggested already in the context of discussing relations between states, presuppose that once these ideological objectives are attained, all else, chiefly the lives of individuals, can go on, subject to such limitations and constraints which follow from the nature of the new regime. The nations of Eastern Europe, while they had systems of government imposed upon them, were not expelled from their homes nor were they prevented from continuing to speak Polish or Hungarian. The Arab–Israeli conflict is *not* ideological in this sense. No change of heart on the part of Israelis would make their national existence legitimate from an Arab point of view. What is at issue here is not only what we have been discussing so far, that is, self-understanding of Islam as the only legitimate framework for political existence, there is also a further consideration, not mentioned before. It is that the Muslim self-understanding *includes* a very specific understanding of their adversary. Jews, like Christians, are regarded as *dhimmîs*, i.e. members of tolerated religions (Lewis, 1960, *passim*). Much of the Arab propaganda about the so-called Golden Age of Muslim–Jewish coexistence is based on the memory of historical times when this stratification was institutionalized and lived by. A great part of Arab bitterness about Israel has its psychological roots here; Muslims find it offensive to have to treat *dhimmîs* as if they were of equal standing, as demanded by the basic assumptions of the international system, and it is even more offensive for them to be beaten by *dhimmîs* on the field of battle.

The rule of violence, as the lesser part of the general rule of reason, is to be abandoned as soon as the fundamental law of nature, the law of peace, has a realistic chance of prevailing and of taking over. This is the lesson of Hobbes. In the light of all I have been saying so far, it seems that given that the chances of peace are slim and precarious, violence, or more precisely its pursuit, is the most rational thing Israelis can do. This rather sweeping statement leaves open, of course, the amount and kind of violence that must be expended to keep Arab violence, which appears to Israelis permanent and inexorable, within 'reasonable' bounds, which will prevent it from doing more harm than inevitable. This is the most general background of the debate which is, again, as old as Jewish settlement in the country. It is the debate about 'what to do about' Arab violence. There are various schools of thought, there are hawks and doves, but the basic assumption of all is the same factual premiss: Arab violence is there and it is not likely to go away. It has no aim the adoption of which on the part of Israel would placate its perpetrators and thus Israel's relating to Arab violence is always in the nature of symptomatic treatment. True enough, there are people in Israel who speak of 'solving' the problem, as if it were an ordinary inter-nation or inter-state conflict but, significantly, those who sincerely think this way are not very numerous. The reason for this is simple enough. Historical experience shows that hostility and violence is constant while the rationalizations or, shall we say, the reasons which are offered in supporting them, change with time and circumstance.

At the present time there is a strong case made out for the Palestinian Arab demand for self-determination. It is a good case and I venture to say that if Israelis did not think that the attainment of this objective would be fatal for them, they would be enthusiastic in embracing the idea of a Palestinian state, so as to bring to an end a hundred years of unstructured violence. The fact of the matter is that confidence is slow in being born in the Middle East and given that Israel is allowed, by demography and geography alike, to make just one fatal mistake, the current campaign of the PLO to persuade Israelis that they mean no harm is not likely to be very successful.

Being on the receiving end of violence is not an Israeli experience for which Arabs must take all the blame. Before the advent of the century-old conflict over Israel/Palestine, Jews have been habituated to one-sided violence by a long and unfortunate history of dispersion. Pogroms, like gas chambers, are just the more distinctly ugly faces of a long-standing tradition, both in Christendom and Islam, which has regarded equal rights for Jews as impudence, to use the term sanctioned by the usage of the Church in this very context. Correspondingly there arose among Jews not only fear of violence but also, more relevant to our present concerns, a belief that there is something like a law of history that Jews are singled out to be victims of violence. The theological doctrine of chosenness has this inverse face too: chosen, i.e. singled out for violence. Against this background it is comprehensible that in her resolve never again to be singled out, Israel sometimes reacts to acts in ways which are arguably not proportional to the deeds that provoke them. Proportionality, as is well known, is one of the requirements international law sets for acts of self-defence, if they are to be justifiable. What I am suggesting is that, against the background I am sketching it is reasonable for Israelis, in the sense given to this notion by the right of Nature of Hobbes, to act in this way. The latest terrorist incursion is always seen as a link in a long chain and thus reaction to the event itself may well be rather excessive. I am not arguing here, not by any means, that all Israel does is all right. The task I set myself is to convey to the reader the essentials of an Israeli perspective on violence. Note, *an* Israeli perspective and not *the* Israeli perspective; what I say is not shared by many of my compatriots. Thus from this point of view, I am saying that massive retaliation seems to many Israelis as a sort of settling of accounts after the bill has been running up for a while. It is part of what I am trying to convey here that this 'a while' has deep roots in history and in the not always conscious self-understanding of Israelis whose historical memories are inescapably Jewish.

If the reader has succumbed by now to a measure of gloom then I have not completely failed in this chapter. All the same, as it would be unfair to leave matters in a condition of total despondency, I shall attempt to say something speculative about better prospects, if any; is there a way to stop the circle of violence between Arabs and Israelis? While what I have to say is hypothetical and speculative, it is no less realistic for that. I am attempting to articulate some of the conditions which will have to be satisfied if violence is to stop, or at least to be reduced to 'normal' proportions. The logic of what I have to offer is analogous to the old Hungarian joke about the ways the Soviets can be got out of Hungary. 'There are two ways,' Hungarian wisdom has it, 'the natural and the miraculous. The natural way is that the Hungarian people will rise and drive the Russians out; the miraculous way is that they will go home on their own initiative.' Here too, I wish to suggest, there are two ways out of the present situation. One internal and other external. Let me sketch both of them; it will emerge that these two ways do indeed cross each other at the crucial point.

The internal solution would be for the Israeli–Arab conflict to reduce in size and to metamorphose into a 'normal' conflict between states. Over the decades the conflict has had many names and appellations and the latest of these, that 'the heart of the conflict is the problem of the Palestinian people', is *but* the latest in a series of descriptions which, from an Israeli point of view, all seem but so many dissimulations and cover-ups of a profound and implacable hostility. This internal spontaneous reduction in dimensions is what I would term, in the light of all I have said so far, the miraculous. For it would be truly miraculous if the parties to this conflict of almost unstructured violence could, of their own accord and without outside help, rid themselves of habits of thought and feeling which have been shaping their destinies for a century. The more promising approach is to involve outside powers. The difficulty here is that, given the background with which we are by now familiar, it must be manifest to all that those outsiders are indeed honest brokers. Israel is not likely to put its fate into the hands of powers it cannot trust. It all comes back to the general rule of reason of Hobbes. If peace cannot be secured then exercising the right of nature is the *most* rational thing to do. In order to avoid this undesirable consequence a way out of the impasse, proposed by outsiders, must have a supreme attraction. Now, this sort of attraction can be of two kinds. It can be the supply of what Warrender (1957) has called, in the context of Hobbes, the 'validating conditions' for the actual operation of the laws of nature. He meant by this that the sovereign, by concentrating power in his own hands, creates conditions in which it is safe for people to desist from violence.

In the international realities these conditions can be none other than *credible* guarantees. This is the point where the two routes cross each other; the name of this crucial point is credibility. Whether any such credible guarantees are possible or forthcoming is the great question of the future as far as the conflict under discussion is concerned.

There is, of course, another way of making an offer 'attractive'. It is to make an offer impossible to refuse. In plain English this amounts to posing a mortal threat to whoever refuses to accept. From the Israeli point of view, this possibility always looms in the background and it relates to the so-called Massada complex. This is a matter which requires some elaboration.

Making an offer which cannot be rejected *is* to make clear to the addressee that if he rejects it his situation will be much worse than if he accepts. In other words, even in compelling a party to submit there must be at least the promise of being spared. That this cannot be relied upon has been made clear enough throughout history. The victor may also slaughter the vanquished (Aron, 1981). So it may not be that rational after all to submit. What is known as the 'Prisoner's Dilemma' is in essence the 'game' in which being killed while the adversary lives on is less desirable than mutual destruction. In the light of all I have been saying so far, it should need no argument to establish that Israel could never prefer her own destruction *alone* to her own destruction *together with* the destruction of whomever it may be. Israel is capable of spreading destruction in a formidable measure. Therefore, it cannot be rational to put her into the corner where the only choice she has left is acquiescing in her own destruction *or* augmenting this with the destruction of others. Clearly, under such dismal circumstances, the latter option is more rational (Kenny, 1985). The fortress of Massada was the last Jewish stronghold in the anti-colonial war against the Roman Empire. Its outnumbered defenders preferred suicide to slavery. They were powerless to effect *mutual* destruction, so they could destroy only themselves. Israel, while in serious trouble, is not powerless.

It might be objected at this point that the trouble is just that: Israel is far too powerful and she abuses her power to inflict injustice on others. Let me explain how all this appears from the Israeli perspective. The difference between Arabs and Israelis in this conflict is, when it comes to the most basic of all considerations, that Arabs have hope while Israelis have none. I mean by this the following: Arabs believe that if they make some more effort then, at some time or other, they will ultimately be successful and Israel will disappear. In the context of this grand hope, the price that will have to be paid for its realization is devoid of all significance for those who entertain it. The late President Sadat was speaking sincerely when he had said, long before he made peace, that he would readily sacrifice a million Egyptians to get Sinai back. There *is* this Arab hope of liquidating Israel. By contrast, Israelis have no hope that, at any time in any future, their country will be free of Arab presence. This creates deep frustrations which manifest themselves, at the individual level, in emigration and, on the political level, in the emergence of marginal extremist political parties which advocate the expulsion or the 'transfer' of Arabs into other countries. Needless to argue that none of this is serious. In the light of this contrast of hope and hopelessness, Israel's power is suddenly illuminated in a new light. I would like to conclude this outline of an Israeli perspective on violence by saying something on this point.

Outside observers, such as viewers of television in other parts of the world, regularly behold Israeli soldiers in full battle gear chasing, catching, beating and arresting stone-throwing youngsters. The contrast between the powerful Israelis and the powerless Palestinian could not be clearer. And yet, I am suggesting that in the light of what I have just said about hope, this visual impression is not the whole picture and it is not how it appears from the Israeli perspective. Israelis see stone-throwing kids as deadly dangerous not only because they pose immediate danger to life and limb but *chiefly* because Israelis know that those kids, like the women there, in the first line of stone-throwers, are just the *first* line and behind it there stretch endless other lines, such that there will always be another line behind the one which has been made ineffective. It is this confrontation with unstructured and unending violence which is so hopeless. It is paradoxical but true. While the army and the police are certainly stronger than the stone-throwers, it is the latter who effect the siege. Conor Cruise O'Brien (1986) was highly perceptive when he gave the title *The Siege* to his book dealing with Israel's existential problems.

All this leads us back to Hobbes and to the general rule of reason. Israelis, like Hobbes, hold that the best thing is to live in peace. Their pent-up yearning for peace was dramatically expressed in the explosion of enthusiasm for President Sadat, the enemy of only yesterday, when he came to Jerusalem to talk peace. But Israelis, like Hobbes, also hold that the worst thing is to go under. There is no way back from death, not for individuals and not for states. Given that, Israelis, like Hobbes, hold that the next best thing, until the time peace comes, is to live by the right of nature. After all, our enemies live that way and glory in it.[2]

Notes

1. I would like to emphasize that this title is meant literally. This chapter is *not* about possible *political* solutions. If I wrote about *that*, this would be a very different chapter.
2. Cf. Hobbes, 1958, p. 273, where Hobbes states his views about foreign relations: 'And every Sovereign hath the same Right in procuring the safety of his People, that any particular man can have, in procuring the safety of his own Body.'

Bibliography

Aron, R., 1981. *Peace and War; A Theory of International Relations*. Malabar, Florida: Kriger.
Clausewitz, C. von, 1982. *On War*. Harmondsworth: Penguin Books.
Hobbes, T., 1958. *Leviathan*. Oxford: Oxford University Press.
Kant, I., 1927. *Perpetual Peace*. London: Sweet and Maxwell. (First published in 1795).
Kenny, A., 1985. *The Logic of Deterrence*. London: Firethorn Press.
Lewis, B., 1960. *The Arabs in History*. New York: Harper Torchbooks.
O'Brien, C.C., 1986. *The Siege. The Saga of Israel and Zionism*. London: Weidenfeld & Nicholson.
Shennan, J.H., 1974. *The Origins of the Modern European State 1450–1725*. London: Hutchinson University Library.
Warrender, H., 1957. *The Political Philosophy of Hobbes: His Theory of Obligation*. Oxford: Oxford University Press.

10 In Europe's Shadow: Zionism and the Palestinian Fate[1]

Shiraz Dossa

For Palestinians, decline and fall represent the true face of their historical reality in this century. The Palestinian condition has indisputably become more intolerable with the march of time. This truth is now widely conceded, but there is a crucial fact missing in the wide-ranging scholarship on the Palestinian situation: the Palestinian condition is partially the legacy of the antinomian impulses for *recognition* and *power*, long acknowledged as springs of human action by such philosophers as Hobbes, Hegel and Nietzsche. Unless the Zionist strategy for dealing with the Palestinians is understood as a Hegelian desire for recognition conjoined with a Nietzschean will to power, the pathos of the Palestinian condition is neither conceivable nor fully intelligible. This is the underlying argument of the following reflections on the contemporary fate of the Palestinians.

I

The striking thing about the Zionist strategy is its Hobbesian ruthlessness, its stance of moral neutrality: its palpable purpose is dominating Palestinians. Mass killing of Palestinians outside Israel is condoned and even encouraged. But this is not the primary aim. Like the infamous butchery at Deir Yassin (1948), the managed horror of Sabra and Shatila (1982) was intended to serve as a new warning of the tenacity of Zionist resolve.[2] 'Sanctioned massacre'[3] of civilians is permitted under the guise of eliminating Palestinian terrorists, even though outright genocide is disallowed. Such lurid dreams are officially *verboten*, understandably, since they evoke memories of the 'final solution' launched against the European Jews.

But the realization that there is a 'moral' limit to this venture, paradoxically, has lent impetus and legitimacy to the strategy of political Zionism. For as long as this strategy neither utilizes the exact methods, nor claims the vast numbers of the Hitlerian genocide, Jews can continue to sustain their image of themselves as morally blameless. The failure on the part of countless Jews to recognize the European provenance and the European confines of their new ethics has licensed a deadly moral blindness toward the Palestinians—toward a people who played no part in the *European* Holocaust.[4]

Though there are numerous honourable Jews opposed to it,[5] the revisionist Zionist strategy and ethics enjoy the tacit or explicit support and approval of the mass of Jews around the world. Still, it would be unfair to the dissenting minority and to proponents of spiritual Zionism, like Martin Buber and Judah Magnes, to paint the Zionist strategy as a Jewish strategy. Fairness demands, as well, that Jews who acquiesce in it be distinguished from the protagonists and the troops of political Zionism.

Shorn of all self-serving masks, the Zionist strategy is one of aggressive ethnocide. Contrary to genocide, ethnocide is humane in the absolute sense: it does not seek physically to wipe out the whole people. Instead the ethnocidal strategy attempts systematically and efficiently to destroy the national and cultural identity of the targeted group. Philosopher Monroe Beardsley's (1976, p. 86) definition of ethnocide is painfully pertinent in this context. He describes ethnocide as

> the commission of acts of specified sorts with intent to extinguish, utterly or in substantial part, a culture. Among such ethnocidal acts are the deprivations of opportunity to use a language, practice a religion, create art in the customary ways, maintain basic social institutions, preserve memories and traditions, work in cooperation towards social goals.

Judged in these terms, there can be no doubt that Zionist conduct toward Palestinians has been ethnocidal in the most exacting sense, prior to and especially after 1967. Unequivocal evidence adduced by both Jewish and non-Jewish scholars is too overwhelming to justify a less damning conclusion.[6] Indeed, in the aftermath of the recent murderous invasion of Lebanon and the unceasing expansion of Jewish settlements on Palestinian land in the West Bank, it is arguable whether the Zionist strategy is not distinctly genocidal.

Whether a specific strategy is genocidal in nature is a question which defies easy resolution. Leo Kuper has argued that genocide entails the intention to commit genocide. If such intent cannot be established beyond all doubt, then the charge of genocide is tantamount to an unjustified assertion (Kuper, 1981, p. 87). Though Kuper is fully aware that denial is a sure method of 'evading responsibility' he is disinclined to press the case for genocide unless the intent to engage in genocide is plainly demonstrable.

By contrast, philosopher Jean-Paul Sartre is much less sanguine in his attitude toward mass killings. Sartre contends that it is sheer sophistry to predicate genocide on provable intention—for intention is an essentially contestable issue and cannot be irrefutably established. Sartre argues convincingly that genocidal intention should be inferred from the substantive conduct and the tangible consequences of specific policies. Using the American war in Vietnam as his example, Sartre concludes that the US intention to commit genocide was 'implicit in the facts'. Furthermore, the facts could not have been different because they encased 'the only possible relationship between an overindustrialised country and an underdeveloped country, that is to say, a genocidal relationship' (Sartre, 1971, pp. 545, 547).

Sartre's conclusion is perhaps too emphatic, perhaps too certain. Still, it is hard to deny the general truth underpinning his argument. In that case the question that needs to be raised is whether the relationship between an advanced Zionist Israel and the considerably weaker Palestinians is genocidal? In the classical and historical meaning of genocide, the answer is negative, even though there are now visible strains of genocidal conduct evident in the Zionist–Palestinian relationship. The Zionist strategy is, in essence, ruthlessly ethnocidal in its virulent commitment to dispossess, dominate and humiliate the Palestinians.

Falling back on this strategy was a logical necessity. Having resolved to establish and maintain a *Jewish* state, the incoming European Jews had only two real alternatives: either totally liquidate the Palestinian people or reduce them to wholly passive subjects under Zionist control and tutelage. For 'moral' reasons already considered, the first alternative was officially unacceptable. The Zionists were therefore obliged to pursue the path of political domination and to acquire the national capacity to unleash unbounded violence against Palestinians at will.

In the context of the grand Zionist purpose, this peculiar strategy was as inevitable as it was necessary. For as Maxime Rodinson (1968, Ch. 9, pp. 213, 219) has tersely put it, the conflict between the Palestinians and the incoming Western Jews (as distinct from the ancient Jews) 'appears essentially as the struggle of an indigenous population against the occupation of part of its national territory by foreigners'. To realize and sustain an exclusivist Jewish nation-state, the European foreigners had no choice but to destroy the Palestinians as a national and cultural unit. In Rodinson's words, 'this is as undeniable as it is obvious'.

II

Though the political wish to dominate is crucial and palpable, it does not exhaust the intellectual scale and the 'moral' reach of the Zionist strategy. The core of this strategy is achieving domination and sovereignty in a manner which elicits Palestinian acquiescence in the justice of the Zionist ambition. What is at stake is the willingness of the Palestinians to grant the moral validity of Zionist purpose, to assent to the truth of Jewish mind over Palestinian matter. In a nutshell, the real aim of the Zionist strategy is mastering Palestinians.

This strategy is distinguished and impelled by two fundamental themes: Jewish desire for recognition and Jewish fear of powerlessness. In a precise sense, both impulses are European in origin and both constitute Jewish responses to their horribly tragic fate on European soil during World War II. To understand the contours of the Zionist strategy, it is essential to grasp the salient thrust of Hegel's dialectic of lordship and bondage and of Nietzsche's doctrine of the will to power.

For Hegel, the transition from human consciousness to articulate self-consciousness entails a battle between people on the spiritual as well as the concrete level. This necessary conflict between people is both intellectual and political, simultaneously mental and material. Hegel depicts this process as the struggle for recognition which historically has culminated in lordship for the few and bondage for the vanquished. To be master is to wield visible power and to be recognized as the superior by the defeated (Hegel, 1967, Ch. 4, Sect. 3, pp. 228–32).

Hegel construes lordship as the initial step in the humanization of mankind: it is the basis of self-discovery and self-knowledge. As Hegel sees it, the question is whether one is to be master or slave. But to become master requires the compliance of the conquered: the master self is vindicated externally. The quest for mastery thus imposes a cutting limitation on the outcome of the struggle for recognition. Hegel harbours no illusions that the struggle ends in death for the vanquished in the normal course of events (1967, pp. 232–3). On this primordial level, history is a Hobbesian spectacle of unending destruction and death: a veritable state of nature. But there is no possibility of recognition in this state, simply because the dead can recognize no one. This is the intrinsic limitation characterizing the untempered pursuit of mastery.

But in Hegel's analysis, the self-consciousness in search of recognition bifurcates into a lesser and a higher kind of intellectual and moral awareness. While the lesser kind remains wedded to the exigencies of its Hobbesian universe, the higher self-consciousness repudiates killing in favour of the mastery of the defeated. This necessary condition for securing recognition presupposes moral equality between the recognized and the recognizer, which is, ironically, inconceivable in the context of mastery and slavery. Unwilling to concede the humanity of the vanquished, the master can never be certain of his own humanity because he cannot cease doubting the worth of the recognition forced from the defeated. For the same reason, the master is equally uncertain of his knowledge of himself and of his claim to moral prestige (Hegel, 1967, pp. 233–40).

Mastery thus serves to thwart the master's primary desire to be recognized by one whom he recognizes as fully human. The vanquished heeds the master out of fear and loathing, not because he truly respects him. Inevitably the master comes to realize the moral failure of his mastery: he is denied the prize he most covets. For Hegel, mastery is no more, and no less, than a vital moment in the struggle for recognition. Mastery cannot be the final end.[7] That privilege will be the legacy of a world in which there will be neither masters nor slaves, the world where the struggle for recognition will be between equals—between citizens in the Aristotelian sense.

For the Western and Westernized Jews who ventured into Palestine, their principal need was to be recognized in the Hegelian manner. That, in essence, was the true purpose of their settlement in the land of the Palestinian nation. For in their places of birth in Europe the Jews were largely unrecognized and despised as a group, though many were successful and respected as individuals. Jews lacked full recognition as members of their political communities and as human beings entitled to the rights and privileges enjoyed by their Christian compatriots. Despite the accomplishments of the Enlightenment, the status of the Jews was perennially in question. In this decisive sense, the European Jews were politically and morally homeless: they were reviled as an abnormal parasitic growth on the body of the European polity and on the European race (e.g. Arendt, 1958, Chs. 1–4; 1978, Part I).

Not surprisingly then, the Jewish aim in Palestine was stridently to erase their European failure, to preclude repetition of their European fate: in a word, *to solve their European problem on Oriental territory*. Strangely and tragically, these Jews resorted to a strategy in which the Palestinian residents did not figure at all. To ignore the factual presence of a people who were there and who had inhabited Palestine for a millennium and more, was as politically absurd as it was morally bizarre.[8]

Far more damaging and consequential is the human failure entailed in the Zionist strategy. This failure is incarnated in the fact that the Jews, in choosing to remain Europeans in a profoundly Oriental milieu, have never been accepted as Middle Eastern. Once disdained as Asiatics in Europe, they are now despised as European conquerors and desecrators of the Muslim Orient. In Hegelian terms, Jewish consciousness of themselves as Jews depends on more than a unilateral decision on their part. Palestinian acceptance is fundamentally and finally necessary in validating the legitimacy of their presence in Palestine. Indeed, Palestinian approval is undeniably crucial in securing a haven where Jews can feel at home in the Arab Orient.

That is exactly what has eluded them. The Jews are still homeless in the real sense, in spite of their redoubtable and proven skills in the arts of war and destruction. Jewish self-esteem and identity are still precarious in their own eyes, notwithstanding their routinized arrogance and braggadocio. They are still linked too closely to their memory of Nazism to allow them to establish a normal relationship with their new world.

Their mastery of Palestinians has denied modern Jews the recognition they so passionately desire. As Hegel had foreseen, recognition of the master by the vanquished is deeply unfulfilling because of the questionable human status of the latter. For Jews, therefore, passive Palestinian recognition is inadequate, and cloying reverence is equally unsatisfactory. To be recognized implicitly or explicitly by those in bondage necessarily casts doubt on the moral calibre of the masters. Within the debilitating circle of mastery and slavery, there is no hope of true recognition for the master, and no possibility of recovering humanity for the vanquished.

What is left when the master rejects the counsel of Hegel's higher self-consciousness is the passage of mastery to its logical extreme. Flanked by the failure to gain recognition, the project of mastery transforms itself into the will to power for its own sake.[9] In effect, Nietzsche supplants Hegel because the master fears nothing more than the sense of powerlessness. Visible trappings and displays of power become crucial in validating the master's feeling of mastery, but there is no real purpose to the accumulation and exercise of power. The willed purpose which drives the master and justifies the new strategy is the pretext of survival and security.

In Nietzschean terms, the will to power usurps reason in the name of sheer life, which has no purpose other than itself. Hovering on the threshold of nihilism, the will to power inexorably engenders irrationality. Fearing the absence of power and lacking a valid purpose, the master is free to produce his own meaning or range of meanings, which are all equally meaningless. In defending and advancing exclusively the claims of life, as Nietzsche knew so well, everything is permitted, everything is justifiable, and everything becomes meaningful (Stern, 1978, esp. Ch. 5; Heller, 1968; pp. 173–98).

Unlike Hegelian lordship, the Nietzschean will to power entails the kind of mastery which is permanently violent and relentlessly destructive. For this doctrine of power has no transcendent purpose or sensible end in view. In contrast to the limits inherent in the Hegelian struggle for recognition, the will to power has no consciousness of a proximate *telos*: it constitutes its own justification. Not constrained by moral interdictions outside itself, the will to power necessarily slides into tragically destructive domination. In the words of Stern (1978, p. 85), 'conquest remains at the heart of the doctrine. Only where it finds no opposition is the "will to power" not destructive.'

Since 1967 the Zionist project of mastering Palestinians has palpably inclined toward absolute conquest. On the occupied West Bank, in Gaza, and in Lebanon, the Palestinians are systematically denigrated and dehumanized, their lands and their water taken at will, their villages destroyed, their sacred places desecrated, their music and literature disgraced, their lives disrupted, their persons violated, their political aspirations denied—that is, when they are not being imprisoned, tortured and killed for 'security' reasons.[10] This catalogue of crimes committed against the Palestinians unequivocally testifies to the Zionist will to power.

In the Muslim Orient, the Zionists desire nothing less than the total political and moral conquest of the Palestinians. If the Palestinians will not vanish, then the Zionists will ensure that they are no longer visible as a nationality. And if the Palestinians become unrecognizable as Palestinians, as the people displaced and dispossessed by the incoming Jews, then they will cease to be a political problem for the Zionists. But like the European Jews, the Palestinians refuse to become invisible, to disappear as a national community, to abandon their cultural identity, to repudiate their legitimate claims to a homeland in Palestine.

Few historical injustices have produced so tragic a result for the victims and so tenuous a victory for the conquerors. This tragedy is ineffable in more than the usual sense: it is a tragedy of epic scale because the Zionist protagonists are themselves the accidental remnant of a European vision of wilful mastery and destruction. That this Jewish remnant is incapable of understanding the moral meaning of the Zionist programme of conquest, irrevocably completes the tragedy.

Postscript (May 1989)

In the four years that have elapsed since this chapter was written, nothing has changed for the better in the human condition of the Palestinians. Nietzsche's influence on sustaining and furthering the Zionist strategy, its will to power, has not diminished. Since the spontaneous start of the *intifada* (uprising) in the West Bank and Gaza in December 1987, 460 Palestinian men, women and children have been murdered for daring to resist the occupation.

To judge by the brutality of its response, Israel has genocide in mind: it is no longer entitled to the benefit of the doubt. In its 17 February (1989) report, the UN Human Rights Commission condemned Israel for its 'savage treatment' of the Palestinians. The Commission charged Israel with:

- Killing Palestinians, including children
- Crippling youths by breaking their bones
- Savagely beating and maltreating women
- Torturing detainees
- Throwing gas bombs into houses, mosques and hospitals, causing death by suffocation
- Imposing curfews and military sieges intended to destroy towns and villages [*The Globe and Mail*, 19 April 1989]

UN charges are only the tip of the horrors faced by Palestinians: these and many more similar actions have been documented and validated by other sources.[11] Such conduct is so common inside and outside the occupied territories that the Norwegian commander of UNFIL (UN Interim Force in Lebanon) recently 'likened Israelis to Nazis'. Even Amnesty International, which is usually solicitous of Jewish sensibilities to a fault, has accused the Israeli government 'of condoning the killing or wounding of Palestinians by its troops' in the West Bank and Gaza (*The Globe and Mail*, 18 February 1989).

I think we can now speak of Israeli racism and fascism with full justification. By any standard we may choose, the organized hatred and killing, the routine beatings and insults, the standard pattern of abusing and torturing, of Palestinians that began in 1967, intensified in 1982, and unleashed with full force in 1987, is tantamount to fascism in theory and practice. That European Jews were nearly wiped out by Nazi fascism is not sufficient reason to think that Jews can never espouse fascism for their own purposes. Israeli conduct today towards the Palestinians is in its accurate meaning fascist.

No people, in principle, is immune to the virus of fascism, not even the remnants of its original victims. But the West, and mainstream

Christian thinkers and institutions, continue to think of Israel as innocent and decent despite massive evidence to the contrary. On one level, this is clearly a form of secular penance for the Holocaust, but it is buttressed, on another level, by the strong anti-Muslim, anti-Arab ethic central to the Western sensibility since the Crusades (Dossa, 1988, pp. 515–28).

In Israel itself, Jewish opposition to the occupation and to incipient fascism is increasing. But the position of the establishment and the majority is still anti-Palestinian to the core. Last December, PLO Chairman Arafat renounced terrorism and recognized Israel's 'right to exist' in language and terms acceptable to the US, which then agreed to talk directly with the PLO—a radical change in American policy. Israel's reaction to this huge concession was predictably negative.

In an interview on French television on 2 May 1989, Arafat declared that the 1964 PLO Charter, which is committed to the elimination of Zionist Israel (one of its provisions), was now 'null and void'. Prime Minister Shamir's reaction, through his spokesman, was typical: 'We know that Mr Arafat is a chronic liar.' (*The Globe and Mail*, 15 December 1988; 3 May 1989).

Nothing that the PLO does, including meeting the basic demands of a state that has been oppressing its people for 40 years, is enough. At the time of writing, Nietzsche's doctrine of the will to power and destruction is the official policy of the survivors of the Holocaust towards its victims in the occupied West Bank and Gaza.

Notes

1. An earlier version of this chapter was published in *Arab Studies Quarterly*, Fall 1984. In this chapter the terms 'Zionism' and 'Zionist' denote revisionist or political Zionism, as distinct from religious or spiritual Zionism.
2. The complicity of the Begin government, and specifically of Ariel Sharon, in sponsoring the Sabra-Shatila massacre has been established beyond doubt. For an honest discussion, see Ahmad (1983, pp. 31–40); and Lamb (1983, pp. 10–11).
3. This is Kuper's (1981, p. 87) term.
4. For a cogent and penetrating analysis of this issue, see Israeli writer Boaz Evron (1981, pp. 16–26).
5. Suffice it to mention the close to 400,000 members of the Israeli 'Peace Now' movement; Noam Chomsky, I.F. Stone, Alfred Lilienthal, Israel Shahak, Uri Davis, Daniel J. Amit, Boaz Evron, Jacob Timerman and Mark Lane.
6. For details see Chomsky (1982, Chs. 9–12; 1983, pp. 7–19); Jiryis (1976); Lilienthal (1978, esp. Chs. 4 and 5); Lustick (1980).

7. For a lucid argument in support of this view, see Kojeve (1969, Ch. 1, pp. 3–30).
8. In *Israel and the Arabs*, Rodinson (1968, pp. 7–21, *passim*) provides a thoughtful discussion of this issue. For a knowledgeable and provocative unravelling of the connection between the Zionist viewpoint and the discipline of Orientalism, see Said (1979; 1980, esp. parts 1 and 2). For a critical consideration of Said's thesis, see Dossa (1984).
9. Nietzsche's doctrine of the will to power is scattered throughout his writings, but it is stated most explicitly in Nietzsche (1968, Book III, Parts I–III; 1969, first two essays).
10. In addition to the works cited in Note 6, see the devastating indictment of Israeli crimes in Sean McBride *et al.* (1983). In his review of this report, the late Richard Arens (1983, p. 108) concluded that 'Israeli responsibility for war crimes and crimes against humanity is established beyond reasonable doubt.'
11. For details see for example, A. Cockburn in the *Nation* (21 November 1988, pp. 520–1); and the *Nation* (17 April 1989, pp. 506, 535, 536); Chomsky (1984). Most of the information and facts cited by Cockburn and Chomsky were obtained from Israel newspapers, journals and writers.

Bibliography

Ahmad, E., 1983. 'The Public Relations of Ethnocide', *Journal of Palestine Studies*, vol. 12, no. 3.

Arendt, H., 1958. *The Origins of Totalitarianism*. New York: Meridian Books.

Arendt, H., 1978. *The Jew as Pariah*. New York: Grove Press.

Arens, R., 1983. 'Review on McBride et al., 1983', *Journal of Palestine Studies*, vol. 13, no. 1.

Beardsley, M., 1976. 'Reflections on Genocide and Ethnocide', in R. Arens, ed., *Genocide in Paraguay*. Philadelphia, Penn.: Temple University Press.

Chomsky, N., 1982. *Towards a New Cold War*. New York: Pantheon Books.

Chomsky, N., 1983. 'The Middle East and the Probability of Nuclear War', *Socialist Review*, no. 70.

Chomsky, N., 1984. *The Fateful Triangle: United States, Israel and the Palestinians*. Montreal: Black Rose.

Dossa, S., 1984. 'Under Western Eyes: Islam and the Arab Orient', in T.Y. Ismael, ed., *Canadian–Arab Relations*. Ottawa: Jerusalem International Publishing House.

Dossa, S., 1988. 'Auschwitz and the Palestinians: Christian Conscience and the Politics of Victimization', *Alternatives*, vol. 13, no. 4.

Evron, B., 1981. 'The Holocaust: Learning the Wrong Lessons', *Journal of Palestine Studies*, vol. 10, no. 3.

Hegel, G.W.F., 1967. *The Phenomenology of Mind*. New York: Harper Colophon.

Heller, E., 1968. 'The Importance of Nietzsche', in *The Artist's Journey into the Interior and Other Essays*. New York: Vintage.

Jiryis, S., 1976. *The Arabs in Israel.* New York: Pantheon Books.

Kojeve, A., 1969. 'Introduction', in A. Bloom, ed., *The Reading of Hegel.* New York: Basic Books.

Kuper, L., 1981. *Genocide: Its Political Use in the Twentieth Century.* Harmondsworth: Penguin Books.

Lamb, F.P., 1983. 'The Kahan Commission and International Law', *Middle East International*, 18 March.

Lilienthal, A., 1978. *The Zionist Connection.* New York: Dodd, Mead & Co.

Lustick, I., 1980. *Arabs in the Jewish State.* Austin: University of Texas Press.

McBride, S. *et al.*, 1983. *Israel in Lebanon.* London: Ithaca Press.

Nietzsche, F., 1968. *The Will to Power.* New York: Vintage.

Nietzsche, F., 1969. *On the Genealogy of Morals.* New York: Vintage.

Rodinson, M., 1968. *Israel and the Arabs.* New York: Pantheon Books.

Said, E., 1979. *Orientalism.* New York: Vintage.

Said, E., 1980. *The Question of Palestine.* New York: Vintage.

Sartre, J-P., 1971. 'On Genocide', in R. Falk *et al.*, eds., *Crimes of War.* New York: Vintage.

Stern, J.P., 1978. *Nietzsche.* Glasgow: Collins/Fontana.

11 European Values after the 'Euromissile Crisis'

Matthias Finger

A 'cultural revolution' took place in Europe between 1981 and 1983, that is, during the three years the new European peace movement was most active. Ever since, concepts such as 'Europeanness', 'European (cultural) identity', and 'European values' have flourished. Since the beginning of the 1980s, European politicians have once again liked to talk about the 'Europeanization of Europe' and envisage all manner of projects to give form and structure to this slogan. Peace researchers likewise promote the idea of 'European security' (e.g. Jahn *et al.*, 1987).

But the question remains: are these projects, slogans, concepts and approaches a real answer to a much more uneasy feeling, sometimes even an awareness among Europeans since the beginning of the 1980s that something is wrong with Europe and its future? Should one not, before coming up with concrete proposals, try to understand what this uneasy feeling was, and probably still is, all about? But rare are the researchers and the philosophers who, in my opinion, really try to go to the very root of the problem (e.g. Hettne, 1988; Morin, 1987; Petitjean, 1987).

It is a fact that, motivated by a fear for their own survival, Europeans started, at the beginning of the 1980s, to ask questions about the identity and the future of Europe: what was Europe going to be? Was it to become a future nuclear battlefield of the two superpowers, or was there space left for an alternative?

Probably for the first time in history, Europeans also became aware of the fact that they had lost control over their own destiny: Europeans were and are no longer the masters of their 'own house'. And this awareness emerges after centuries of European hegemony and expansion: after having conquered the planet, and after having passed on the European model of conquest to other nations, Europe is now the first victim of the very process it had initiated. In other words, are the two superpowers not just the mirror in which Europe is actually confronted with its true face?

Unfortunately, the military dimension of European hegemony and expansion is only the tip of the iceberg. The nuclear and military threat to the survival of Europe should therefore not be separated from all the other threats which, almost daily, are experienced by Europeans. I think here not only of the destruction of the environment, particularly advanced in Eastern and Western Europe, but also of the threats to Europe stemming from high-technology accidents. If the new European peace movement has crystallized around and focused on the question of the nuclear annihilation of Europe, support for it certainly also stems from a much more general awareness among Europeans of a community created by the risk towards civilization.

It is true that the cultural revolution at the beginning of the 1980s, which underlies a more general awareness of the specificity of Europe, was triggered by the new European peace movement (e.g. Finger, 1989). This movement opposed the implantation of 572 Euromissiles in Western Europe as decided by NATO's double-track decision in December 1979. Although this movement had its most spectacular expression in Western Europe, a correspondingly profound 'cultural revolution' has also been taking place in Eastern Europe.

It is the underlying assumption of this chapter that a better understanding of the new European peace movement, and therefore of what happened at the beginning of the 1980s, is one of the keys to a better understanding of today's talk of the identity, the values and the future of Europe.

Europe, source and victim of the process of militarization

The inadequacy of the actual theories of peace and war

If we go on looking at the problem solely in terms of 'conflicts', 'wars' and at most in terms of 'arms races', we miss the essence of the very process that is going on under our eyes. With such conceptual categories we always end up describing at most an exponential accumulation of arms, whereas the only conceivable solution to that is a state of inter-state management of conflict and wars. Consequently, such conceptual categories, as well as their underlying theories, lead precisely to a political solution (by the state) of a process of which the state is the very motor.

On the other hand, there are, at the present moment, no alternative conceptual tools or theories available. The two theories on which the above-mentioned concepts are based are both *theories of modernization*;

unfortunately, both of them separate the military from the civil, where it is implied that the military can and has to be controlled by the civil. To illustrate this, let me recall the actual existing two main theories of modernization, which determine the two prevailing approaches to war and peace.

There is on the one hand an 'optimistic' theory or interpretation of modernization. This is still today the most widespread among the political establishment, even if fewer and fewer people actually believe in it. This interpretation considers modernization as a linear process of rationalization. Societies progress and develop from the simple to the complex, from the primitive to the civilized, from the underdeveloped to the developed, from a non-industrial to an industrial state. This is a process which progresses in steps, and whose result is an organized society, able to decide entirely on its own aims and its own evolution. The motors or the instruments of this modernization are political, scientific and economic institutions, including the social sciences. Significantly, this optimistic interpretation sees its main steps as the Enlightenment, the French revolution, the industrial revolution, and the scientific and technological revolutions.

One speaks, within this interpretation of 'wars' and 'conflicts' among nation-states. However, the main periods of war in Western history are considered as being accidents—an archaism of the old regime—which do not affect the underlying evolution towards industrial 'civilization'. 'War' is considered as regression, a sign of immaturity, even as an obstacle on the road to progress. This is generally the interpretation of politicians and scientists, in particular of researchers in the social sciences, since their professional activities strive, by definition, towards the promotion of a rational society, managed by the political system on the basis of scientific expertise. Consequently, war appears in this interpretation as a problem of scientific and political control and management which, unfortunately, is not yet sufficiently developed.

There exists on the other hand a 'critical' theory or interpretation of modernization. One finds it mainly in the intellectual establishment, in particular among leftist intellectuals. The philosophical foundations of this critical interpretation are about the same as in the previous interpretation: modernization is considered as fundamentally good, as long as one does not forget its ultimate aim, that is, the emancipation of mankind. In order to achieve this aim, a rational organization of society, supported by science, economy and state politics, is necessary.

This interpretation mainly criticizes the fact that the instruments of emancipation—science, technology, industry and the state—have become the very ends of the process. In other words, the ideals of modernity, as expressed by the Enlightenment and the French

Revolution, have been perverted parallel to the process of modernization itself. Modernity has been perverted because the instruments of emancipation have become the ends; and these instruments have become the ends because society is organized according to power relations. Within this process of perversion, science as well as technology, and above all the state and industrial production, gradually lose their emancipatory potential, since they are said to be more and more controlled by a powerful minority whose aim is to stay in power. Therefore these emancipatory forces are no longer able to develop their full potential; they are somehow 'hindered'.

Consequently, this critical interpretation no longer speaks of isolated 'wars' and 'conflicts', but of an 'arms race'. This arms race is the very expression of the perversion of means into ends, a perversion which results from power relations. Within this interpretation the arms race is therefore not the result of an accident, but the product of the institutionalization of power relations.

Nevertheless, this interpretation does not consider the arms race as the central question in modernization. It is only an epiphenomenon, which will disappear when power relations have been abolished. So, ultimately, the arms race appears in this interpretation as a political problem in the traditional meaning of the word: a problem which can be solved on a political level and by political means. Here too, as in the previous interpretation, 'wars'. 'conflicts' and even the 'arms race' can be 'subjectively appropriated' and therefore managed.

According to which underlying theory of modernization—optimistic or critical—one chooses, there exist different reasons which lead to war, that is, either accidents or a 'deliberate build-up of armed forces' (Lodgaard, 1986). Accordingly, the management of wars will have to be different. If these two currently dominant interpretations offer a simple and coherent interpretation of modernization, they do not on the other hand offer an adequate understanding of the role the 'military' or rather the 'war system' plays within our highly industrialized societies. If the optimistic interpretation simply does not offer an explanation of the actual military phenomenon at all, the explanation offered by the critical interpretation is obviously not sufficient to account for today's phenomenon of a profound and global militarization.

The new European peace movement and the 'Euromissile crisis' emerged at the beginning of the 1980s within this theoretical vacuum, which is somewhat perplexing. The perplexity results mainly from the commonsense observation that, in reality, the military is today, at least in our highly industrialized societies, at the core of a system which integrates technological innovation, industrial growth, the management of natural resources and scientific progress. The military has, moreover, invaded all dimensions of national space, and determines, to a large extent, relations between the nation-states. Rare are the domains of the political and the economic life of a state where military considerations are absent. One must even admit that the military has by now substantially affected our culture and therefore each person's life. This situation must also be seen as a result of a process of (European) history with its wars of the past, as well as with the values related to the army. And this socio-historical phenomenon cannot be considered an accident, nor as a perversion of a fundamentally good idea. This is the general context of the 'cultural revolution' of the early 1980s; and this is also the situation against which many Europeans more or less intuitively react.

Towards a new theoretical framework

Since World War II we have seen the emergence of new theories which no longer try not to distinguish between the 'civil' and the 'military'. One of the first authors to have called into question the separation between industrialization and 'war' is the economic historian John U. Nef (1950), who fundamentally questions the idea that industrialization could, one day, abolish war. In fact the opposite will be the case: the process of industrialization will lead humanity to an ever more generalized war, both on the economic and on the technological, but also on an intellectual and a moral level. From now on, 'war' is no longer an isolated phenomenon which concerns only a fraction of society; it engulfs the totality of society. In other words, 'war' becomes the central problem of modern civilization.

This opinion is also shared by the French architect Paul Virilio (1976; 1977; 1983), who, in a more philosophical and more essayist language, has described, since the beginning of the 1970s, this process towards what he calls 'Pure War'. In the same perspective of a radical inversion of the traditional positivist and liberal theory of war, one must also mention the historical vision of Serres (1974), in particular his famous concept of 'thanatocracy'.

The American historian William McNeill (1982; 1963) has a more economic and technological approach, but comes to similar conclusions: militarization is no longer separable from modernization. These and other works, whether they put the accent on the evolution of ideas, on economy, on the political system, on science or on technology, show to what extent we are today part of a process which leads Western civilization towards militarization and total war. Such a perception cannot but relativize the ideas of progress and modernization generally associated with the 'Western civilizatory process'.

For some years these general historical considerations can also be based on detailed sociological and political–scientific knowledge which has come up with more operational concepts such as 'military–industrial complex', 'garrison state', 'warfare state', 'military establishment', and so on. Among them the concept of a 'military–industrial–scientific complex' is certainly the most interesting, since it puts the accent on the interrelation of the state, industry, science and technology (Clarke, 1971; Koistinen, 1980). All these concepts imply a general process which is the opposite of the traditional liberal vision of war as a temporary phenomenon, bound to disappear thanks to industrialization and progress towards modernity. These concepts see the highly industrialized societies as typically being militarized societies. Politics is totally powerless when it comes to preventing or controlling this process; the opposite is the case: it is an integral part of this very process.

If we wish to attain an adequate understanding of the problem, Europe must be considered as being part of this process of militarization = modernization: Europe is not only the most industrialized, but also the most militarized, continent in the world. Moreover, Europe is at the origin of this process, and in the 'Euromissile crisis' Europe also features as its first victim. And this despite the fact that Europe is also the continent with the greatest tradition of democracy and human rights.

Such a perception of the problem and of the role of Europe is totally incompatible with the two currently prevailing theories of modernization. For them, as for most people, in particular the developing countries, 'modernization made in Europe' even today seems the only possible model. This is also the position of those philosophers who today monopolize thinking and 'discourse' on modernity (e.g. Habermas, 1984).

On the other hand, however, such a position is totally unacceptable to the few intellectuals who are close to the movements and who have tried to reflect intellectually on the phenomenon and the process they are opposing. The works of Bahro (1987), Kaldor (1981), Schell (1982; 1984), and Thompson (1982) must be considered as the very rare ones where a new theory of modernization is currently being elaborated. All these authors help us to understand better how militarization and modernization actually interrelate. It is of course understandable that the political establishment should look askance at such a new theory of modernization, but it is less understandable that intellectuals should do so. It is my conviction that one cannot understand today's talk of European values without looking more closely into the link between militarization and modernization and especially into its particular relation with Europe.

Europe, continent of militarization=modernization

In all the significant writings on the history of civilization (e.g. Elias, 1969; McNeill, 1963), Europe always appears as a compulsory stage on the road to 'civilization'. In the same way, Europe is also a compulsory stage on the road to worldwide militarization, as well as to the worldwide destruction of the biosphere. Let us recall the main, typically European stages, which make modernization an increasingly military process.

The first stage is probably the constitution of the modern state since the Middle Ages, with its conquest and its defence of territory. As early as 1832 Clausewitz résumèd this relation between the state and war in his famous sentence: 'War is a continuation of state politics by other means.'

The second stage is the scientific revolution, through which science becomes associated with the military and the arms race; this is the beginning of a process which makes war, and in particular its preparation, more and more scientific.

The third stage comprises the political revolutions, of which the French revolution is an example; they define the nation-state as the core unity of militarization. Ever since then the citizen has been a soldier, and therefore personally concerned with war. This is the beginning of a process which makes war more and more total.

The fourth stage is the industrial revolution, which makes militarization part of the cycle of industrial production, and which moreover links industrialization to the arms race. Ever since then militarization has ceased to be separable from industrial production (and consumption).

Militarization is therefore the result of an amalgam between the stage, science and industry, the three factors which are at the same time the main forces of modernization, as well as the main pillars of modern civilization. In other words, militarization is linked to the very nature of the process of modernization, a process which is not perverted, but which is military to the roots of its rationality.

With World War II yet another new, fifth, stage of militarization probably set in, characterized by the production and the use of nuclear weapons, as well as by the division of the world into two blocs. These are linked and probably reinforce each other.

The years since World War II must be understood as the period of 'militarization *par excellence*'. In the situation of bloc logic all the potentialities of militarization, as contained in the nation-state, in science, in technology and in industry are, so to speak set free. Politics has favoured this process and the result is a Europe which is by now the most militarized continent in the world.

Considering this, what can Europe offer today besides a reaction against its own threatened annihilation? Before coming up with an answer to this question, one must recall that Europe has—because of this very process of militarization=modernization—undergone a profound cultural transformation. Very probably only a cultural transformation of the same kind and of the same depth will offer the slightest chance of stopping or even reversing this process of militarization = modernization.

What 'culture' do we mean, then, when we talk today of 'European culture'? Is it the one before or after this 'cultural transformation'? The German philosopher Georg Picht (1984, pp. 224–5) at least has a clear answer:

> Europe has done everything to destroy its own cultural tradition. This self-destruction begins with the preliminaries of the French Revolution, continues through the beginnings of capitalism and the machine age and culminates in the technical industrial revolution. I have to add that the Europeans, in the years after World War II, seem very decided to terminate this self-destruction.

In other words, the process of militarization = modernization has not promoted but destroyed European culture. I would argue that what we today consider in Europe as our main cultural achievements are probably but the survivals of a culture that has not yet been destroyed. Moreover, this reflection applies not only to our cultural, but also to our natural, environment; says Picht: 'We all have to see that the ecological crisis reflects what happens to nature when the construction of Europe takes place on a large scale' (1984, p. 227).

Let us summarize: today's European culture is affected by this (originally European) process of militarization=modernization. What does that mean? Ellul (1964, pp. 95–6), sets the tone:

> What seems certain to me is the fact that an eventual crisis of Europe is a crisis of the world. In other words, we will not solve the problems of the world anywhere else than in Europe. . . . We are therefore responsible twice: for the crisis, which has been caused somehow by us and responsible to find the answers and to use the means we have.

And Picht (1984, pp. 228–9) sees 'Europe as some sort of community of cultural solidarity', to which only an 'extreme danger or crisis can give birth'. And what Picht said in 1979 has in my opinion comes true in the early 1980s. The 'Euromissile crisis' gave rise to some sort of European cultural solidarity or 'cultural identity'. It is the cultural solidarity of those who are doomed by a process of militarization=modernization for which they are historically responsible but over which they have lost control. In particular it became clear to the Europeans in East and the West that:

- Europe had become an 'armaments dumping ground';
- that it was a 'crucial epicentre of peace and war';
- and that Europe itself had lost control over the whole situation. [Thee, 1985]

In other words, the beginning of the 1980s was the first time that Europeans had to face the result of a process of militarization=modernization which was born in Europe but which is now out of European political control. To what kind of 'European solidarity and identity' will this feeling of a crisis in Europe lead? In order to answer this question, let us now look into what exactly the new European peace movement reacted against at the beginning of the 1980s.

'European identity' as a reaction

The previous section outlined a general theoretical framework which can help us to understand the emergence of the new European peace movement as well as today's talk of European values. In this section I shall try to describe in a more detailed manner exactly what, concretely, the various main issues the new peace movement has raised are. I also want to examine how these issues are perceived in the aftermath of the so-called 'Euromissile-crisis', and what kind of 'peace' can be expected from the various perceptions of these issues?

The new European peace movement's view of the 'Euromissile debate'

In a previous work (Finger, 1989) I have distinguished, within the new European peace movement, nine different ways of looking at the 'Euromissile debate'. Two out of those nine ways are, to my mind, the most important. The first, because it is somehow at the 'argumentational core' of almost all the others. The second, because it has appealed to the greatest number of Europeans, in particular to citizens and peace activists in Eastern Europe. Both ways of looking at the 'Euromissile debate' are complementary and not contradictory; together they give a good picture of what the new European peace movement at the beginning of the 1980s was all about.

The first view sees Europe as the future battlefield of the two superpowers. Its main point was criticism of the Reagan administration, which was accused of preparing a nuclear first strike against the Soviet Union. On the technological level, this preparation takes the form of a 'first strike capability', whereas on the strategic–doctrinal level it takes the form of the idea of 'decapitation' of the USSR. This strategic doctrine actually means a rupture with the traditional logic of deterrence.

Moreover, this view presumes that the United States is preparing a limited nuclear war, planned to take place on European ground; in other words, Europe would become the battlefield of the two superpowers. This also means that Western Europe can no longer be considered as being protected by the USA and by NATO, since it will be used by the latter as an (American) nuclear platform in order to threaten and to attack the USSR. For Europe to be available for this purpose, the United States not only has to hide its plans from the Europeans (citizens and governments), it also has to undertake a vast public relations campaign in order to manipulate European public opinion. This idea is best expressed in one of the first appeals of the West German peace movement by Karl Bechert on 18 August 1980:

> The American protection takes a nebulous shape: the planning of defence within NATO has not yet been able, and will not be able this time, to protect, be it only a single European state, in particular not West Germany, to say nothing of Berlin. In a war, whether with conventional or with nuclear weapons, Europe will be completely destroyed by its own 'Defence'.
>
> The destruction of Europe is the price of the defence of the United States. I tell you: defend yourselves! Do you want to be killed in a Third World War? Do you still believe in protection by NATO? Have you still not understood that you will have the honour to die for the United States of America?

The second, complementary, view stems from the European Nuclear Disarmament campaign (END). It takes as its point of departure the previous view: if Europe is to become the future battlefield of the two superpowers, this is seen as the consequence of the logic of deterrence, of the Cold War and of the existence of the two military blocs. According to this way of looking at the problem, the arms race, which will lead to a nuclear war in Europe, is pursued exclusively between the two superpowers, and Europe is, so to speak, its victim. Mary Kaldor, in a text presented at the third END convention in Perugia, Italy, in 1983, gives a perfect account of this view:

> The nuclear arms race in Europe is the political expression of the bloc system. 'Deterrence' is supposed to prevent nuclear war in Europe by threatening horrible retaliation. Instead, the conflict in Europe is maintained by this very threat. And this conflict offers the reason for the existence of the two blocs and

for maintaining the zones of influence of the USA and the USSR. The Soviet tanks offer a legitimacy to the American nuclear arms and the other way round.

And E.P. Thompson explained at a private conference in Budapest on 9 September 1982:

If the actual Cold War—the hostile attitude of the two blocs—still continues for 20 more years, this will not automatically lead to the final holocaust, even if this is probable. But it will certainly lead to two profoundly disturbed economies and to two mutilated cultures, to two contradictory societies in a state of war, governed by leaders who are intolerant fanatics for 'security'. And that is why this will lead to a diminution of liberty and the rights of each citizen.

Rudolf Bahro thinks that this not only dangerous but fundamentally totalitarian evolution is already crystallized in the structures and institutions (Bahro & Freyhold, n.d.):

The two blocs are in reality a dragon with two heads, which maintain the people of Europe, of Northern American, of the Soviet Union and of the whole world under the threat of total destruction and so prevent any movement which wants to liberate itself from their influence. Neither the 'Russians' nor the 'Americans', nor the Warsaw Pact, nor NATO is alone the enemy. It is not enough either to add them together and to compare them. The problem lies in the structure of the Cold War which links both, and within which they are both completely dependent on each other.

In this argumentation, the two blocs or the two superpowers have an obvious interest that the arms race and militarization continue, since this reinforces their hegemony, in particular over their own (European) allies. Instead, a third way, for example an autonomous Europe, would threaten these hegemonies, as well as the Cold War structure which legitimizes them.

This idea of 'Europe as a third force' can be found in the whole new European peace movement and more and more among Europeans. Most of the time, this movement does not think of a Europe of nation-states and governments, since they actually owe their existence to the two superpowers, and since they are therefore completely submissive to them. Instead, such a Europe should be built by European people from the East and West, united in their geography, in their history and in their common culture. The commitment to peace has therefore to come from the citizens at the grass-roots level, through autonomous movements, to begin with, within each European country. This idea has been called '*détente* from below'. In order to achieve *détente* from below, the Europeans should practise 'cultural solidarity'. Says Thompson: 'since the destruction of the continent is at stake,we should decide together and act as Europeans'. Doing so is the only chance to avoid annihilation. Moreover, Thompson declared in Budapest,

> . . . our situation is not only dangerous. It is not normal and absurd. We are separated by plane or by train only a few hours from the other. We share many elements of a common history and a common culture. There is no geographical frontier which separates us. . . . Every time we accept in our heads the false separations of the Cold War we are guilty of mutual distrust.

Let us conclude this second way of looking at the 'Euromissile crisis' with Bahro (Bahro & Freyhold, n.d.):

> With the refusal of the logic of the arms race, of the bloc logic, starts this 'Renaissance' of a political culture which embraces all of Europe, and which this continent needs to find an answer to the biggest challenge of the world's history.

In brief, there are three core arguments of the new peace movement's way of looking at the 'Euromissile crisis': first, Europe will become the future battlefield of the two superpowers: second, in order to avoid this, Europe has to emancipate itself, mainly through '*détente* from below'; third, this will lead to a new cultural solidarity and identity in Eastern and Western Europe.

I will now look at how things were perceived in the literature after the new peace movement declines, i.e. after autumn 1983.

Europe in the aftermath of the Euromissile crisis

In the aftermath of the Euromissile debate several authors have tried to conceptualize the 'crisis of Europe' as they perceive it; the most interesting of them are Johnstone (1984), Palmer (1987) and Senghaas (1986). One can identify in their works mainly two factors which are said to make up for the 'crisis of Europe'; both can be traced back to the new European peace movement's view.

The first factor seen as contributing to the 'crisis of Europe' stems from the fact that Europe is 'occupied' (Western Europe by the USA through NATO, and Eastern Europe by the USSR either directly or through the Warsaw Pact). The main decisions on the future of Europe are therefore taken somewhere other than in Europe. This point is made mainly by Palmer, who also shows that the crucial influence of the USA in Western Europe has not only a military, but also an economic aspect, although it might be easier for Europe to achieve economic than political independence.

If the 'crisis of Europe' is appraised in these terms of 'domination by the superpowers', then the following two questions arise.

- Will the independence of Europe (or American disengagement from Europe) 'take place by mutual consent over a significant period of time and be negotiated in an atmosphere of relative accord, or will it be the product of a major crisis in the Atlantic system'?
- And 'if Altanticism is crumbling, what is to take its place?' [Palmer, 1987, pp. 18–19]

In any case, if one sees the 'crisis of Europe' in terms of Europe's domination by the superpowers—in particular Western Europe by the USA—it is very likely to seek an alternative in the idea of a strong Europe, i.e. of a Europe as a third superpower. However, the analysis which underlies this idea seems to me weak, and Western Europe politicians who would like to draw public support for such a project must not forget that the new European peace movement, though it has raised the point of the domination of Western Europe by the United States, would not admit the idea of a Western European superpower.

The second point generally made in the aftermath of the Euromissile crisis regards the 'crisis of Europe' as the result of the bloc logic, of Cold War between the superpowers, and of the corresponding doctrine of deterrence. This point does not focus on the domination of Europe, but on its division, that is, on the fact that Europe is unnaturally split into two blocs, a problem which is most acute in Germany. The author in the new European peace movement who has contributed most to this argumentation is E.P. Thompson; he has coined the particularly strong term of 'exterminism' to account for this militarization resulting from Europe's division into two blocs (Thompson, 1982). Exterminism is closely linked to the existence of the two blocs and the Cold War, as well as to the existence of nuclear weapons; Thompson shows that these, by definition, do not produce stability but fuel a never-ending arms race.

An analysis of this type—though a less dynamic one—is today generally admitted in the literature; the actual situation of Europe is now said to be the result of World War II, and this mainly for the following two reasons (Bracher, 1979):

- Europe, once the subject of world history, has now become its object;

— the formerly sovereign nation-states are now replaced by rigid blocs.

It is evident that analysis of the new European peace movement has considerably influenced peace researchers (Antola, 1984; Väyrynen, n.d.), and increasingly also mainly radical politicians, particularly in Germany, Scandinavia and Eastern Europe. These people, like the new European peace movement, also state that, although since World War II divided into two blocs and pushed into a Cold War dynamics, Europe has always aspired to overcome this 'un-European' situation, for example by constantly seeking *détente*: '*Détente* is par excellence a European product: it has aimed to transcend East–West dissociation by associative measure in the economic, political and socio-cultural domains, to build-down the East–West bloc structure' (Thee, 1985, pp. 4–5).

However, it remains extremely obscure in the name of what Europe should overcome this un-European situation. It is therefore no longer, as in the previous point, a matter of what Western Europe shall oppose to the domination of the USA. The question is now much more complicated, since one has also to ask what would replace the two blocs. This is a very difficult question, if one remembers for example that nation-states like the two Germanies are, as such, the product of the Cold War and of the bloc logic. Bracher (1979) and many others think that *détente*, if it came about, would probably favour the re-emergence of the old pre-war European nation-state system.

This is implicitly and sometimes even explicitly also the vision of many concrete 'post-bloc' projects for Europe, in particular those which oppose (political) confrontation to (economic) co-operation (e.g. HSFK, 1982). In other words, *détente* should favour economic development; the Europe of the blocs is to be replaced by a Europe of business. But will a return to the pre-war ideal of the European nation-state systems, eventually combined with the prospect of economic development, be a sufficiently solid basis for an identity and a future for Europe? Will it be a solid answer to the 'crisis of Europe' as perceived in the aftermath of the Euromissile debate?

Many Europeans would not accept a pre-war European nation-state system, eventually with an economic development perspective, as a sufficiently radical answer to this crisis. On this point, these Europeans are moreover supported by the Green movement. They analyse 'Europe's crisis' not so much in terms of the domination of Western Europe by the United States, nor in terms of the result of a bloc logic, but in terms of the bankruptcy of politics: politics, and in particular state politics, has been unable to control the arms race and, more generally, militarization. The European states are considered as much responsible for this process as are the superpowers. In consequence, we find ourselves today in a situation where Europe is the most heavily armed and the most nuclearized continent of the world, the continent where nuclear annihilation is most likely. For the Europeans (peace activists and intellectuals) who make this point, neither a strong Europe, nor a pre-war European nation-state system would be an alternative.

In search of the theoretical foundations of a European cultural identity

As we have seen, a European cultural identity cannot be the result simply of a reactivation of a Europe of the past, but must be elaborated, probably against some achievements of 'modernization', in particular against the nation-sate. But what concrete project for Europe results from considering the 'crisis of Europe' as the result of the bankruptcy of politics?

In order to come up with an answer, I suggest we go back to the way the new European peace movement has looked at the 'Euromissile crisis': it holds militarization=modernization responsible for Europe's present situation, and (state-) politics is considered part of that process. An alternative can therefore only come from below the level of the state, that is, from '*détente* from below'. Kaldor (1985), one of the rare peace researchers who has tried to follow up this line of thought, comes up with 'transforming the state'.

In other words, for many peace activists, the road to peace in Europe passes through a redefinition of their relation to (state-)politics. This redefinition can only be the result of a cultural transformation, since (state-)politics is, at least since the French revolution, part of the 'cultural' process of militarization = modernization. In this section I will explore, from a theoretical point of view, what such a transformation might look like.

Let us summarize the possible perspectives for 'peace' in Europe and the future of Europe according to what is considered to lie at the origin of the 'crisis of Europe'.

First, if the 'crisis of Europe' is seen as the result of the domination of the two superpowers, a possible perspective might be a strong Western Europe.

Second, if the 'crisis of Europe' is seen as the result of the bloc logic and the Cold War, then a possible way out might be some pre-war European nation-state system.

Third, if the 'crisis of Europe' is seen as a result of the bankruptcy of (state-)politics, then a possible remedy might be 'Europe as a cultural entity and identity', based on a new relation to (state-)politics.

As I have shown in the first section, the only intellectually coherent perspective for Europe is the third i.e. 'Europe as a cultural entity and identity', the result of a *détente* from below'. But what concrete form is this 'European cultural identity' going to take, and what 'peace-building measure' do we have today at our disposal in order to make this perspective come true?

In fact, as shown in the first section, today's two dominant ways of looking at war and peace cannot consider 'peace' in any other way than as the state management of conflicts. It is therefore not surprising that the main intellectual, theoretical and conceptual instruments for promoting peace or rather 'security' remain, even today, rooted in the idea and in the very process of modernization. According to this idea security can be obtained through or brought about by more armament; *détente* between blocs; arms control; disarmament (of the blocs); and co-operation (Albrecht *et al.*, 1972, pp. 184–5).

As a consequence of this, 'peace in Europe' (as elsewhere in the world) continues to be seen as a question of 'European security, that is, as a result of negotiations between nation-states (e.g. Dean, 1987). Peace in Europe as the result of a build-down of the European nation-states themselves—not only as a result of the build-down of a bloc—does not seem to be imaginable (yet).

But this 'European security' approach has no answer to the culturally new way of looking at the 'crisis of Europe' as it arose at the beginning of the 1980s. In particular it has no answer to the problem the new European peace movement calls the 'bankruptcy of politics', that is, to the nation-state's incapacity to find the solutions to the militarization = modernization process.

Intuitively this inadequacy of the current peace perspectives in Europe is also familiar to many in the political, but mainly in the intellectual, establishment. And this explains why the idea of a European cultural identity is gaining ground even within these establishments. Intuitively, many Europeans know that the European nation-state system (be it pre- or post-war) is incompatible with a European cultural identity; they know that a cultural identity cannot be brought about, nor promoted, by the state or politics. One might thus ask a most central question: How to develop the common cultural foundations of European civilization instead of dividing the continent? But nobody in the political and intellectual establishment today has an answer to this question, mainly, in my opinion, because the theories of 'war and peace' still actually dominant do not offer us a different approach. And while—since the beginning of the 1980s—writings and projects about and for ('peace' in) Europe are proliferating not only among politicians but also among intellectuals, most of these writings add no new arguments and remain within the traditional conception of war and peace criticized earlier. We therefore have to go back in history to find a theoretically sound and solid alternative conception of a European cultural identity.

Denis de Rougemont: from personalism to federalism

There does exist one school of thought which reflected profoundly on Europe and its future long before the Euromissile crisis, that is, back in the inter-war period. This is a mainly French school of philosophers –writers like Paul Valéry, Emmanuel Mounier, Alexandre Marc, Denis de Rougemont and others. The latter three are generally considered to be the founders of the philosophical school of 'personalism'.

I will concentrate here on the Swiss–French philosopher and writer de Rougemont (1906–86), mainly because his main preoccupation is Europe, and also because he is the intellectual and founding father of the only institutions hitherto to have concerned themselves with Europe's cultural dimension. These are the Centre Européen de la Culture (Geneva) founded in 1949, and the Institut d'Etudes Européennes (Geneva).

Moreover, Denis de Rougemont was involved in the creation of the European Cultural Foundation, founded in 1954 in Geneva (today in Amsterdam). He is therefore a crucial figure, and at least some aspects of his philosophy may well be of use if we seek a better conceptualization of the eventual political outcome of the 'crisis of Europe' as perceived since the Euromissile debate. Denis de Rougemont is a prolific writer; here I shall concentrate on those writings which directly relate to our topic.

The point of departure of the personalist philosophy is the question of the relation between person and things. Personalists believe that the movement should be from persons to things and not the other way round, as is the case in modern society. The person is a 'concrete human being in action', gifted with spirit, this of course including a religious dimension. The person is the measure of everything; as such, it must be opposed to the individualized and massified individual. Therefore, the movement must be from the person to society, and not from society to the person. One may comment that this is in fact a Christian (Protestant) and therefore highly anthropocentric vision of the person.

Denis de Rougemont (1946) makes this conception of the person the point of departure for his project for Europe. This project is rooted in the central question of the relation between the person and politics. In this matter, de Rougemont's whole conception could also be résuméd in the slogan: 'Politics as if the person mattered!'. He seeks to define politics from the viewpoint of the person and not that of the political system. The main enemy of such a perspective is the nation-state, which goes along with growing individualism; says de Rougemont: '*C'est avec la poussière des individus que l'Etat fera son ciment*' (1932, p. 198). As opposed to that he suggests that

> . . . true politics could not be anything other than an expression of the person. [True politics] is rooted in the man as an active, creative and responsible person vis-à-vis the community. . . . From this definition of politics it results that everyone, inasmuch as he/she acts as a person, finds him/herself committed in true politics. [de Rougemont, 1946, p. 253]

Opposed to the state with its giantism, de Rougemont wants to go back to a 'human scale': to the level where the life and the actions of a person have real meaning. He therefore wants to go back to the commune and the community.

There is, implicitly at least, a certain critique of modernity in the philosophy of de Rougemont: for example he shows very clearly how individualization and the state go together and reinforce each other. But, conversely, this is also true of the opposite movement: if the person is to have a say in politics, the power and the role of the state will have to be diminished, which in turn will reinforce the role and the status of the person in politics.

Nevertheless, de Rougemont fails to see that the problem lies not only between the person and the state, but more generally within the process of militarization = modernization, of which growing individualism and the very stronger state are only two aspects. De Rougemont therefore neglects the role of science, of technology, of the army and the economy, which are of course also 'perverted' along with the militarization = modernization process. This means that the re-evaluation of the person implies the redefinition not only of his/her relation to politics, but also of his/her relation to the economy, to science, to technology, to defence, and so on. And this more general redefinition of one person's relation to the militarization = modernization process can be observed, today, in many grass-roots movements, in particular in the Green movement. Unfortunately, de Rougemont has never been really concerned with the movements; rather, his main question pertains to the translation of his conception of the 'person' into political structures.

De Rougemont thought that the political structure which not merely respects but promotes the person, is federalism. Federalism is the 'political projection of personalism'; it is this political structure which allows the expression of the diversity of those cultures of which the person is the core. Federalism 'does not mean the federal grouping of nation-states, but the splitting up of nations into much smaller unities' (Ellul, 1984, p. 97). This smaller unity is the 'region', which is 'not a small-scale nation-state' (de Rougemont, 1970, p. 181).

The idea of the person and its new relation to politics therefore leads de Rougemont, via federalism, to the idea of a Europe of regions, the only political form which respects and promotes the cultural identity of Europe. And this cultural identity is the only identity Europe has:

> Europe's unity is above all a cultural one. [De Rougemont, 1948, p. 151]
> Its name is 'cultural pluralism.' [De Rougemont, 1970, p. 31]

But the nation-state destroys this very identity; says de Rougemont: 'If it is true that the diversities, even the contradictions of our culture, have been the motor of our history, the modern nation-states have brought only misfortune to Europe' (1970, p. 61).

If this is true, the nation-states will have to be deconstructed in order to allow this diversity and pluralism—which forms the actual cultural unity and identity of Europe—to re-emerge. And this is a process: only beyond the nation-state will we find a European cultural identity, of which—according to de Rougemont—the two main aspects are the concept of the 'person' and the plurality and diversity of local and regional cultures. This is, in my opinion, what is at stake when we speak of about the identity and the future of Europe. Of course the literature on European identity and European culture is huge, and I have not explored it in detail. Nevertheless, it seems to me that all authors agree on essentials. For Denis de Rougemont (1984, p. 236) 'What distinguishes our culture from others is the extraordinary diversity of roots.'

And for the German philosopher Hermann Lübbe (1985, p. 200) it is the 'multitude and the closeness of regional cultures' which characterizes Europe. Building Europe therefore means making roots in these regional cultures in order to create a political structure which will in turn promote this very European cultural identity. The effects of such a process will be worldwide, says de Rougemont (1970, p. 104):

> European civilization, which has become a worldwide one, is in fact only threatened by the disease it has produced and spread itself.

It is in its sources, at the centre of its creative vitality, it is in Europe, where this disease has to be exorcized.

Because what threatens us from outside also undermines us from inside.

Denis de Rougemont would probably agree that today's threat is not only called 'bloc-logic' or 'domination of Europe by the superpowers', which are only epiphenomena, it must at least also be seen as the 'bankruptcy of (nation-state) politics'. Therefore, if Europe wants to survive, it needs not only *détente* and security concepts, but a deconstruction of the nation-state, and therefore a new relation of the person to (state-)politics. This is what a great number of Euromissile grass-roots activists and citizens in Europe have in common with de Rougemont.

De Rougemont after the 'Euromissile crisis'

I want to put de Rougemont's intellectual contribution into the context of the 'Euromissile crisis'. It is my belief that since what happened in Europe at the beginning of the 1980s de Rougemont's philosophy has actually acquired new and much stronger significance.

To begin with, one has to consider that there probably exists a parallel between the beginnings of the 1980s and the period before and during World War II, when Denis de Rougemont elaborated his philosophy. Both are periods of 'profound crisis' in Europe. And at both moments, Europe faced a 'crisis of civilization', which required, in order to be overcome, nothing less than a 'cultural revolution'.

The only realistic attitude at such moments is that of 'active pessimism', whose only possible political translation can be a 'politics of despair'. These concepts seem to me to fit, more than ever, the actual situation; they are views which were shared by a great number of Europeans in the early 1980s. These Europeans did not so much feel they were living in an 'economic community' as in a 'community of risk'. It could be that the experiencing of life in a 'European community of risk' furthered the 'politics of despair'. The immediate outcome of such a 'politics of despair' is a search for a new relation to (state-) politics, that is, a redefinition of 'politics, as if the person mattered'.

If de Rougemont's conception is right and still applies, this would mean that a new relation of the person to politics can only be rooted in local and regional cultures, in so far as they have not yet been destroyed by the state and more generally by the militarization = modernization process. And this process should ultimately lead to a European federation below the nation-state, whose unity is its cultural diversity and its cultural richness. There are at least four reasons why, I think, de Rougemont's conception perfectly applies today. In particular it applies to this tendency of the new movements and of grass-roots activists, whose main slogan is: 'The personal is political!'

First, activists in these movements, whether the peace or the Green movement, or citizen groups, share with de Rougemont the idea that (state-)politics is contrary to the personal. Second, they also share the conception of a political commitment of responsible people with a moral, an ethical and a religious dimension. For them political commitment can stem only from the person; it is therefore neither Left nor Right. What counts is the authority of the better argument, rooted in one person's life, not the number of voters. Third, they share, then, the communitarian and local dimension of political commitment. True political commitment can only be defined on a human scale. They finally share with de Rougemont (1946, p. 189) the idea of the crucial role of education, when he says that 'it is not the masses which have to be touched, but each person, one after the other—by educating them.'

But if these activists share with de Rougemont the premisses of their political commitment, they are on the other hand not very clear as to the concrete outcome of this commitment. De Rougemont's conception helps to clarify here: that would mean that at least part of the new movements and citizen groups are actually working towards the deconstruction of the nation-states into a 'European federation of cultural regions', since only this type of political structure allows a new relation of the person to politics.

Unfortunately this project of a 'European cultural identity' has never been clearly formulated, either by the movement or by the intellectuals. And this despite numerous conferences and publications on 'Europe's cultural identity' and its contribution to peace in Europe since the 'Euromissile debate' (e.g. Bender, 1981). Most of the writings are more confusing than enlightening, since nobody has actually reflected on the reasons why everybody, today, is so fascinated by 'Europe' and its European values. If the writers had either looked more closely into the new movement, or at philosophically more solid approaches, such as that of de Rougemont, they could, in my opinion, have avoided two of the main errors which can be found throughout most of this literature about Europe.

The first error is to confuse elite and local/regional culture; if the first survives and sometimes even promotes modernization, the second is destroyed by it. But this local/regional culture is precisely the only one which is capable of serving as the roots or the basis on which a European identity can be built.

The second error is to forget that the build-up of a European cultural identity is a process—and not a reactivation of past ideals; it is a process which cannot be separated from the definition of (state-) politics, and therefore from the redefinition of the person's relation to it. It cannot be achieved without a fundamental cultural transformation, challenging the whole militarization = modernization process.

Conclusion: a cultural transformation towards peace in Europe?

According to de Rougemont, a way out of the 'crisis in Europe' cannot be achieved without the build-up of a 'European cultural identity', which in turn cannot be achieved without the establishment of a new relation between the person and (state-)politics. This means at the same time a fundamental transformation of the militarization = modernization process. But will Europe be able to come up with an alternative to the very process it has set in motion?

I have tried to show that the new European peace movement of the beginning of the 1980s must be considered, first as a reaction against this process, and second as an attempt to come up with some alternatives, in particular with alternatives to militarization. Of course, social movements are always only an expression, so to say a momentary crystallization, of underlying socio-cultural transformations. Movements will therefore be able to go only as far as such transformations have reached among the citizenry in general. As yet, however, the socio-cultural transformations which have emerged with the 'Euromissile debate' are not very well conceptualized.

As a consequence, most of the concepts, ideas and slogans for peace in Europe—even if they have sometimes been endorsed and advocated by the new European peace movement—often fail to translate the very nature of the underlying socio-cultural transformation,which is much more about the relation of the person to (state-)politics than about concrete projects. I therefore think that the new European peace movement has used most of the slogans and concepts 'for peace in Europe' not so much out of conviction but in the absence of coherent alternative ideas.

Among these concepts one must therefore clearly distinguish between two different types: there are, on the one hand, 'alternative security concepts' for Europe, whereas on the other hand one finds 'alternative conceptions of the relation between the citizen and politics'. This also covers the distinction made between 'negative' and 'positive' peace or between 'security' and 'peace'. Some think that the concept of a 'non-provocative defence' must be located in between.

As for alternative security concepts, they proliferated after the 'Euromissile crisis'. The main notions are an American- and Soviet-free Europe; a nuclear weapon-free Europe; zones of troop and armed forces reduction; nuclear weapon-free zones; and all kinds of concepts which guarantee defence and do not favour (surprise) attacks, etc.

What all these alternative security concepts have in common is that they do not actually require the citizen to alter his/her relation to politics, in particular not to the state, nor to question the process of militarization=modernization. It is obvious that by promoting such concepts neither European values nor a European cultural identity will be furthered.

On the side of 'positive peace' there exists a variety of less concrete proposals; most of them take the form of social of civilian-based defence, of which Gene Sharp (1985) is probably the main theorist. Although Sharp does not state this explicitly, this kind of 'defence' can only be built in the long term through education, on the basis of a new relation of the person/citizen to politics and to the nation-state. As says Mechtersheimer (1987, p. 335), one of the rare peace researchers who himself seeks a form of 'positive peace', such a peace in Europe cannot be achieved without a cultural (i.e. a value) transformation, leading ultimately to a 'peace culture'. This is a transformation which cannot be promoted by the state, but probably only against the state:

> With which state could such a politics be achieved? Certainly not with the actual one, which is characterized by all the attributes of nationalistic behaviour. Probably: with no state at all, since the state, in order to justify its existence, must practise precisely the actual politics of conflict and war. The chance of realization (of this peace culture) lies on a social level, where the state, at most, can act supportively.

Social and civilian-based defence without a cultural transformation of the citizen's relation to (state-)politics is therefore an illusion, and to implement such a defence (as is being studied in some Western European countries) prior to this cultural transformation is certainly a perversion of the very idea of social defence. The probably outcome of this process will be a strengthened local and community life and therefore a strengthened European cultural identity and solidarity. In other words, no social 'defence' without a strengthening of local and regional cultures and identities and no cultural identity without the deconstruction of the (European) nation-states.

There exists yet another concept: the concept of a 'non-provocative defence', translated politically and militarily into the idea of a 'structural non-aggression capacity'. The main promoters of this concept would like it to be situated between negative and positive peace. Galtung (1984) has come out very strongly for this idea, which seeks to combine conventional military, para-military and non-military defence, giving Switzerland as an example. But, to my opinion, Switzerland is the worst example there can be, since it is probably one of the rare countries in the world where the process of militarization = modernization has penetrated even the remotest part of every citizen's social, economic and even cultural life (e.g. Pestalozzi, 1982). And if one looks at how the idea of a 'structural-non-aggression-capacity' is now being introduced into traditional defence concepts (e.g. Dialog 1987), one must conclude that the concept of 'non-provocative defence' is probably just another version of 'negative peace'.

In conclusion one must say that almost all intellectuals—and most of the peace researchers—who have elaborated and promoted concrete proposals for peace in Europe still cling to 'negative peace' and to 'alternative security concepts'. Hylke Tromp, Director of the Institute of Polemology at the University of Groningen, concludes: 'Almost all the alternative proposals to actual security policy take place within the framework of the traditional paradigm of international relations' (Tromp, 1985, p. 101).

And this is the paradigm which insists that the nation-state remains the central actor for peace.

As I have tried to show in this chapter, nation-states will not be able to promote a type of peace which would strengthen European cultural identity and solidarity and which would be an answer to many Europeans' concern for the future of Europe, a concern which has arisen in the aftermath of the 'Euromissile crisis'. The new European peace movement which, together with the philosopher Denis de Rougemont, has probably best crystallized this concern, underlines the fact that such an answer can only stem from a profound cultural transformation which will inevitably leave neither the nation-state nor more generally the militarization=modernization process untouched.

Or conversely a profound cultural transformation, leading to a redefinition of the citizen's relation to (state-)politics, is a necessary condition for building up a European cultural identity based on new European values. And such values are certainly necessary if we want to stop, not to say reverse, the (originally European) process of militarization=modernization.

But will Europe still have the necessary (cultural) resources to pursue such a profound cultural transformation? And where else would these resources come from, if not from locally rooted people joining citizen groups and grass-roots movements?

Bibliography

Albrecht, U., *et al.*, 1972. 'Is Europe to Demilitarize?', *Instant Research on Peace and Violence*, vol.2, no.4.

Antola, E., 1984. 'Peaceful Change as a Model for Europe', paper presented at the conference on 'Peace and Security Processes in Europe', Siuntio, 7–9 September 1984.

Bahro, R., 1987. *Logik der Rettung. Wer kann die Apokalypse aufhalten?* Stuttgart: Weitbrecht.

Bahro, R. & M. von Freyhold, n.d., 'Charta für ein atomwaffenfreies Europa', manuscript.

Bender, P., 1981. *Das Ende des ideologischen Zeitalters. Die Europäisierung Europas.* Berlin: Severin & Siedler.

Bracher, K-D., 1979. *Europa und Entspannung.* Frankfurt: Ullstein.

Clarke, R., 1971. *The Science of War and Peace.* London: Jonathan Cape.

Cultural Roots of Peace, GDI papers, no.34. Rüschlikon, Switzerland: Gottlieb-Duttweiler Institute.

Dean, J., 1987. *Watershed in Europe.* Lexington, Mass.: Lexington Books.

Dialog, 1987, no. 10.

Elias, N., 1969, *Uber den Prozess der Zivilisation.* Berne: Francke.

Ellul, J., 1964. *The Technological Society*, New York: Knopf.

Ellul, J., 1984. 'Interview', in *L'Europe et les intellectuels.* Paris: Gallimard.

Finger, M., 1989. *Paix, Peace, Pace . . . Les dix bonnes raisons de s'engager pour la paix.* Lausanne: Loisirs et Pedagogie.

Galtung, J., 1984. *There Are Alternatives.* Nottingham: Spokesman.

Habermas, J., 1985. *Der philosophische Diskurs der Moderne.* Frankfurt: Suhrkamp.

Hettne, B., 1988. 'European Perspectives Project 1986–87. Concluding Report', *PADRIGU Papers*, University of Gothenburg.

Hessische Stiftung Friedens- und Konfliktforschung, (HSFK), 1982. *Europa zwischen Konfrontation und Kooperation. Entspannungspolitik für die 80er Jahre.* Frankfurt: Suhrkamp.

Jahn, E.; P. Lemaître & O. Waever, 1987. *European Security–Problems of Research on Non-military Aspects.* Copenhagen: University of Copenhagen, Centre of Peace and Conflict Research.

Johnstone, D., 1984. *The Politics of the Euromissiles.* London: Verso.

Kaldor, M., 1981. *The Baroque Arsenal.* New York: Hill & Wang.

Kaldor, M., 1985. 'Transforming the State', *Bulletin of Peace Proposals*, vol.16 no. 4.

Koistinen, P., 1980. *The Military–Industrial Complex.* New York: Praeger.

L'Europe aujourd'hui, 1985. Neuchâtel, Switzerland: Baconnière.

Lodgaard, S., 1986. 'The North–South Dimension of European Security', *PRIO-Report*, no.1.

Lübbe, H., 1985. 'Die grosse und die kleine Welt. Regionalismus als europäische Bewegung', in W. Weidenfeld, ed., *Die Identität Europas.* Bonn: Bouvier.

McNeill, W., 1963. *The Rise of the West.* Chicago: University of Chicago Press.

McNeill, W., 1982. *The Pursuit of Power.* Oxford: Blackwell.

Mechtersheimer, A., 1987. 'Das neue Denken. Eine Anmerkung zur Friedensdiskussion', *Dialog*, no.10.

Morin, E., 1987. *Penser l'Europe*. Paris: Gallimard.

Nef, J.U., 1950. *War and Human Progress*. New York: Norton.

Palmer, J., 1987. *Europe without America*. Oxford: Oxford University Press.

Pestalozzi, H.A., 1982. *Rettat die Schweiz–schafft die Armee ab*. Bern: Zytglogge.

Petitjean, A., 1987. 'L'Europe, continent de l'avenir', *Science-Culture-Info*, 14 May.

Picht, G., 1969 *Der Mut zur Utopie*. Munich: Piper & Co.

Picht, G., 1980–1. *Hier und Jetzt*, 2 vols. Stuttgart: Klett-Cotta.

Picht, G., 1984. 'Interview', in *L'Europe et les intellectuels*. Paris: Gallimard.

Rougemont, D. de, 1932. *Politique de la personne*, Neuchatel, Switzerland: Baconnière.

Rougemont, D. de, 1946. *La Politique de la personne*. Paris: 'Je Sers' (first published in 1932).

Rougemont, D. de, 1948. *L'Europe en jeu*. Neuchatel, Switzerland: Baconnière.

Rougemont, D. de, 1962. *Les chances de l'Europe*, Neuchatel, Switzerland: Baconnière.

Rougemont, D. de, 1965. *Fédéralisme culturel*, Neuchatel, Switzerland: Baconnière.

Rougemont, D. de, 1970. *Lettre ouverte aux Européens*, Paris: Albin Michel.

Rougemont, D. de, 1984. 'La culture commune des Européens et le débat Est–Ouest', *Cadmos*, no.26–7.

Schell, J., 1982. *The Fate of the Earth*. New York: Avon.

Schell, J., 1984. *The Abolition*. New York: Knopf.

Senghaas, D., 1986. *Die Zukunft Europas*. Frankfurt: Suhrkamp.

Serres, M., 1974. 'Trahison: La Thanatocratie', in M. Serres, *Hermes III*. Paris: Minuit.

Sharp, G., 1985. *Making Europe Unconquerable*. London: Taylor & Francis.

Smith, D. & E.P. Thompson, eds, 1987. *Prospectus for a Habitable Planet*, Harmondsworth: Penguin Books.

The European Heritage: Unity and Singularity, 1984. Geneva: Centre d'études pratiques de la négociation internationale.

Thee, M., 1985. 'The Arms Race and the Fate of Europe', *PRIO-Paper*, no.2.

Thompson, E.P., 1982. *Beyond the Cold War*. New York: Pantheon.

Thompson, E.P., *et al.*, 1982. *Exterminism and Cold War*. London: Verso.

Tromp, H., 1985. 'Alternativen zur gegenwärtigen Sicherheitspolitik und die Friedensbewegungen', in A. Skuhra & H. Wimmer, eds., *Friedensforschung und Friedensbewegung*. Vienna: VWGÖ.

Varis, T., 1984. 'Europeanizing Peace', *Current Research on Peace and Violence*, vol.3, no.4.

Väyrynen, R., n.d., 'Omens of a New European System', manuscript.

Virilio, P., 1976. *L'insécurité du territoire*. Paris. Stock.

Virilio, P., 1977. *Vitesse et politique*. Paris: Galilée.

Virilio, P., 1983. *Pure War*. New York: Foreign Agent Series.

12 Is There a New Germany Coming?

Johan Galtung

Let me try to formulate some points about my own attitude to Germany, meaning by that both Germanies. But my experience is mainly with the Western part, and relatively typical of a citizen of one of the many countries occupied by Nazi Germany.

I came out of the war 14 years old, shocked like everybody else. My father had been in a German concentration camp. My sisters, who had worked in the resistance movement, had barely managed to escape to Sweden. The family consisted for a couple of years of my mother and myself. Norway came out of the war without major scars, but every family had stories similar to mine.

However, it would be entirely dishonest to say that I hated Germany. I guess that what later became Johan Galtung the peace researcher, peace activist, pacifist had a basis in some ability to distinguish between Germany and Nazi-Germany, Germans and Nazis. I can still vividly remember how shocked I was by the slogan 'the only good German is a dead German.' But I was also shocked by what my father reported one of those days in spring 1945 before the capitulation came, when he was asking one of the concentration camp guards, at the time rather demoralized, what would happen to Germany. The answer was: 'After the war we shall systematically make ourselves beloved.'[1] Must have been a rather bright one, that one.

I was one of the first Norwegians to *really* travel to Germany, in 1949. I had been through by train the year before, had seen Hamburg in ruins, had verified that 'the allies have done a good job', had felt only remorse and shock. But in 1949 I managed to get the permission to hitch-hike around (my sister was working in the International Refugee Organization in Frankfurt). I talked with everybody, high and low. I had good luck: very close to Rüdesheim I was trying to get a lift, and a big bus filled with young people stopped. They were high-school students (*Abiturienten*) out with their favourite teachers, celebrating that their studies in high school (*Gymnasium*) were about to come to an end. They were simply stopping to get rid of some of the wine they had tested and tasted rather amply the night before (the uncle of one of them was the owner of a major wine cellar). But in the general commotion they got me into the bus. I spent three days with them, went to their home town, talked with their parents. Not a small number of the fathers were directors of steel industry in a small Ruhr district town.

What I heard shocked me profoundly. They saw the world so differently from how we saw it from the outside. The fathers saw themselves as the forerunners in the fight against Communism. They had all participated actively one way or the other in Nazism. They were all rich. Bolshevism inside and outside had been the threat, and continued to be the only real threat. Hitler had made two mistakes: to turn against the West, and to be 'so rough' with the Jews. He should have been either more discrete, or else have tried to make the Jews his friends. One day the rest of the West would learn to appreciate what he had done. In the mean time the Germans had to keep a low profile. ('Das hätte der Adolf bestimmt besser gemacht' (Adolf Hitler would surely have done it much better) was the comment at a somewhat skimpy 4 July fireworks in Frankfurt, 1949.)

The heaviness of the talk, the intensity of the voices, the somewhat puffy red faces, I will never forget. Nor do I easily forget that when I found people who had been on the right side, meaning the Left side, they looked very much the same and talked very much in the same pompous way – the manner that I later on tried to describe in some detail as 'Teutonic' (Galtung, 1980, Ch. 8).

The experience made me sick and tired of Germany. In the period of fifteen years between 1950 and 1965 I must have been in Germany dozens of times. But I always travelled as quickly as possible, usually by night, making a minimum of stops. I could not stand it when Germans came up to me with the usual 'Are you a Norwegian? A wonderful country, I was there during the war, really nice girls!'[2] I must have heard that dozens of times. What annoyed me was not so much the memory of the past as their lack of ability to understand that this was not the thing to say! That total *Antennenlosigkeit* (insensitivity)!

I should add that during the following fifteen years I heard this decreasingly often, now almost down to zero. I guess not so much because the *Antennenlosigkeit* has diminished as basically because the Hitler generation is getting old and has retired socially and/or biologically. However, I remember a couple of things from those first fifteen years.

Dachau, June 1955: I came on my motorbike, got out, trembling with emotion. Outside was a bulky Mercedes, with bulky Germans, the car radio on, playing 'Three Coins in the Fountain'. Somehow we started talking. I reported some of my feelings. 'Six million gassed? Rather exaggerated, impossible. A couple of thousand perhaps.'[3] That people develop defence mechanisms against one of the most horrendous crimes in history is not exactly surprising. But would it not have been easier to accept it, and draw the appropriate conclusions, as many other Germans did?

September 1957: motorbike again, leaving West Berlin, through East Berlin on the way to the Sassnitz ferry. We lost the road somewhere north of Sachsenhausen concentration camp (Oranienburg), looked at the map, were approached by a nice family on a motor cycle and a side-car. They were all working for the ubiquitous *Handelsorganisation*, all members of the only party, the SED (Party of Socialist Unity). They invited us home. We stayed overnight, talking the whole night through. There was certainly no problem concerning rejection of Nazism. It was total, and absolutely genuine. And they had rather good reasons. But I was amazed at the way in which they accepted the crimes on the Soviet side. The inventiveness, the factual distortions in connection with Stalinism, the mysticism connected with the construction of their own mirage, the *Arbeiter- und Bauernstaat* (the 'worker's and farmers' state')! Till in the morning some grey light broke. It was dawn, misty, and some cages with rabbits appeared in the garden outside the house; it turned out that they were collectively owned, those rabbits, not only for the meat, but also for the wool. Somehow they may be able to spin a couple of solid and nice gloves out of that wool. The co-operative was very much praised: 'We think this is the solution, not only for Germany, but for the whole world!'[4] I looked at the rabbits. The rabbits looked at me. We both saw the future in a somewhat dim light.

The next fifteen years I experienced the European student revolt very closely. I generally shared their views and was with them in several countries, in terms of what they were against, usually unimpressed with their efforts to be constructive.

6 May 1968: Fumiko and I were marching with the students up the Champs-Elysées in Paris, sitting down on the Place de l'Etoil in one of the hundreds or thousands of small discussion groups, trying to understand what was going on. I was professor at the University of Essex and participated actively in that connection. Some of my own writings were attacked and rightly so. I learned a lot from it, often much more than from any colleagues.

But what shocked me in Germany was the way in which German groups inclining towards Marxism behaved in exactly the same way that the bearers of Nazi values had done. It was verticality and hierarchy. Women were rarely recognized. Extreme fanaticism, dogmatism. And those cold eyes, with no love for anything, only hatred directed against the system. No understanding of how deeply they themselves were a part of the deep culture and structure they abhorred in its Nazi manifestation and had internalized its values. All my social science experience tends to convince me that it is at the level of deep structure and deep culture, collectively and individually, that interesting things are located. My assumption was continuity, that there was something basic underlying both German Fascism, meaning Nazism, *and* German Marxism.

In a sense I was not surprised when in 1972 I came to a relatively innocent political science meeting in Berlin and was met by Maoist groups (*K-Gruppen*) with big posters: 'Galtung, Agent des amerikanischen Imperialismus, raus!' (Galtung, American Imperialist, go home!) I went up to them and said: . . . 'That is simply not true. I give you two hours to prove it and then you either produce evidence or you apologize. If neither, then you are simply a louse.'[5] They preferred the characterization of *Laus* (louse). After quite some 'debate' they left, with their megaphones. I remained. My colleagues at the Freie Universität said that that was the first time it had happened. But they also added it was a little bit easier for me since I could after all leave Berlin the next day. True.

In other words, in those years I felt rather strongly that this so-called second Germany coming up was quite similar to the first, and wrote my first article on the Teutonic style. The reaction was interesting. It was rejected by about ten journals and magazines, all of them saying the same thing: 'Most interesting, but this is not exactly the moment to publish it.' I became *persona non grata* on the Left, being very explicitly not only not Marxist, but in a sense anti-Marxist. I have always seen Marxism as a brilliant analysis of capitalism, a philosophy of history that will forever place Marx at the top to those trying to shed some light on the vaster dimensions of time and space. An indispensable method, but somewhat empty when it comes to visions of alternatives, and a poor guide, strategically speaking, for political action because of its one-sidedness. Marx is one among many, but for them he was the sole source of wisdom, and everything had to be accepted. That was what the German Marxists had done, and more in the West than in the East. After all, the West Germans did not have to live with it.

I was Carl von Ossietzky Professor in Peace Research, the first one, in Bonn 1973. Again a fascinating experience, but not so much because of the many politicians who, regardless of party, were more or less of the same basically and profoundly German type. I remember a party with members of the foreign policy committee of the Bundestag, who wanted to discuss views on *Ostpolitik*. One of them, after three to four hours of discussion, asked me whether on the basis of the discussion I could guess who were from the Christian Democratic Union (CDU) and who were from the Social Democratic Party (SDP). I got only 50 per cent correct!

It was not the politicians and the establishment, but the students who were interesting. Here something new was evidently coming. There were people who rejected not only the ideology of the establishment and their more pompous style of behaviour; they started rejecting the deeper ideology and the deeper structure. They were changing to new ways of life. There were communes (*Wohngemeinschaften*), although the house-rules (*Hausordnungsregeln*) sometimes looked like the rules of military barracks. But there were efforts to come to grips with something deeper. I do not think that they themselves were, or still are for that matter, in any sense aware of how *German* that thing was against which they were fighting. It is certainly still not my experience that Germans are capable of recognizing their own Germanness. On the contrary, in 1983, at the 50th anniversary of Hitler's coming to power in East Germany they discussed Nazism as Fascism, as the last stage of capitalism in crisis, universalizing Nazism as a phenomenon subject to some kind of natural law. And in West Germany they trivialized Nazism in very general politological terms, as a question of a parliamentary system that was too weak; and illegal action by some people who simply were exactly that, 'illegal', extra-parliamentarian. The German aspect of Nazism disappeared in perspicacious, sharp-witted analysis (*scharfsinnige Analysen*). Most disturbing for those who hoped for an agonizing reappraisal.

And at the same time a real 'second Germany' (*zweites Deutschland*) was coming. I wrote these lines right after the highly successful 'Nuremburg Tribunal against First Strike and Mass Destruction Weapons in the East and the West', 18 to 20 February 1983, organized by the Green Party (*Die Grünen*). The Germans in that room were of the type who would have stood up against Nazism. I was not so convinced about many of the Marxist revolutionaries I found in the late 1960s and early 1970s. The deep culture of their thinking, and the deep structure of their behaviour, were so similar to Nazism that it might only have been a question of changing some rhetoric.

But what impressed me about the new generation was not so much their concrete stand against nuclear weapons, whether nuclear armament is seen as an effort to obtain nuclear disarmament (plainly ridiculous) or as a preparation for a nuclear war that can be won (plainly criminal). What impressed me was the way they combined this with a number of other very concrete stands without becoming the victims of the all-too-German temptation to weave it into a tightly spun pyramid of deductive thinking, with some mystical faith on top. I have discussed it with many of them. They report that it is very tempting to put together such an ideology and, I would add, particularly on German soil (*auf deutschem Boden*). But somehow, at least so far, they see the tremendous value of trying to build a movement as a federation of single-issue movements, certainly with some kind of common nucleus but perhaps one which is best left to the intuitive level and not raised to the level of basic dogma.

And then, the style of behaviour. Maybe it had to start with informal dress, with long hair, turning bourgeois styles of self-presentation upside down. Maybe it had to start with rejection. And maybe some of it has to continue that way. But non-organization is how an enormous amount of things get done. I have seen it so often. Of course there is preparation behind it all. Of course there are quarrels, groups that make their views known in no unceratin way, realists (*realos*) and fundamentalists (*fundamentalos*). Of course sometimes it breaks up. But in few places have I seen conferences where all the sessions are introduced with a little tune played on a flute or on a harp, soft instruments, where there is a sense of tranquillity, bordering on meditation (without the people knowing it themselves) coming over the faces in the crowd. Small and large conflicts are resolved gently, not pushed under the carpet. If these were the people who handled relations with the Soviet Union much of the East-West conflict would evaporate. And let me only add to that statement (which I am prepared to defend in detail, but on the assumption that the new generation—and not only among die Grünen—*are* as realistic in their perception of the Soviet Union as they express in writing and in talking) that I am rather amazed by the ability to combine informality and friendliness with an efficiency that I have never found when confronted with big organizations in Germany, be they blue or red.

Of course these people are young. Of course they have a surplus of education which they can invest in highly talented, well informed political action. Anybody who want can compare a Green political speech with a red and a blue. Try to eliminate the rhetoric in all three places, and compare what remains. There is so much more content in the Green versions; considerably more rhetoric in the other two.

The interesting point is to what extent the same process of not only de-Nazification (*Entnazifizierung*) but of something broader, let me call it de-Teutonization (*Entteutonisierung*) takes place in East Germany, with the usual lag that one would expect given the general, centre–periphery gradient running West–East in Europe in general, and in Germany in particular. I remember very vividly my own experience in September 1968. I was invited to a meeting of the East German Christian Democratic Union on solidarity with Vietnam, a field where I had been quite active in addition to work for the recognition of East Germany, against the Hallstein doctrine. There were testimonials, including some from East Germans who had received letters from relatives in West Germany telling about unemployment. One had even been in the transit room of a West German airport and could report 'a warlike atmosphere'. I managed to get up to the rostrum and started talking. But my credentials came to nothing: as they could not predict the end of my talk which would have compared Vietnam and Czechoslovakia, they dragged me down before I got that far. The whole issue became quite ugly. The discussion in the car from Weimar to Schönefeld had sufficient drama to fill a play or two. So, one Teutonism was superseded by another: *There is but one truth.* And the language, the voice, all that anger that is somehow released: Where does it all come from? Those red, puffy faces. . . .

But what I have seen of the East German peace movement in East Berlin is different, not only in point of view, but also in deep ideology and style of behaviour. I admire them. It must be tough. But that is where the hope lies. They will remain blue and red in their organizations for some time, these Germanies. But a greening of the German spirit is clearly on its way.[6]

So I do not think there is much reason to fear that the Germans will start marching again: Germans East or West, North or South, or all four as they did last time. What we might be afraid of would not be a German inclination to sacrifice others so much as the inclination to sacrifice themselves, the 'spirit of self-sacrifice' (*Opferbereitschaft*) often referred to. It is as if the Germans feel that they have been born under a sign of ambiguity. On the one hand they are chosen, seeing themselves as more gifted than others, as carriers of a transcendent civilization, produced by the Germans, but bequeathed to humankind as a whole. It is a heavy responsibility. Whatever happens there have to be *Germans* around to interpret Kant, Schopenhauer and Nietzsche; Goethe and Schiller—or Marx and Engels or Habermas. That responsibility became particularly clear in 'Das Teutonenjahr 1983', celebrating Luther, Wagner, Marx and Hitler, all four in one year! There is a German message, a mission. The duty to undertake this mission of bringing the message to the world easily also becomes a right to do so.

But there is the darker side to the inheritance, the dark forces hidden in the German tribe, collectively and individually. The Beast (*Das Tier*) is seen as not far away. When it appears in Nazi form as the blond beast (*die blonde Bestie*) the implication is that nature has run her, sometimes cruel, course with the Germans. Atavism is hidden in the collective subconscious, deep forces that may come up again. Who knows. Drama is given unto the Germans, jubilant (*himmelhoch jauchzend*) but also grieving (*zum Tode betrübt*), not unmixed bliss, happiness, enlightenment and peace, for instance in the Buddhist sense of nirvana (*Erlösung*). Of course, other people—such as Anglo-Saxons, Nordic people, US people, maybe most Latins, not to mention non-Europeans—may not understand this. There is a German sense of destiny. Those to the East and France, however, they understand. Their destiny has been to be invaded, standing in the way of the German destiny.

I interpret the German *Angst* as an *Angst* the Germans have about themselves. By believing in these darker forces and a destiny with which one cannot argue, Germans may run into the vicious circle of self-fulfilling predictions. If a total war should once again be on the horizon, *my Angst* would be that the *German Angst* would make them nod with recognition, *here it comes*, destiny catching up with us, rather than really fight it. Should a nuclear holocaust come, the Germans would not only sacrifice themselves, but also be heroes in the holocaust. Like the incredible German women who, during the spring of 1945, with defeat around the corner, in a society ravaged by war, with the men either dead or away on the fronts in the east and the west, in the north and the south, carried the burden of keeping society going. They would probably do it again if called upon, as part of their destiny. Here the Germans under Nazism differed fundamentally from the Italians under Fascism. The Germans went on to the bitter end. The Italians saw the writing on the wall, withdrew and/or escaped to the mountains.

Most important and encouraging in German youth today in general, and the Green wave in particular, is not necessarily the political stand but the underlying ethos. They are less victims of this general German mystique I have attempted to explain here. They are less willing to sacrifice themselves and others for the sake of abstract principles. Rather, so many of them seem to be filled with love of life, and love of love, not with the self-hatred which is always a condition for self-immolation and extreme acts of sacrifice. And this, needless to say, has much to do with their alternative way of life, particularly when they are able to build their own institutions, less vertical, certainly filled with rivalries and competition, but not with that hatred that springs from repression.

I would also tend to think that the older Germans tendency to develop sharp enemy images (*Feindbilder*) replete with *Angst* and hatred at the world level is a projection of experiences at the micro-level, in the high number of vertical, collective and exclusive organizations that together constituted Germany, and still are the social reality for much of conservative Germany. They have good reasons for hating youth: why should young people be entitled to all that love when they were not?

To this one may add an important question: why should the green generation be different? Why should they represent a discontinuity at this point in history, if it is correct, as stated earlier, that a certain German cosmology is very deeply embedded in the collective and individual German mind? To this I will try three answers, all of them tentative, as a summary.

First, a true German reaction, on German soil, against Nazism certainly did not start in 1945, nor in 1955. A number of people had to retire biologically or at least socially in order for such a reaction to come. A number of young people had to be born and grow up and achieve sufficient maturity to understand what had happened, yet not feel that they had to be defensive about it. Maybe the first clearly anti-Fascist generation came at the end of the 1960s, and for various reasons in a Marxist form. Maybe the second came towards the end of the 1970s, and then in a green form—certainly also inspired by the TV series *Holocaust*, like the film on Gandhi filled with shortcomings, yet of tremendous pedagogical value. The third, the fourth, the fifth and so on waves of anti-Nazism and deeper understanding are still to come. They will come; driven by the many anniversaries. Germans will learn to see their past more adequately than the former president of the Bundestag, Tenninger, did in 1988. In other words, a steady progress in understanding what Nazism was about may lead to clearer tendencies of dissociation, of distance between oneself and anything Nazi. There will be reversals of the trend as evidenced by the debate among West German historians in 1988 on the origins of Nazism (*Historikerstreit*). But I nevertheless expect the general direction to be as indicated.

Second, the first wave of anti-Nazism was Marxist and was anti-Nazi in content but certainly not anti-Teutonic in form. It was of short duration, among other reasons because its structure was out of touch with the tendency towards horizontal and individualistic forms of social organization. And it failed to answer a number of important questions about ecological degradation; alienation in socialist society; emancipation of women; the emergence of a technocratic class under socialism; the lack of a peace theory in Marxism and peace practice among socialist countries; the insensitivity to non-Occidental culture. At the same time its model of future society was not only unclear but also partly repulsive. Whatever the reason, consciously or unconsciously the 1968 wave may have led to a deeper rejection of authoritarianism, refusing to be party to a struggle whereby one authoritarian system is supposed to replace another.

Third, after the catastrophic experience of the Nazi wave, and after the Marxist wave came the green wave itself. One of its characteristics is as a loose federation of single-issue movements; the futures movement, the peace movement, the feminist movement, the alternative way of life movement, the citizen's action movement (*Bürgeninitiativen*) of any kind, the ecological movement, and so on. Somehow they all seem to agree that none of them should be *the* important one and the others secondary in significance. They should all be on an equal footing, on an 'I shall support-you-if-you-support-me' basis. The movement was pluralistic and has managed to remain so even after the Green Party was founded. The movement has served as a setting for this loose federation, even bringing its issues and its discourse into one of the citadels of the classical Germanic traditions, the parliament, the Bundestag in Bonn.

This horizontal, pluralistic structure is reflected in the field of political theory. Each issue brings in much theory formation in addition to data, criticism and constructive ideas. But so far nobody has come up with a generally acceptable, teutonically shaped, ideological pyramid where everything is neatly deduced from first principles, complete with enemy image (*Feindbild*), crisis and catharsis. There have been efforts in this direction, and there will probably be more. If they should succeed, and one of the issues is seen as more basic than the others, then there is always the danger that the corresponding movement will be seen as the leading movement, using that theory to gain ascendancy over the others. It will insist that 'our issue has to be attended to first, then time will come for the other issues', substituting for a circular model of many small steps a linear model of one big step that will—on paper—bring the solution of all other problems in its wake. And in practice it will probably end in catastrophe.

Should this happen I would feel more frightened again. But I would feel even more frightened if the very same people who did this should also develop that combination of self-hatred and other-hatred that was so rampant in the older generation, deeply anchored in vertical, collective and exclusive organizations all over Germany, and highly compatible with German sentimentality, *Gemütlichkeit*.

So, let us wait and see. But not passively. And not with a spirit of self-righteousness or vengeance. For we are all in it, we Europeans with our superpower neighbours, as part of that expansive, exploitative Occident. And it is certainly in the interests of all of us that Germany manages what the world hopes and expects: getting out of the bondage and clientelism under the superpowers without creating a new superpower, within or without a coming European Union.

Notes

1. 'Nach dem Kriege werden wir uns systematisch beliebt machen.'
2. 'Sind Sie Norweger? Eine wunderbares Land, ich war dort während des Krieges, dort gab es wirklich schöne Mädchen!'
3. 'Sechs Millionen vergast? Das ist ziemlich überzogen, das ist eine Unmöglichkeit. Einige tausend vielleicht.'
4. 'Das glauben wir ist die Lösung, nicht nur für Deutschland sondern für die ganze Welt!'
5. 'Du das ist ganz einfach nicht wahr. Ich gebe dir zwei Stunden, Beweismaterial zu finden und dann kommst du entweder damit oder du entschuldigst dich. Wenn es weder Beweise noch Entschuldigungen gibt, ja dann bist du ganz einfach eine Laus.'
6. For 'the German spirit', see my effort to define *homo teutonicus* and *homo hitlerinicus* in my *Hitlerism, Stalinism, Reaganism: Three Variations on a Theme by Orwell*, forthcoming.

Bibliography

Galtung, J., 1980. 'Deductive Thinking and Political Practice: An Essay on Teutonic Intellectual Style', in *Papers on Methodology*. Copenhagen: Ejlers.

Index

Adisa, J. 112
Africa
and Hegel 101–2
as negation of Europeanism 111–13
perspective on peace 110–25
and savagery 113–16
Agbaje, A. 112
Aho, James 15–28, 73
Airas, P. 70
Albrecht, U. 181
Alexander the Great 4, 81
Aluko, O. 112
America *see* United States
Amin, Idi 88
Antola, E. 179
Arabs
and Israel 147–52
and rule of violence 149–50
war with Israel 148–51
Arafat, Yassir 163
Arendt, H. 159
Aristotle 4, 102
Arminius 83
Aron, R. 152
Asia, and Hegel 102–4
St Augustine 8
Austria 134

Bacon, Francis 80, 88
Bahro, Rodolf 171, 176, 177
Bantu 115
Beardsley, Monroe 156
Bechert, Karl 175
Becker, Ernest 15, 17, 20, 24–5
Bell, D. 105
Bender, P. 186
Berger, Peter 18, 19, 22
Berlin, I. 93
Bloom, A. 94
body politic, re-establishing 46–7
bomb (nuclear)
deterrent, degeneration of 42–7
overvaluation of 41–2
and revelation 47–53
sign 29–57
Botha, P.W. 115
Bracher, K.-D. 178, 179
Buber, Martin 156
Burke, Edmund 8, 58–79
and America 63–7
and East India Company 70
and France 67–9
and India 60–6
as international theorist 59–60
and peace 60–7
and Regicide Directory 67–9, 73–5
and Sons of Light and Sons of Darkness 69–76
and war 67–9
Burkert, Walter 29, 33–4

Cassirer, Ernst 97, 99
Cesaire, Aime 107
Chaiand, G. 13
Chernus, Ira 11, 121
Chomsky, Noam 96, 107

Churchill, Winston 83
Chydenius, John 2, 8, 12
Cicero 81
Cicourel, A. 19
Clarke, R. 171
Clausewitz, Carl von 145–6, 172
Cohn, N. 22
common humanity and dualism 10–13
concentration camps 194
Confucius 16
contradictions in religion 3
Cortes, Donoso 82
Cox, J. 119

Dalby, S. 59
Dean, J. 181
Demandt, Alexandr 80–90
Demosthenes 4
Derrida, Jacques 107
Descartes, René 92
deterrent, degeneration of bomb as 42–7
dialectic of heroism 17
Diamond, S. 110. 118. 121
Dobzhansky, T. 23
Donelan, M. 59
Dossa, Shiraz 5
  on Hegel 91–109
  on Zionism 155–65
Dostoyevski, F. 83
Douglas, Jack 19
Dowling, D. 51
Drake, H.A. 81
dualism
  amd common humanity 10–13
  modes of thinking 2–7
  roots of in Europe 1–14
  traditions, relevance of 7–10
Duras, M. 53
Durkheim, Emil 23

Eisenmenger, Johan 23
Elias, N. 172
Ellul, J. 173
enemy: Schmitt's concept of 80–90
Enlightenment
  and Europe 93–4
  and Hegel 97–8
Eppler, E. 140
'Euromissile Crisis' 166–91
  and de Rougemont 182–7
  Europe after 177–80
  and peace movement 174–7
Europe
  de Rougement on 182–7
  dualism, roots of 1–14
  and the Enlightenment 93–4
  identity 174–80
    cultural 180–7
  and militarization 167–74
  and neoconservatism 96–7
  and savagery 111–13, 120–3
  values after 'Euromissiles Crisis' 166–91
Europeanism: Africa as negation of 111–13
Eusebius 86
evil and violence 15–28

Falk, Richard 107
Fanon, Franz 107
Feldmayer, Kurt 127–9, 139, 141
Ferguson, F. 44
fetishes 24–5
Finger, Matthias 121, 166–91
Forbes, Duncan 101
France
  and Burke 67–9
  as 'evil' 72–6
Frank, A.G. 96
Freud, Sigmund 32, 33, 34, 52
Freyhold, M. von 176, 177
Friedman, Bernhard 130–3, 141
Fülberth, G. 138

Galtung, Johan 10, 11, 189
  on god 9, 12
  on New Germany 192–202
Gay, Peter 2
Geertz, Clifford 93–4
Gelasius I, Pope 12
genocide: and Israel 156–7

George, S. 96
George, Wesley 23
Germany
  conservative views on 126–43
  Feldmeyer on 127–29
  Friedman on 130–3
  identity of 128
  Jaspers on 138–41
  Marxism in 193, 194–5, 201
  and NATO 129, 132
  neo-nationalism 133–4
  New 192–202
  raison d'état of 136–8
  Stürmer on 136–8
  Willms on 133–6
Ghadaffi, Col. M. 88, 147
Girard, René 7, 29, 33, 34, 35–6, 45, 50
Goedesh, Herman 22
Goffman, E. 20
Gorbachev, Mikhial 30, 47, 131
Grant, G. 93
Greece
  classical era 3–6
  Political Oratory 4, 6
Greenleaf, W.H. 58–9

Habermas, J. 171
Hacke, C. 132
Hamman 93
Hansen, E. 111–12, 113
Harle, Vilho 1–14, 121, 123
Hastings, Warren 70
Heck, Bruno 131
Hegel, Georg Wilhelm Friedrich 91–109, 155
  on Africa 101–2
  on Asia 102–4
  and Hegelianism 105–7
  on India 102–3
  and non-Europeans 101–4
  and philosophy of history 97–100
  and reason 100, 101
  and zionism 158–60
Hegelianism, transcending 105–7
Heidegger, Martin 32–3, 35, 98
Heller, E. 161
Herder 88, 93, 97
Herodotus 5
heroism
  dialectic of 17
  sociology of 15–17
  violence and reification 18
Hess, J.C. 128, 133
Hettne, B. 166
Hitler, Adolf 83, 84, 87, 193
Hobbes, Thomas 81, 86, 98, 155
  on peace 144–5, 151
  on role of reason 150, 153
  on war 49–50
Horkheimer, M. 119
Howe, R.W. 114, 115, 122
HSFK 179

inculcation *see* sedimentation
India
  and Burke 60–6
  and Hegel 102–3
infitada of December 1987 162–3
Irwin, J. 21
Isocrates 6
Israel
  and Arabs 147–52
  and genocide 156–7
  and violence 144–54
  see also zionism

Jahn, E. 166
Japan 11
Jaspers, Karl 138–41
Jesus Christ 12
Johnstone, D. 177
Jokisalo, Jouko 126–43
Joly, Maurice 22
Jünger, Ernest 87

Kafka, Franz 36, 38, 50
Kaldor, Mary 171, 175, 180
Kant, Immanuel 82, 84, 88, 92, 97–8
Katz, J. 22
Kenny, A. 152
Kerckhove, D. 44
Khomeini, Ayatollah 88

Kirkpatrick, Jeane 106
Kissinger, Henry 106
Kohl, Chancellor H. 131
Koistinen, P. 171
Kramnick, I. 59–60, 69–73, 77
Kundera, Milan 106
Kuper, L. 156
Kühnl, R. 131, 133–4

Laski, Harold 60
Leggewie, C. 133
legitimation 20–1
Lévi-strauss, Claude, on the savage 116–18
Lewis, B. 149
Lodgaard, S. 109
Lorenz, Konrad 83, 85–6
Lowith, K. 98
Luckman, Thomas 18, 19, 22
Luther, Martin 83
Lübbe, Herman 184

Machievelli 86
McNeil, William 170, 172
Macpherson, C.B. 58, 60, 71
Magnes, Judah 156
Mahoney, T. 67, 71–2
de Maistre 86
Manicheism 24–7
Marc, Alexandre, 182
Marshall, P.J. 61–3
Marx, Karl 54
Mazuri, Ali 107
Mead 119
Mechtersheimer, A. 188
Mehan, H. 47
Meyer, Eduard 83, 84
militarization
  of Europe 167–74
  and modernization 172–4
Miller, D. 58
Mommsen, Theodor 83
Morin, E. 166
Mounier, Emmanual 182
Muslim world 6
myth-making 21–2
Märtz, P. 133

Naipaul, V.S. 102
naming and meanings 19–20
Nandy, Ashis 107
Napoleon Bonaparte 83
Nathanson, C.E. 59
NATO 129, 132
Naumann, Friedrich 83
nazism 195, 197–8, 200
Nef, John 170
neo-nationalism in Germany 133–4
Nero 86
Nietzsche, Friedrich 24, 31, 98, 155, 158, 160, 162
Nnoli, O. 112
nuclear weapons *see* bomb

O'Brien, Conor Cruise 153

Paine, Thomas 69
Palestine Liberation Organization, and Israel 163
Palestinians
  infitada of December 1987 162–3
  killing of 155–6
  state and zionism 155–65
Palmer, J. 177–8
Parkin, C. 71
Pascal, Blaise 81, 86
Paul (Saul) 9, 86
peace
  African perspective on 110–25
  and Burke 60–7
  Hobbes on 144
  movement
    in East Germany 198
    in Europe 31. 174–7
  and overvaluation tendency 41–2
  theories, inadequacies of 167–70
peace movement 31
  and 'Euromissile Crisis' 174–7
  and overvaluation of bomb 41–2
Pestalozzi, H.A. 189
Peterson, Erik 86
Petitjean, A. 166
Philip of Macedon 4
Picht, Georg 173
Plamenatz, John 100

Plato 33
Polanyi, K. 93
postmodernism and Third World
94–7
Pranaitis, Justin 22

racism and Hegel 101–2
Rageau, J.-P. 13
raison d'état of Germany 136–8
Reagan, Ronald 47, 131, 174
Regicide Directory (France) 67–9,
73–5
reification
process of 19–24
and violence 18
revelation and bomb 47–53
ritual 23–4
and animal stories 36–41
Robinson, C. 107
Rodinson, Maxime 6–7, 9, 157
Rohling, August 22
Rorty, Richard 94, 95–6
Rosenbauer 133
Rougemont, Denis de 182–7
Rousseau, Jean-Jacques 50, 54
Rubenstein, R.L. 93
Ryan, W. 21

Sadat, President Anwar 152, 153
Said, Edward 107
Salih, M.A. Mahomed 110–15
Samson 16
Sartre, Jean Paul 116–17, 157
on the savage 116–17
savage/savagery
and Africa 113–16
analysed 116–20
concept of 110–11
and Europe 111–13, 120–3
resuscitation of 120–3
Schabert, T. 105
Schachnasorow, g. 141
Schapera, I. 114–15
Schell, J. 171
Schlegel, Friedrich von 103
Schmitt, Carl
concept of state 80–6
and the 'enemy' 87–90
Schwartz, R. 21
Scott, R. 19
sedimentation (inculcation) 22–3
Seeck, Otto 81
Senghaas, D. 177
Serres, M. 39, 170
Shamir, Yitzhak 163
Sharp, Gene 188
Shennan, J.H. 146
Shover, N. 21
Skelley, J. 47
Skolnick, J. 21
Smith, J. 39
sociology of heroism 15–17
Sons of Light and Sons of Darkness
and Burke 69–76
Soviet Union 11, 129, 135, 197
Spengler, Oswald 82, 84, 87
Spivak, Gayatri 107
state
emergence of 82
pluralistic 85
Schmitt's concept of 80–90
universal 83–4, 87
Stern, J.P. 161
Stürmer, Michael 136–8, 139
Sudnow, D. 19
Szasz, T. 19

Thee, M. 174
thinking, dualistic modes of 2–7
Third World 91–2
and Hegelianism 105–7
and postmodernism 94–7
Thompson, E. 43, 44, 171, 176, 177,
178
Thucydides 80, 81
De Tocqueville, A. 82
Toynbee, Arnold 91–2, 94–5
tradition
dualism, relevance of 7–10
problem of 31–6
and ritual 36
Tromp, Hylke 189

United States 11, 129, 135
  and Burke 63–7

Valéry, Paul 182
Vihlo, Harle 58–79
violence
  construction of 15–28
  and Israel 144–54
  and reason 149
  and reification 18
Virgil 81, 83, 84
Virilio, Paul 170
Volkan, V. 49
Voltaire 92, 97
Vähämäki, Jussi 29–57
Väyrynen, R. 179

Walker, R.B.J. 107
Walsh, W.H. 98. 101. 102
Walzer, M. 105
war
  and Burke 67–9
  Clausewitz on 145–6
  First World 7, 87
  Second World 84, 87
  theories, inadequacies of 167–70
  theories, new 170–1
Warrender, H. 151
Weber, Max 83
Weber, Samuel 42, 56
Weiler, Gershon 144–54
Wells, C.M. 83
Wiarda, H.J. 105
Wight, M. 59
Willms, Bernard 133–6, 140–1
Wolin, S. 97

Xenophon 5–6

zionism
  and Palestinian state 155–65
  strategy of 158–61